THE INDIVIDUALIZATION
OF PUNISHMENT

PATTERSON SMITH

REPRINT SERIES IN

CRIMINOLOGY, LAW ENFORCEMENT,
AND SOCIAL PROBLEMS

PUBLICATIONS

No. 1. Lewis, Orlando F. *The Development of American Prisons and Prison Customs, 1776-1845.*
No. 2. Carpenter, Mary. *Reformatory Prison Discipline.*
No. 3. Brace, Charles Loring. *The Dangerous Classes of New York.*
No. 4. Dix, Dorothea Lynde. *Remarks on Prisons and Prison Discipline in the United States.*
No. 5. Bruce, Andrew A., Albert J. Harno, Ernest W. Burgess, & John Landesco. *The Workings of the Indeterminate-Sentence Law and the Parole System in Illinois.*
No. 6. Wickersham Commission. *Complete Reports, Including the Mooney-Billings Report.* 14 Vols.
No. 7. Livingston, Edward. *Complete Works on Criminal Jurisprudence.* 2 Vols.
No. 8. Cleveland Foundation. *Criminal Justice in Cleveland.*
No. 9. Illinois Association for Criminal Justice. *The Illinois Crime Survey.*
No. 10. Missouri Association for Criminal Justice. *The Missouri Crime Survey.*
No. 11. Aschaffenburg, Gustav. *Crime and Its Repression.*
No. 12. Garofalo, Raffaele. *Criminology.*
No. 13. Gross, Hans. *Criminal Psychology.*
No. 14. Lombroso, Cesare. *Crime, Its Causes and Remedies.*
No. 15. Saleilles, Raymond. *The Individualization of Punishment.*
No. 16. Tarde, Gabriel. *Penal Philosophy.*
No. 17. McKelvey, Blake. *American Prisons.*
No. 18. Sanders, Wiley B. *Negro Child Welfare in North Carolina.*
No. 19. Pike, Luke Owen. *A History of Crime in England.* 2 Vols.
No. 20. Herring, Harriet L. *Welfare Work in Mill Villages.*
No. 21. Barnes, Harry Elmer. *The Evolution of Penology in Pennsylvania.*
No. 22. Puckett, Newbell N. *Folk Beliefs of the Southern Negro.*
No. 23. Fernald, Mabel Ruth, Mary Holmes Stevens Hayes, & Almena Dawley. *A Study of Women Delinquents in New York State.*
No. 24. Wines, Enoch Cobb. *The State of Prisons and of Child-Saving Institutions in the Civilized World.*

Publication No. 15: Patterson Smith Reprint Series in
Criminology, Law Enforcement, and Social Problems

The Individualization of Punishment

By RAYMOND SALEILLES
Professor of Comparative Law in the University of Paris and in the College of Social Science

WITH AN INTRODUCTION BY GABRIEL TARDE
Late Magistrate in Picardy and Professor of Philosophy in the College of France

Translated from the second French edition by
RACHEL SZOLD JASTROW

With an Introduction by
ROSCOE POUND
Professor of Law in Harvard University

Montclair, New Jersey
PATTERSON SMITH
1968

*Copyright 1911 by Little, Brown, and Company
Reprinted 1968, with permission, by
Patterson Smith Publishing Corporation
Montclair, New Jersey*

Library of Congress Catalog Card Number: 68-55781

GENERAL INTRODUCTION TO THE MODERN CRIMINAL SCIENCE SERIES.

At the National Conference of Criminal Law and Criminology, held in Chicago, at Northwestern University, in June, 1909, the American Institute of Criminal Law and Criminology was organized; and, as a part of its work, the following resolution was passed:

"*Whereas*, it is exceedingly desirable that important treatises on criminology in foreign languages be made readily accessible in the English language, *Resolved*, that the president appoint a committee of five with power to select such treatises as in their judgment should be translated, and to arrange for their publication."

The Committee appointed under this Resolution has made careful investigation of the literature of the subject, and has consulted by frequent correspondence. It has selected several works from among the mass of material. It has arranged with publisher, with authors, and with translators, for the immediate undertaking and rapid progress of the task. It realizes the necessity of educating the professions and the public by the wide diffusion of information on this subject. It desires here to explain the considerations which have moved it in seeking to select the treatises best adapted to the purpose.

For the community at large, it is important to recognize that criminal science is a larger thing than criminal law. The legal profession in particular has a duty to familiarize itself with the principles of that science, as the sole means for intelligent and systematic improvement of the criminal law.

248630

GENERAL INTRODUCTION

Two centuries ago, while modern medical science was still young, medical practitioners proceeded upon two general assumptions: one as to the cause of disease, the other as to its treatment. As to the cause of disease, — disease was sent by the inscrutable will of God. No man could fathom that will, nor its arbitrary operation. As to the treatment of disease, there were believed to be a few remedial agents of universal efficacy. Calomel and blood-letting, for example, were two of the principal ones. A larger or smaller dose of calomel, a greater or less quantity of bloodletting, — this blindly indiscriminate mode of treatment was regarded as orthodox for all common varieties of ailment. And so his calomel pill and his bloodletting lancet were carried everywhere with him by the doctor.

Nowadays, all this is past, in medical science. As to the causes of disease, we know that they are facts of nature, — various, but distinguishable by diagnosis and research, and more or less capable of prevention or control or counteraction. As to the treatment, we now know that there are various specific modes of treatment for specific causes or symptoms, and that the treatment must be adapted to the cause. In short, the individualization of disease, in cause and in treatment, is the dominant truth of modern medical science.

The same truth is now known about crime; but the understanding and the application of it are just opening upon us. The old and still dominant thought is, as to cause, that a crime is caused by the inscrutable moral free will of the human being, doing or not doing the crime, just as it pleases; absolutely free in advance, at any moment of time, to choose or not to choose the criminal act, and therefore in itself the sole and ultimate cause of crime. As to treatment, there still are just two traditional measures, used in varying doses for all kinds of crime and all kinds of persons, — jail, or a fine (for death is now employed in rare cases only). But modern science, here as in medicine, recognizes that crime

also (like disease) has natural causes. It need not be asserted for one moment that crime is a disease. But it does have natural causes, — that is, circumstances which work to produce it in a given case. And as to treatment, modern science recognizes that penal or remedial treatment cannot possibly be indiscriminate and machine-like, but must be adapted to the causes, and to the man as affected by those causes. Common sense and logic alike require, inevitably, that the moment we predicate a specific cause for an undesirable effect, the remedial treatment must be specifically adapted to that cause.

Thus the great truth of the present and the future, for criminal science, is the individualization of penal treatment, — for that man, and for the cause of that man's crime.

Now this truth opens up a vast field for re-examination. It means that we must study all the possible data that can be causes of crime, — the man's heredity, the man's physical and moral make-up, his emotional temperament, the surroundings of his youth, his present home, and other conditions, — all the influencing circumstances. And it means that the effect of different methods of treatment, old or new, for different kinds of men and of causes, must be studied, experimented, and compared. Only in this way can accurate knowledge be reached, and new efficient measures be adopted.

All this has been going on in Europe for forty years past, and in limited fields in this country. All the branches of science that can help have been working, — anthropology, medicine, psychology, economics, sociology, philanthropy, penology. The law alone has abstained. The science of law is the one to be served by all this. But the public in general and the legal profession in particular have remained either ignorant of the entire subject or indifferent to the entire scientific movement. And this ignorance or indifference has blocked the way to progress in administration.

The Institute therefore takes upon itself, as one of its aims, to inculcate the study of modern criminal science, as a pressing duty for the legal profession and for the thoughtful community at large. One of its principal modes of stimulating and aiding this study is to make available in the English language the most useful treatises now extant in the Continental languages. Our country has started late. There is much to catch up with, in the results reached elsewhere. We shall, to be sure, profit by the long period of argument and theorizing and experimentation which European thinkers and workers have passed through. But to reap that profit, the results of their experience must be made accessible in the English language.

The effort, in selecting this series of translations, has been to choose those works which best represent the various schools of thought in criminal science, the general results reached, the points of contact or of controversy, and the contrasts of method — having always in view that class of works which have a more than local value and could best be serviceable to criminal science in our country. As the science has various aspects and emphases — the anthropological, psychological, sociological, legal, statistical, economic, pathological — due regard was paid, in the selection, to a representation of all these aspects. And as the several Continental countries have contributed in different ways to these various aspects, — France, Germany, Italy, most abundantly, but the others each its share, — the effort was made also to recognize the different contributions as far as feasible.

The selection made by the Committee, then, represents its judgment of the works that are most useful and most instructive for the purpose of translation. It is its conviction that this Series, when completed, will furnish the American student of criminal science a systematic and sufficient acquaintance with the controlling doctrines and methods that now hold the stage of thought in Continental Europe.

Which of the various principles and methods will prove best adapted to help our problems can only be told after our students and workers have tested them in our own experience. But it is certain that we must first acquaint ourselves with these results of a generation of European thought.

In closing, the Committee thinks it desirable to refer the members of the Institute, for purposes of further investigation of the literature, to the "Preliminary Bibliography of Modern Criminal Law and Criminology" (Bulletin No. 1 of the Gary Library of Law of Northwestern University), already issued to members of the Conference. The Committee believes that some of the Anglo-American works listed therein will be found useful.

COMMITTEE ON TRANSLATIONS.

Chairman, JOHN H. WIGMORE,
>*Professor of Law in Northwestern University, Chicago.*

ERNST FREUND,
>*Professor of Law in the University of Chicago.*

MAURICE PARMELEE,
>*Professor of Sociology in the State University of Missouri.*

ROSCOE POUND,
>*Professor of Law in Harvard University.*

ROBERT B. SCOTT,
>*Formerly Professor of Political Science in the State University of Wisconsin.*

WM. W. SMITHERS,
>*Secretary of the Comparative Law Bureau of the American Bar Association, Philadelphia, Pa.*

INTRODUCTION TO THE ENGLISH VERSION

WHEN Sir James Stephen spoke, not without praise, of the absence of general theories good or bad which distinguished the law of England, he stated a half-truth only. It is true that in Anglo-American law, more than in other systems, juristic theories come after lawyer and judge have dealt with concrete cases and have in some measure learned how to dispose of them. But it is also true that such theories go before our law-making, as they precede law-making elsewhere. They are developed consciously or subconsciously before the legislator, or under our system of case law the judge, formulates the rules by which future causes are to be governed. Hence we have a general theory of crime and of punishment in our Anglo-American common law and in our penal codes; and, although we are coming to have legislation here and there proceeding upon other theories, the latter fits with difficulty into a system of legislation and of judicial decision in which that general theory is consistently developed. Moreover, thinking men have agreed long ago that it is not a good one. For the theory of our common law and of our penal codes is the classical theory. This theory, intrenched in our bills of rights and in common-law juristic thinking, as well as formulated in our penal codes and the decisions construing them, is to-day a formidable obstacle in the way of modern legislation, as the conflict over construction of statutes requiring action at one's peril, the fate of the statute of Washington as to the defense of insanity, and the constitutional difficulties encountered by probation laws abundantly bear witness. Not many years ago a learned Supreme Court released a child from a reformatory on the ground that a reformatory was a prison, that commitment thereto was necessarily punishment for crime, and hence that such commitment could be warranted only by criminal proceedings of a formal type, conducted with due regard to constitutional safeguards. The rise of Juvenile Courts, justified to the lawyer by the fortunate historical circumstance of the jurisdiction of the Chancellor over infants, has now accustomed us to courts of criminal equity for the youthful offender; but attempts to introduce any system of individualization for the adult will have to wrestle a long time with constitutional provisions.

Professor Saleilles' account of the relation of the classical theory to French penal legislation should be of especial interest in America. Substantially all that he says as to the Penal Codes of 1791 and 1810 applies equally to our criminal legislation. For the New York legislators had the French Code of 1810 before them. Livingston's discussions, based on French sources, were known to them, and the theories on which the French legislation proceeded were familiar and congenial. It follows that the American criminalist has little to add. Perhaps two points deserve notice. In the first place, the desire to preclude arbitrary judicial action was especially strong in America because in the hands of appointees of the Crown the criminal law had been found an efficient engine of political and religious persecution. Unhappily, our law as to misdemeanors had developed in the court of Star Chamber, and the contests between the common-law courts and the Crown in the seventeenth century had convinced the next age that there was no safety except in hard and fast legal formulas applied mechanically. So sure of this were the lawyer and the publicist of the end of the eighteenth century, that in our bills of rights they gave us political and philosophical charts, to which all future governmental action must be made to conform, and they believed them to be merely declaratory of doctrines inhering in the very idea of justice. The popularity of the common law in America did not extend to the substantive part of the criminal law. Very early by legislation or judicial decision our commonwealths began to adopt the doctrine that there must be chapter and verse of the written law behind every punishment. Thus the unfortunate political conditions that have made the Star Chamber a synonym for arbitrary and oppressive administration of punitive justice will long stand in the way of a revived "court of criminal equity." But in France also the classical theory was a reaction against abuse of absolute power. In consequence the American reader will find the author in sympathy with the views which have come to us through our legal history. For our experience has not been unique. It is an inherent difficulty in the administration of punitive justice that criminal law has a much closer connection with politics than has the law of civil relations. There is no great danger of oppression through civil litigation. There is constant fear of oppression through the criminal law. Not only is one class suspicious of attempts by another to force its ideas upon the community under penalty of prosecution, but the power of a majority to visit with punishment practices which a strong minority consider in no wise objectionable is liable to abuse and, whether rightly or wrongly used, puts a strain upon criminal law and administration. All criminalists must reckon with this difficulty. Perhaps American lawyers insist upon it unduly, to the exclusion of other points of no less importance. But revolutionary France had the same ideas, and by consequence the author canvasses the very objections and discusses the very requirements of legal policy which we also must consider.

Secondly, we must take account of the part played by Puritanism in the development of Anglo-American law. The relation of Puritanism to the common law is quite as important a part of the philosophical history of our legal system as the relation of Stoic philosophy to Roman law is part of the history of that system. In each case we have to do with the dominant fashion of thinking upon fundamental questions during a critical period of growth. The two growing periods of our legal system, the two periods in which the rules and doctrines that obtain to-day were formative, were the classical common-law period, the end of the sixteenth and beginning of the seventeenth century, and the American common-law period, the period of legal development in America that comes to an end after the Civil War. But the age of Coke was the age of the Puritan in England, and the period that ends with our civil war was the age of the Puritan in America. Indeed, he had his own way in America. Here he was in the majority and made institutions to his own liking. It is no accident, therefore, that common-law principles have often attained their most complete logical development in America. Hence the contribution of individualist religious dogma to the criminal law was much greater in America than in France. The individualization in practice which was permitted by the canon-law conception of searching and disciplining the conscience was wholly alien to the Puritan. For above all things he was jealous of the magistrate. If moral questions were to be dealt with as concrete cases to be individualized in their solution, subordination of those whose cases were decided to those who had the power of weighing the circumstances of the concrete case and individualizing the principle to meet that case might result. His idea of "consociation but not subordination" demanded that a fixed, absolute, universal rule, which the individual had contracted to abide, be resorted to. "Nowhere," says Morley, "has Puritanism done us more harm than in thus leading us to take all breadth and color and diversity and fine discrimination out of our judgments of men, reducing them to thin, narrow, and superficial pronouncements upon the letter of their morality or the precise conformity of their opinions to accepted standards of truth." But this is exactly the method of the classical theory in criminal law. Indeed our common-law jurists have taken it to be fundamental in legal theory. Thus, Amos says: "The same penalty for a broken law is exacted from persons of an indefinite number of shades of moral guilt, from persons of high education and culture, well acquainted with the pro-

INTRODUCTION TO THE ENGLISH VERSION xv

visions of the law they despise, and from the humblest and most illiterate persons in the country." And, be it noted, he states this as a matter of course, with no hint that we may attain anything better. Thus political events and the Puritanism of nineteenth-century America tightened the hold upon us of a theory which on other grounds for a time was accepted everywhere. For to find a proper mean between a system of hard and fast rules and one of completely individualized justice is one of the inherent difficulties of all administration of justice according to law. And in the movement to and fro from the over-arbitrary to the over-mechanical, the eighteenth and nineteenth centuries stood for the latter.

More recently throughout the world there has come to be a reaction against administration of justice solely by abstract formula. In France it appears as a newer and freer method of interpreting the codes. In Germany it takes the form of agitation for "*freie Rechtsfindung.*" In England it is manifest in Lord Esher's farewell speech, in which he thanked God that English law was not a science, in Sir John Hollams's protest against treating the private controversy between John Doe and Richard Roe, not as a cause in which justice is to be done primarily, but primarily as a means by which to settle the law for other litigants, and in the wider discretion which is now accorded to the bench in order to give fuller power of doing justice. In the United States it is manifest in a tendency toward extra-legal attainment of just results while preserving the form of the law. To a large and apparently growing extent the actual practice of our application of the law is that jurors or courts take the rules of law as a general guide, determine what the equities of the cause demand and contrive to find a verdict or render a judgment accordingly, wrenching the law no more than is necessary. Occasionally we find a judge owning frankly that he looks chiefly at the ethical situation *inter partes* and does not allow the law to interfere therewith more than is inevitable. Many appellate courts are suspected of ascertaining what the broad equities of a controversy require and justifying a result in accord therewith by the elaborate ritual of a written opinion. Complaint of this is not uncommon wherever lawyers discuss recent decisions among themselves, and at least one bar association has made it the subject of a resolution. The movement for individualization in criminal law is but a phase of this general movement for individualizing the application of all legal rules.

The chief reliance of our system toward individualizing the application of law is the power of juries to render general verdicts, the power to find the facts in such a way as to compel a different result from that which the legal rule strictly applied would require. Probably this power alone has made the common law of master and servant tolerable in American jurisdictions in the twentieth century. Yet exercise of this power, with respect to which, as Lord Coke expressed it, the jurors are chancellors, has made the jury a most unsatisfactory tribunal in many classes of cases, and, in view of the practice of repeated new trials, which this power has in large part occasioned, a most expensive one. In criminal causes this is even more marked. Exercised in homicide cases, it led to the situation Mark Twain satirized when he called upon the legislature to make insanity a crime. In order to be able to procure convictions at all in cases of homicide, many of our jurisdictions leave the penalty to the jury. The penal code of California has such a provision, and a collection of criminal cases published recently by the chief of police of San Francisco enables us to see how the power has been exercised. As one studies the cases he can see to a certain degree that broad lines were drawn by the juries, even if crudely. But one of these lines which is most apparent is between picturesque murder, however brutal, and brutal murder without the picturesque element. Then, too, the cases show that the choice of penalty depends very largely on the temper of particular juries. For example, Goldensen, a boy of 19, who suddenly killed a girl of 13, was hung, while Hoff, who brutally murdered a woman who had employed him, having been sentenced to be hung on the first trial, on a second trial, granted for an error of procedure, was imprisoned for life. In the cases of murder for gain or incident to robbery this is even more apparent. The so-called " gas-pipe " murderers, who were robbers, were hung. So was Kovalev, an escaped Siberian convict, who murdered for gain. But Sontag and Evans, professional bandits, who had committed a long series of train robberies, had killed many and shot many more, were imprisoned for life. So in the case of Dorsey, a stage robber and murderer. Experience elsewhere has been the same. Obviously the crude individualization achieved by our juries, and especially by leaving the assessment of penalties to trial juries, involves quite as much inequality and injustice as the mechanical application of the law by a magistrate. Unchecked jury discretion upon the whole is worse than the unchecked magisterial discretion from which the classical school sought to deliver us.

What we have to achieve, then, in modern criminal law is a *system* of individualization, and that this is possible we have the warrant of the experience of courts of equity. In equity we have a system of legal individualization. Every rule has a margin, more or less wide, which admits of discretion in its application to individual causes. As Lord Eldon put it, the doctrines of equity "ought to be as well-settled and made as uniform almost as those of the common law, laying down fixed principles but taking care that they are to be applied according to the circumstances of each case." In equity, too, we have a system of judicial individualization. There is not, as at law, a stereotyped form of judgment which must needs be rendered in every case; but the court has wide powers of adapting the decree to the concrete cause and of doing what will most subserve the ends of justice therein. For the individualization in equity in our system is in its administration rather than in its substance, except as its substance allows this. That rights of property, which are constantly involved in our equity litigation, have not suffered in any wise under such a régime, argues that rights of personal liberty, of which we are at least no less tender, do not require hard and fast formulas administered mechanically in order to receive full protection. We must not overlook that to-day publicity is the most effective check and balance upon the magistrate. There is much less need of the elaborate tying-down to which our fathers subjected him.

It will be urged that there are constitutional provisions which preclude any system of legal or judicial individualization in criminal law in this country. But Professor Saleilles seeks to guard the very interests which our bills of rights are designed to maintain. Hence in large part his discussion of the means of attaining a system of individualization are applicable to us also. Moreover, "unconstitutional" is ceasing to be a word to conjure with. Not long ago we were wont to say "unconstitutional" as Mr. Podsnap said "not English." To-day we are not so sure that the end of the eighteenth century spoke the last word on all fundamental questions of our polity. Where but a short time since it was a commonplace to say that amendments of the federal constitution came only through civil war, we now contemplate complacently speedy and peaceful alterations therein without any pressing exigency. As to State constitutions, which are chiefly involved, we are likely to see change become quite easy enough in the near future when there is anything which reasonably demands it.

With respect to the author, it should be noted that he is primarily a lawyer, writing from a lawyer's standpoint and appreciating, as sociologists and lay criminalists do not at all times appreciate, the purely legal problems of which the lawyer is so acutely aware. As professor in the Faculty of Law of Dijon and afterwards in the Faculty of Law of the University of Paris, his chief labors have been in the field of comparative law, in which he has published, among others, the following important works: Étude sur les sources de l'obligation dans le projet de code civil allemand (1889); Du réfus de paiement pour inexécution de contrat; Étude du droit comparé (1893); Étude sur la théorie générale des obligations dans la seconde rédaction du projet de code civil allemand (1895, 2d ed. 1901); Les accidents du travail et la résponsabilité civile (1897); De la déclaration de volonté (1901); De la possession des meubles; Étude de droit allemand et de droit français (1907). As to his sociological teaching at the College libre des Sciences sociales, it will be enough to refer to the appreciation by M. Tarde in the preface to the first edition of the present work.

ROSCOE POUND.

HARVARD LAW SCHOOL.

AUTHOR'S PREFACE TO THE SECOND EDITION

THE first edition of this essay in criminal economics having been exhausted, I was requested to prepare a second. It was difficult to resist so flattering a demand. The text needed thorough revision; and notes and a considerable bibliography were required to place the work in line with the legislative reforms of the past decade, as well as with the movements of thought in legal and sociological literature to which congresses devoted to criminology and related disciplines have given expression. I found it difficult to take up the revision, inasmuch as, for the past ten years, I have transferred my teaching from criminal to civil law, and more particularly, to comparative civil law. It has thus been impossible for me to follow so carefully as formerly the evolution of ideas and systems, or to digest the literature that has accumulated in this field. The state of my health has also required urgent husbanding of my resources and an avoidance of over-exertion. I therefore decided upon a compromise.

So far as concerned the field of criminal law, it seemed to me that this book, however inadequate, sufficiently well represented the initial stage of a movement that has left its mark upon the history of opinion. It appeared at a time when jurists were confronted, on the one hand, by unprofitable essays in the field of abstract law, and, on the other, by dangers threatened by reformers, ready, in their disregard of the judicial attitude, to replace law by sociology. They thus attempted to establish a "middle ground," in which effort they may be said to have achieved creditable success.

This new spirit found expression in recent legislative reforms and support in congresses of criminology, but it was left for the initiative of medical associations (such as that of Geneva, 1907) and the contributions of eminent scholars (such as Dr. Grasset of the University of Montpellier) to bring about a more intimate affiliation between law and anthropology, and between law and sociology.[1]

Parallel with this advance, the Italian school, at least in regard to its more extreme tenets, became scientifically discredited. The demands of law and order and security gained ground. Even in the radical socialistic position the conception of law encroached upon the merely empirical attitude towards social realities as accidents, or as responses to the crude demands of impulse. There was a mutual tendency for the law to consider social facts, and for the facts to fall in with the conventions of the law. Nowhere does this tendency appear so convincingly as in criminal law.

The views expressed in this book were first formulated in connection with a popular course which I conducted at the College of Social Sciences; they record the initial stages of a movement that has since then developed to a notable position. To convey an exact impression of the present status of the subject and to indicate in detail the altered developments of recent origin would involve the preparation

---

[1] See certain characteristic passages, particularly the fourth lecture, in "Les Psychonévroses et leur traitement moral," by *Dr. Dubois*, professor in the University of Berne (Paris, Masson). [English translation: "The Psychic Treatment of Nervous Disorders." Funk & Wagnalls Co., 1908.]

of an entirely new book. This is not what I was asked to do. I decided to retain the chapters which had their initiative ten years ago and to look upon them somewhat as an expression of the period, as reflecting a phase of legal thought; for therein lies their worth. In themselves they may now have but slight value ; as an historical document they may still be of use. Therefore I have retained the text almost intact.

On many issues the volume no longer represents the views of contemporary science ; on some issues, it no longer exactly expresses my own opinion, or at least, not as I should now express myself if I were called to give my views. For example, in regard to the application of the indeterminate sentence, I might have other reservations than those presented in 1898.

This explains why the essay retains the character and the form of its first appearance ; it expressed the legitimate position of the period and what I myself held in 1898, — and nothing more. The change of date of the present edition is not intended to indicate a final point of crystallization, either in the advance of opinion or in the conviction of the author, nor to imply that the trend of these studies has lost its plasticity. Though the fundamental positions remain the same, account should be taken of the change of date, if only to indicate that institutions have changed, that laws have been revised, and that the literature has considerably increased. It seemed to me adequate to recognize this by adding brief notes in the text, and particularly at the end of the chapters. These offer not a complete bibliography of the subject up to the present time, but merely an indication of a few of the principal works containing complete references.

For reasons already mentioned I found it difficult to take

up the task of summarizing and compiling; and I accepted the kind offer of co-operation from M. Gaston Morin, my able assistant in the Paris Faculty of Law, whose special interests keep him in touch with the bibliography of criminal law. In associating his work with mine, I followed the example instituted some years ago in the Faculty of Paris by my distinguished colleagues, — MM. Le Poittevin, Garçon, and Thaller. They introduced practical conferences and co-operative research of a distinctly scientific grade, and thus established a profitable collaboration of professors and students, in which the direction of the work retained its recognizable authorship yet left a free and fertile opportunity for individual initiative. It is well to draw wider attention to these first attempts at such co-operation in our Faculties of Law, and to recognize its advantages. This change in method and attitude within the higher legal education bespeaks well for the future.

I appreciate that the advantages of the present collaboration are in my favor. I do not mean to imply that my efforts are on a par with the very successful ventures of my colleagues. I refer to them only to commend their methods and to indicate that I hold it desirable to follow, however remotely, in their footsteps, yet without assuming to a like success, at least so far as my own contribution is concerned. As for the assistance rendered me, of which I have reaped the benefits, I wish to express to M. Gaston Morin my sincere and profound gratitude.

The circumstances that turned my career to a somewhat different line of study and instruction explain my inability to carry out the project contemplated when I first published this book. I referred there to my intention to issue, under the title of "Problèmes de Politique criminelle," a series of legal and sociological studies covering some of the important problems in the science of criminal law. I wished particularly to resume and pursue more thoroughly my first studies upon the question of "La tentative et du délit impossible." I was strongly encouraged by the conclusions accepted on this subject by such authorities as M. Garraud (in the last edition of his text-book) and M. Garçon (in his annotations of the penal code); and, if I may be permitted to say so, by the support thus given to the principles and ideas which I had set forth. I must also mention the excellent contributions to the same subject published in Germany by M. Ernest Delaquis.

But I was particularly drawn to the important problem of "Complicité et du délit collectif," and finally to a very live question of the day, that of "Responsibilité atténuée." My course in Criminal Law for the candidates for the doctorate of law had reached these topics, when I was offered the chair of Civil Law, unexpectedly vacant, from which I soon transferred to the course in Comparative Civil Law.

I promptly realized that it would be difficult to pursue these several lines of study simultaneously, and that my promises were likely to be most imperfectly fulfilled. I am not sure that the volume on Criminal Law will ever appear; and in the present edition I have omitted any reference — which, in any case, would be premature — to what I had proposed to say on the questions there to be considered. As the preparation of this new edition may thus be my last scientific contribution in the field of criminal law, I wish to pay my tribute to one to whom we are largely indebted for the considerable progress of legal science in this field, — one whom I, more than any one else, have particular reason to remember, because it was he who encouraged my first attempts and introduced to the public the book which I now republish. I refer to M. Gabriel Tarde, the distinguished sociologist, a scholar of profound and original views, of fertile imagination and brilliant insight, who opened new paths in many directions and left a permanent impression wherever he ventured. He passed away at a time when his aid would have been most helpful in establishing between the position of the law and that of sociology the reconciliation here favored. In this respect, as in many another, his loss is irreparable. The merit of his services and of the man will be increasingly appreciated as time goes on.

In the compromise which M. Tarde furthered between the principles of abstract reasoning and the data of experience, he effected a service in behalf of criminal law in some respects comparable to that achieved in the field of civil law by the distinguished M. Bufnoir, to whom was dedicated the original edition of this book. It is natural that I now associate with his memory that of M. Gabriel Tarde. To both I express my personal obligation; and to both all future students of civil law will be increasingly grateful. The demands of the social order represented by the rigidity of legal principles as well as by the requirements of individual justice, will ever be recognized; and such requirements will more and more bear the impress of psychology and the principle of individualization.[1]

R. SALEILLES.

PARIS, April 24, 1908.

[1] In addition to the works on Psychiatry cited in this preface, I wish to refer to a new book by *Dr. Dubois*, "L'Éducation de soi-même" (Paris, 1908). [English translation: "Self Control, and how to secure it." Funk & Wagnalls Co.] — See the chapter entitled "L'Acte," p. 38, first edition. See also the important "Traité de Pathologie mentale," published under the direction of *Dr. Gilbert Ballet* (Paris, 1903), pp. 1465, *seq.*

INTRODUCTION

By Gabriel Tarde [1]

As the first volume of a series in sociology to be published under the auspices of the College of Social Sciences, the present book is certain to meet with a prompt and decided recognition. This institution, founded three years ago, has satisfied a real public need; it has become a permanent congress, not of religions but, more venturesomely, of social philosophies. Common points of view are more readily found in Christianity, Buddhism, and Mohammedanism, than in the several doctrines that, from Le Play and Comte to Karl Marx, have been expounded in turn from the same professorial chair in the *rue de Tournon*. Here extremes have met by finding a common ground in the field of practical applications, to which, even more than to theories, the hospitality of this foundation has been extended. It neglects no timely question in the interests of public philanthropy, political economy, and even æsthetics and ethics. Naturally the problem of crime and punishment could not remain foreign to its purpose. The lecturer of this year, assigned to present and discuss these problems, is the author of the present book. His readers will agree with the verdict of M. Saleilles' audiences, that the choice was a happy one.

[1] Late Magistrate in Picardy, Professor of Modern Philosophy in the College of France, and lecturer in the Paris School of Political Sciences, author of "Penal Philosophy" (No. VI, in the Modern Criminal Science Series).—Ed

M. Saleilles presents two qualities rarely combined: the dialectic subtlety of the jurist and the keen analysis of the psychologist and criminologist. His ability as a thinker found a field for expression in the Faculty of Law of Paris.[1] The same quality appears in this volume, in which he carries out his purpose of reconciling a loyalty to moral responsibility based upon the freedom of the will with the advocacy of a punitive system derived from quite different considerations. He forcibly expresses the objections to the conception of free will as a basis of penal condemnation. He mentions the practical difficulty of establishing the presence of freedom; and again he brings forward the paradox that, to be consistent, this view must assert that the first offender should be held most culpable, while the recidivist, having less power to resist as he becomes more hardened, should be exempted from punishment. In brief, it appears that the author, if not definitely siding with the new moralists, such as MM. Cuche, Moriaud, and others, who, notwithstanding their religious convictions, are breaking away from the traditional association of ideas between freedom and responsibility, yet closely approaches their conclusions. In common with them he regards the freedom of the will as having no bearing upon moral or criminal responsibility. It may be that what he retains of the freedom of the will, presumably to appease the popular conscience, is more the name than the reality. While admitting that responsibility implies freedom, he adds that freedom as popularly conceived is simply physiological normality. "What determines the degree of popular indignation is not the measure of freedom which the act implies, but the degree of sympathy or

---

[1] M. Saleilles was recently obliged to undertake the courses in civil law, ably and learnedly presented by his father-in-law, M. Bufnoir. The sudden death of the latter necessitated M. Saleilles' acceptance of a difficult task.

repugnance which the agent arouses," according to his character as revealed in act and speech. This amounts to saying that the popular conscience, in reaching a verdict, is concerned in determining, not whether the incriminating act was freely done (which would be paradoxical, implying that the issue could have been different from what it was, at the moment when it became the issue) but whether it conformed to the permanent and fundamental character of the accused. M. Saleilles rightly says that "the conception of freedom is the same as that of a first cause." Now I know of no jury or court which, before condemning a man, has ever stopped to ask whether he was the primary or only the secondary cause of his act. A real cause is enough. What makes a man's act his own is an inner causality — "a psychic determinism," as M. Fouillée would say. Such issue belongs to every individuality, and to the individual himself, — not to the alleged physical, physiological, and social factors, of which the personality is but the point of intersection. It is also — which is at times overlooked — the subjective fusion and expression of these several conditions.

I do not deny, more than does M. Saleilles, the existence of freedom in a metaphysical sense; but I separate it from the problem of responsibility, where the conception should be retained, at least in outward form. Hence arises the difficulty of reconciling the two conclusions: how, on the one hand, to retain moral responsibility, centering about the freedom of the will, as the basis of condemnation; on the other, to base penal legislation on the very different principle of the individualization of punishment.[1] Thus freedom would be reduced to a mere principle "without

[1] "Responsibility as the basis of punishment and individualization as the criterion of its application: such is the formula of modern penal law." (p. 181).

application"; for it does not determine the severity nor the choice of the punishment. The defendant is judged to be culpable because, by implication, he is judged to have been free; though care is taken not to mention the word "freedom," a caution observed by the Code of 1810, and commended by our author. But it is the permanent character that punitive trea ment should consider. If this be so, it follows that when the crime appears to be the issue not of the true character of the agent but rather of a momentary lapse, punishment should not be enforced; for there is no occasion to reform a character because of incidental conduct. Consequently it would seem more logical to let both the responsibility and the liability to punishment depend upon individual character, and thus responsibility and individualization, far from being contradictory or antagonistic, spring from a common origin. If our author does not quite reach this position, the trend of his characteristic thought brings him near to it. Among the interpretations which he gives to the conception of freedom, the one he favors consists in defining it as an influence upon the personality tending towards a change of character. In this sense, which is acceptable even to the determinists, he notes pertinently that punishment considers future freedom, "the germ of the moral future of the condemned," and must regard this much more than his past freedom — "that which led him towards crime."

The problem is not to proportion the punishment to the material evil done, nor to the degree of criminality involved at the moment of the crime, but mainly to adjust it to the perversity of the agent, to his real criminality, which is to be prevented from expressing itself in further action. This view, which he recognizes as of ancient origin, M. Saleilles (in common with the International Union of Criminal Law) ascribes to the Italian school. He cites the official ecclesiastical decrees that anticipate our psychological criminologists on this point, in that, through their attention to the motive, they regard punishment as a remedial measure, rather than as a debt or an expiation. I confess that I am less surprised to find this view among the theologians than among the positivists. It is strange that when the criminologists of our day, whether naturalists or sociologists, look for the causes of crime, they find only impersonal factors like climate, social environment, season, race, cranial or other anomalies; in brief, they make crime a natural or sociological fact, and depersonalize it. And later, when they come to the problem of the application of their theories to punishment, one is surprised to find them carrying the individualization of punishment to the extreme, as though the individual, who hitherto was of no consequence, had suddenly become all-important. A choice must be made: if we regard it established that punishment should be individually adjusted, we should also agree that crime and criminality are pre-eminently affairs of the individual, and this, notwithstanding the range of surrounding influences and external circumstances; for it is truer that the individual utilizes these than that he is moulded by them. If we persist in believing that the individual does not make his own what he imbibes (in which case there would be no individuality); if we persist in believing and maintaining that the true causes of crime are the impersonal factors constantly present in nature, in history, and in society, then our endeavor should be concentrated upon the reform and improvement of these factors, and not upon the reform and improvement of the individual, who is but the passive servant of their sovereign decrees.

Consequently, the general tendency to adjust punishment to the individual clearly shows that crime is more and more regarded as the result of individual causes and that the individual is held responsible for their occurrence. Responsibility and individualization of punishment are not incompatible; and M. Saleilles need not excuse their association. The two are connected, the one implying the other, and by associating them in his theory he has avoided the contradiction of more radical but less logical positions.

It is unfortunate that in individualizing punishment we assign unequal punishments for like offenses. It is well to recognize the sense of apparent injustice which this inequality cannot fail to present to a large number of the convicted as well as to the uninformed public. Criminal law is admirably defined by our author as "the sociology of crime adapted to the sense of justice." But is not the sense of justice dominantly that of an equality of treatment? So far as possible it is the duty of legislatures, in regulating punishments and in fixing the upper and lower limit within which the discretion of the judge operates, to take account of this fundamental and popular notion of equity. Thus I am entirely in accord with M. Saleilles in recognizing that the individualization of punishment cannot be administered by statute. It is primarily a judicial matter. It is administrative as well, but under the supervision of the judge. Such judicial supervision would be facilitated by bringing the prison administration under the authority of the Minister of Justice, — a reform constantly urged and as constantly postponed. Our author rightly regards the Bérenger law, which becomes better understood the more it is extended, as an admirable beginning of penal individualization by judicial authority. This new and successful law falls in well with the principles advanced in the present volume. As indicated by the official report of 1895 on criminal statistics, we are indebted to it for the arrest and decline of the rising wave of habitual crime, which was apparently beyond control. The law of deportation, which owes its origin to a very different inspiration, is far from having proved equally effective. "Gentleness does more than violence."

G. Tarde.

April, 1898.

AUTHOR'S PREFACE TO THE FIRST EDITION

THE course of lectures which I had the honor to deliver during the past winter at the "College of Social Sciences" on the "Individualization of Punishment" is reproduced, with slight modification, in this volume. As I was addressing a mixed audience, for the most part unknown to me, who presumably were to be my hearers throughout the course, I had to avoid considerations proper to technical instruction and give the lectures a markedly popular character. To an audience somewhat unfamiliar with legal conceptions I could not speak as a jurist; accordingly I kept to the field of general ideas. This will explain certain gaps and shortcomings of the book. I am not unaware of them, but I thought it best to retain the original form of presentation which this work is to reflect. If the scientific aspect has thereby been sacrificed, it may possibly have given place to something more engaging, more individual, and more vivid.

I must add a word of explanation in regard to another matter. The subject, treated exhaustively, would include all the branches of criminal law; for the applications of the principle of individualization have relation to every part thereof. It was quite impossible in a limited course of ten lectures to presume to cover this ground. I had to be satisfied to set forth the principles and expound the system; for such was the scope of the course. This work contains nothing more; it is an exposition of principles.

I have in mind to follow it with a sequel; and in a second work, now in course of preparation and bearing the title "Problèmes de Politique Criminelle," I shall set forth certain applications of the principles of individualization, so far as relates to such topics as limited responsibility, the status of minors, complicity, and habitual crime.

It was my first intention to dedicate this book to the Société Générale des Prisons, under the influence and auspices of which I received my brief training as a criminologist and to which I owe a debt of gratitude. I had informally inquired whether the Society would be willing to accept this tribute, and was about to present my request officially upon finishing the volume, when I was overwhelmed by an inconsolable loss, both personal and in the relation of pupil to master.

Under these circumstances it was natural for me to inscribe this work to the memory of M. Bufnoir. It is true that he was not a specialist in criminal law; but to a mind of his scope none of the branches of legal scholarship was foreign. M. Bufnoir was one of those all-around men who become specialists in whatever they have in hand, and almost in what they are momentarily discussing; and questions of criminology were of interest to him. But there is more to be said. Through the force of his teaching he introduced a method of instruction, cautious and sound, yet plastic, delicate, and nicely adjusted to the requirements of the practical and the social situation. Such a method is an instrument of absolutely general application. It is not limited to the sphere of civil law, but may be extended and more completely and comprehensively developed, wherever the requirements of society, as expressed in abstract legal

PREFACE TO FIRST EDITION

formulæ, demand a more realistic interpretation. Such is the case in regard to criminal law. In common with other branches of law and perhaps most notably of all, criminal law owes much to such disciplines as favor the newer methods of interpretation.

Let me return to considerations of a more personal type. In the progress of this book M. Bufnoir had a personal share. I constantly consulted him in the preparation of my lectures. He knew my difficulties and my hesitations; possibly also my temerity, which he dared not encourage too openly but which he was not displeased to put to the test.

My task is accomplished; but the gifted and versatile man, who guided me in its preparation and whose intimacy I enjoyed, has passed away. His influence pervades the book, and I have inscribed his name upon the dedicatory page. In resuming my work after the shock of such a loss I could not do otherwise. The inscription was more than the tribute of affection and the gratitude of a pupil. The sentiment that inspired me will be understood by every sympathetic reader.

In closing I wish to extend my profound thanks for the auspices under which this essay is to appear. The modest attempt which I present to the public hardly merits the sponsorship of the name of M. Tarde. But I would not forego the privilege; for it is to the volume, as the first of the College of Social Sciences Series that the eminent sociologist has willingly given the stamp of his approval. This, at all events, is the only ground upon which I can conscientiously accept it. For his consideration of the book thus introducing the series, as not unworthy of his endorsement, I tender my cordial and respectful appreciation; and I ask him to accept as well the gratitude of my hearers, who in reality were my collaborators. For in oral instruction that dispenses with a set program and is not governed by the profitless concern for a diploma, such support is a common experience. The course grows by the mutual reaction of mind upon mind, and by the reciprocal sympathy of speaker and hearer. The lecturer does not prepare it in advance, but awaits the inspiration of his audience. Such was the origin of the present book.

R. SALEILLES.

PARIS, March 11, 1898.

LIST OF PERIODICALS REFERRED TO IN NOTES AND TEXT

Annales de l'Énseignement superieur de Grenoble
Annales de l'Université de Grenoble
Annales de philosophie chrétienne
Année sociologique
Archivio giuridico
Bulletin de la Société française de philosophie
Bulletin de l'Union internationale de droit pénal. (Bull. de l'Un. inter. de droit pénal)
Bulletin de l'Union pour l'action morale
Der Gerichtsaal
Deutsche Rundschau
Figaro
Grünhut's Zeitschrift für das privat und öffentliche Recht der Gegenwart
Journal de psychologie normale et pathologique
Kritische Vierteljahresschrift für Gesetzgebung und Rechtswissenschaft
La Quinzaine
Reforme sociale
Revue Bleue
Revue critique de législation et de jurisprudence
Revue de métaphysique et de morale
Revue de Paris
Revue de psychologie sociale
Revue des Deux Mondes
Revue du Clergé français
Revue internationale de sociologie
Revue pénale suisse
Revue pénitentiaire
Revue scientifique
Zeitschrift für die gesammte Strafrechtswissenschaft. (Zeitsch. f. d. ges Str. W.; In connection with Liszt, Z.)

CONTENTS

	PAGE
GENERAL INTRODUCTION TO THE CRIMINAL SCIENCE SERIES	v
INTRODUCTION TO ENGLISH VERSION BY ROSCOE POUND	xi
AUTHOR'S PREFACE TO SECOND EDITION	xxi
INTRODUCTION BY GABRIEL TARDE	xxvii
AUTHOR'S PREFACE TO FIRST EDITION	xxxv
LIST OF PERIODICALS REFERRED TO	xxxix

CHAPTER I

THE STATEMENT OF THE PROBLEM

§ 1. Sociological and Psychological Foundations	1
§ 2. The Subjective and Objective Aspects of Crime	3
§ 3. The Purpose of Punishment: "Zweckstrafe"	8
§ 4. Practical Influences: the Jury	10
§ 5. Types of Individualization	11
§ 6. Queries and Objections: the Schools	13
§ 7. Consistencies and Concessions of Opinion	15
§ 8. The Origin of the Classic School	18

CHAPTER II

THE HISTORY OF PUNISHMENT

§ 9. Introductory: Private and Communal Punishment	20
§ 10. Primitive Punishment as Penalty and as Expiation: the Wergild	23
§ 11. The Growth of Communal Interests and Social Consciousness: the Religious Factor	26
§ 12. Early Views of Objective Crime and Subjective Criminality	30
§ 13. Responsibility, Freedom of the Will, and Sin, as determining Crime	34
§ 14. The Analysis of the Grounds of Punishment; Responsibility in Ecclesiastical Law	39
§ 15. Consequences of the Older Position: its Contrast with the Modern View	42
§ 16. Early Types of Individualization	44
§ 17. The Discretionary Power of the Judge, and Individualization	47
§ 18. The Protection of the Social Interests	49
§ 19. The Classical and Historical Position	51

CONTENTS

CHAPTER III

THE CLASSIC SCHOOL

	PAGE
§ 20. The Eighteenth Century Philosophy of Crime	52
§ 21. Modifications and Concessions of Later Codes	56
§ 22. Advantages and Defects of the Classic System	58
§ 23. The Reaction and the Neo-Classic Transition	61

CHAPTER IV

THE NEO-CLASSIC SCHOOL AND INDIVIDUALIZATION BASED UPON RESPONSIBILITY

§ 24. The Assumption of Free Will: the Fallacy Involved	63
§ 25. Empirical Conditions of Freedom: Premeditation	68
§ 26. Potential and Actual Freedom: Applications	70
§ 27. The Social Regulation of Conduct	73
§ 28. Responsibility Proportioned to the Degree of Freedom; Irresponsibility and its Establishment	75
§ 29. The Basis of Mitigation and of Exemption from Punishment	79
§ 30. The Individualization thus Resulting; Practical and Theoretical Objections	83
§ 31. Remote and Immediate Responsibility	87
§ 32. The Social Responsibility for Crime	90
§ 33. Motives and Impressionism of Juries	93
§ 34. Individualization Resulting from the Variable Attitude of Juries	95

CHAPTER V

THE ITALIAN SCHOOL AND INDIVIDUALIZATION BASED UPON FORMIDABILITY

§ 35. Historical Review of the Italian Movement in Penology	99
§ 36. Practical Situations and Reforms: the Making of the Recidivist	103
§ 37. The Solution Proposes the Personal Consideration of the Offender and his Social Reinstatement	107
§ 38. Gradation by Presumptive Morality and Good Conduct of Offenders: Protest against Promiscuous Association	111
§ 39. Criticism of the Position: its Basis in Law and in Public Opinion	114
§ 40. Purpose and Effect of Punishment: Consequent Status of Crime	116
§ 41. The Types of Criminals and their Individualized Treatment	118
§ 42. Difficulties Attaching to the Position of Lombroso	122
§ 43. A Third Italian School	125
§ 44. The Physical Recognition of the Criminal; Innate and Acquired Degenerate Traits	127
§ 45. Other Phases of Italian Penology; Judicial Diagnosis	132
§ 46. What Italian Penology has accomplished	134

CHAPTER VI

THE DOCTRINE OF RESPONSIBILITY

	PAGE
§ 47. The Moral Issues in Punishment	137
§ 48. The Criterion of Normality; Crime and Insanity; Mental and Moral Maturity	140
§ 49. Preventive Punishments for the Irresponsible	145
§ 50. True Punishments for True Criminals	148
§ 51. A Mediating View	150
§ 52. The Popular and Social Bases of Responsibility; Social Solidarity	152
§ 53. The Subconscious Basis in Feeling and its Logical Justification	157
§ 54. Criminality and Motives; Responsibility and the Moral Nature	159
§ 55. General and Specific Freedom of Action	165
§ 56. Responsibility, Freedom, and the Will	168
§ 57. Freedom and the Principle of Causality	172
§ 58. The Human Will as a First Cause	175
§ 59. Determinism and the Environment	177
§ 60. Freedom Essential to Punishment	179

CHAPTER VII

RESPONSIBILITY AND INDIVIDUALIZATION

§ 61. Freedom in the Penal Codes	182
§ 62. Social and Personal Aspects of Punishment: their Legal Recognition	184
§ 63. The Conception of Punishment	187
§ 64. Society's Interest in Punishment; Crime and Degradation	189
§ 65. The Moral Purpose of Individualized Punishment	192
§ 66. Ecclesiastical Law and Individualization	196
§ 67. Examples in Penance and Clemency for Special Crimes	199
§ 68. Individualization in French Codes; Political Crimes	203
§ 69. Individualization in Deportation	206
§ 70. Individualization in Short-term and Long-term Sentences	209
§ 71. The System of Parole: its Faulty Application	215

CHAPTER VIII

LEGAL INDIVIDUALIZATION

§ 72. Legal Individualization Necessarily General	220
§ 73. Examples of False Individualization	223
§ 74. Approach to Judicial Individualization and the Cases Concerned	227
§ 75. The Proper Education of Magistrates	231
§ 76. The Place of the Jury in Individualization	232

CHAPTER IX

JUDICIAL INDIVIDUALIZATION

	PAGE
§ 77. Older Forms of Individualization	237
§ 78. The Analysis and Place of the Motive	239
§ 79. A Second Interpretation of the Motive: the Psychological Factor	243
§ 80. Difficulties in the Application of the Motive to Punishment	247
§ 81. A Third Interpretation of the Motive: the Moral Status	251
§ 82. Individualization and Political Crimes	253
§ 83. Individualization in the Italian Penal Code	256
§ 84. Principles underlying Individualization; Uniform Punishments	260
§ 85. Legal Individualization for Special Offenses or Circumstances	262
§ 86. The System of Parallel Punishments; Punishment and Social Dishonor	266
§ 87. The Factors entering into the Classification of Criminals	270
§ 88. A Tentative System of Individualization; Static and Dynamic Criminality	274
§ 89. The Detailed Classification of Criminals	278
§ 90. Concessions to other Principles	282
§ 91. Special Types of Individualization	285
§ 92. Possible Extensions of Individualization; Relation to Preventive Measures	288

CHAPTER X

ADMINISTRATIVE INDIVIDUALIZATION

§ 93. The Administrative Treatment	295
§ 94. The Principle of Indeterminate Sentences; the Elmira System	298
§ 95. Modified Indeterminate Sentences adapted to European Conditions	301
§ 96. Difficulties in the Extension of the System	305
§ 97. The Personal and Religious Factors in Reform	308

INDEX 315

THE INDIVIDUALIZATION OF PUNISHMENT

CHAPTER I

THE STATEMENT OF THE PROBLEM

§ 1. Sociological and Psychological Foundations.
§ 2. The Subjective and Objective Aspects of Crime.
§ 3. The Purpose of Punishment: *Zweckstrafe*.
§ 4. Practical Influences: The Jury.
§ 5. Types of Individualization.
§ 6. Queries and Objections: The Schools.
§ 7. Consistencies and Concessions of Opinion.
§ 8. The Origin of the Classic School.

§ 1. Sociological and Psychological Foundations

THERE is at present a general movement having as its purpose to detach the law from the purely abstract formulæ, which, as commonly regarded, hold it aloof from living issues. Sooner or later civil law will no doubt undergo such a transformation. As yet the change affects the field of criminal law alone, and there it has acquired a firm foothold. It is evident why this field was chosen for the initial venture. Of the laws controlling the organization of society the oldest and most inalienable is that of self-protection, whereby each organism and each group of living creatures instinctively rejects such factors as refuse to submit to the conditions of its own existence, directly oppose it, or obstruct its further development. Criminal law may be said to be the formulation into a system of positive legislation of such requirements for the self-protection of society; or, in other words, it may be said to be an instrument of social defense, adapted to the requirements of the sense of justice.

It cannot be too constantly emphasized that the science of sociology is something more than the correlation of facts of experience. Inasmuch as it is a social science, and, indeed, *the* social science, it finds in man at once a determining factor and the objective goal of its pursuit. It considers the conditions of organized groups. But the laws which it discloses have likewise a message for the individual man, in that the individual must take the initiative in their application. Thus, for sociology, man is at once object and subject; and this applies not alone to his specifically social relations but to his entire psychological nature. It is generally recognized that sociology finds its material directly in history and psychology, but until recently psychology has been called upon only for the explanation of the interactions of one man upon another ; and such a restricted psychology is wholly inadequate. The interpretation of social reactions requires a close study of the complete man, with his distinctive and individual psychology. In the depths of human nature lies the latent spark which becomes the motive force, insignificant at the outset but momentous in its issues. Here is to be found the origin of man's personal development as well as of his reactions upon others; here also lies the origin of that other life, which is part of the individual, yet which each individual develops only in his relations with others and which constitutes his participation in the social organism.[1]

In so far as the germ of human evolution is to be found

---

[1] See the excellent lectures delivered by M. Tarde in October, 1897, at the College of Social Sciences, from which source I have borrowed several conceptions and phrases. These lectures have been published under the title "Les Lois sociales" (F. Alcan, last edition 1907). [English translation by H. C. Warren, London and New York, 1899.]

in the psychology of man, it may be held that the sense of justice is, of all the inherent human instincts, the deepest, the most tenacious, and the most distinctive. The tenacity of this sentiment appears in that it persists even among the criminal classes, among those who presumably have discarded all notions of it. They associate more or less transiently in bands or small gangs and hold themselves subject to laws based upon the sense of justice. Such adoption of law and regulation, which is the essential foundation of organized life, is found, not alone among those banded together for a purpose, but even among those who resist the laws of society. The sentiment appears in their insistence upon a fair division of the spoils, in holding to their word of honor, in their legitimized sanction of occasional betrayals, — all these represent the expression of the sense of justice. Their mutual relations, their language, and such convictions as these criminals retain, reflect the same sense of innate justice that prescribes for society what is due to the individual in his relations with others.

Criminology must accordingly consider the essentially social nature of man as well as his individual character; and it cannot neglect so important a factor of human psychology as the sense of justice. Accordingly criminal law may be defined, with sufficient precision and definiteness, as the sociology of crime adapted to the sense of justice.

§ 2. The Subjective and Objective Aspects of Crime

It is the purpose of a relatively recent school — the Italian — to reduce criminal law to an instrument of social protection and to regard it merely as a reaction to the sociological forces conditioning crime. Before proceeding further, it is well to face this position definitely, and to show, along with the measure of support which it finds in practice, the essential inadequacy and chief defects of this Italian school.

The distinctive purpose of criminal law would thus become the economics of social defense; but this formula of the Italian school should be amended by adding: an economics of social defense adapted to the demands of the sense of justice. That criminal law reflects the sociology of crime is sufficiently clear; but the sociology must be such as leaves the heights of abstract science and becomes adjusted to common sentiment, — to ordinary notions that circulate in the body social, to the sense of justice, the distinction between good and evil, and accepted views regarding human responsibility. All this applies no less to the conception of crime than to criminal law.

Crime has been regarded as falling to pathology. It is better to refer it to sociology,[1] for a social product it undeniably is. Crime is a social phenomenon in the nature of a violation of a generally recognized social obligation. It is an outgrowth of social institutions, but consists of an individual disregard of the rights of justice. Criminal law occupies a distinctive position in the group of the social sciences; and every general system of sociology must include an analysis of the social protective function.

The entire province of criminal law must be reviewed from this new approach. A comprehensive and constructive survey of the data, together with an exposition of principles, must be directed to the critical problem of criminology, which is the problem of the individualization of punishment.

The first step is to indicate how the problem arises and what are its main features. Logically defined, crime is a violation of the legally established order. Punishment is

[1] See *Makarewicz*, "Das Wesen des Verbrechens" (Vienna, 1896).

the penalty of such transgression of the law and may be looked upon as a reparation, a kind of compensation through the suffering of the individual for the injury that has been done; as such it is what the Germans call a *Vergeltungsstrafe*. When thus considered, it is the practical consequence of a crime that attracts attention, by which is meant the social disturbance that has been occasioned, the resulting individual or collective harm of which society reflexly feels the effect.

To express these relations in legal language technical phrases have been adopted. In discussion the external aspect of the criminal act is referred to as the "materiality,"[1] or circumstances of the crime; and in so far as we have come under the influence of this terminology, as used in scientific discussions, we speak of it as the "objective" side of the crime.

It is obvious that a school which regards only the consequences of an act — the "materiality" of the crime, or the injury done — disregards the personality of the criminal agent; for this factor does not affect the crime itself. Whoever the criminal, the consequences of his crime remain the same. The punishment is not the expiation imposed upon the individual criminal; it is the compensation for the injury done, and this remains the same whoever the agent may be, and whatever may be the nature of his personal disposition. The law sets the punishment in accordance with the injury done; by which is understood only the *objective* injury. It sentences to months or years of imprisonment, or to penal servitude, or even to death, according to the material gravity of the crime. The person of the criminal is not considered. In the eyes of criminal justice the offender is but an abstract, nameless individual, as later he becomes a mere number in the work-yards of the jail or penitentiary.

[1] This French term has no equivalent in Anglo-American law. It signifies the abstract quality of the act in itself, apart from the mental or moral state of the doer. ED.

Thus conceived, criminal law becomes a wholly abstract construction, taking cognizance only of the crime while ignoring the criminal. In this familiar view a crime becomes a legal abstraction, after the manner of a geometrical construction or an algebraic formula. Upon this abstraction the law develops its procedure and argument. Every technical science has its formulæ, as typically in algebra terms are added, subtracted, or multiplied. But the legal formula lacks one essential term, and that is the intent. This may be represented by $A-B$, A standing for the crime as a whole, as completely accomplished, and B the factor which it lacks of completion. Such penal codes as the Italian, which aim to be strictly logical and quantitatively adaptable, would lessen the punishment in view of such consideration. If a represents the entire punishment corresponding to the factor A, which is the entire crime, and b the fraction of the punishment in proportion to what the crime lacks of accomplishment, the punishment for the attempt would be represented by $a-b$, just as objectively the crime is expressed by the formula $A-B$. What is true of the intent would be proportionately true of joint complicity; in which case, instead of the operation of subtraction, an equation is assumed, $A=B=C$, with correspondingly identical punishments. In the case of a joint crime, the crime of each accomplice may be assumed to be the same, until by a process of civil law a more accurate verdict is reached. Disregarding the nature of the accomplices and their different intentions and their several wills, their participation is equalized in their common crime; and they are alike subject to the same degree of punishment under the principle that the same crime deserves the same punishment.[1] If objection be made to this theory on the ground that it makes the procedure

[1] French Penal Code, art. 59; and the proposed revision, art. 82.

fictitious and artificial, recourse may be had to a law which is regarded as more equitable and which, instead of equalizing, distinguishes the greater and the less, and reduces the punishment of an accomplice, recognizing that his part is but accessory to the principal crime.[1] But the quantitative conception persists.

Examples could readily be multiplied, but it is sufficiently evident that underlying these equations and manipulations of formulæ there are involved living realities, human beings whose moral and social future constitutes a problem. While admitting that the sacrifice of individuals may be of slight importance in comparison with the interests of social order, it is not to be overlooked that society itself suffers through the haphazard application of a mathematical type of administration; for such punishment acts blindly, running the risk of setting free the incorrigible and the pervert and penalizing the semi-responsible and the chance offender. The injustice of the situation is aggravated by the promiscuous intercourse of the prison that itself serves to make perverts and to enlist these several classes in a career of crime.

Be this as it may, the legal and objective view of crime, despite its many concessions, remains the classic conception, or at any rate what is still called the classic conception of crime; for as a thorough-going conception this classic view is hardly more than a tradition of the past. We have indeed reached a point of development at which the several schools are quite ready to assimilate. None the less the distinctive conceptions of the classic school, namely, the tendency to consider the criminal action in its materiality and from its objective side, and, secondly, its distinctive position with reference to responsibility, still merit consideration. Ac-

[1] For example, the Italian Penal Code, art. 64.

cording to this view there would be only crimes and no criminals; somewhat as if a physician were to maintain that there are only diseases and no patients. The two formulæ are of like applicability.

§ 3. The Purpose of Punishment: "Zweckstrafe"

Opposed to this fundamentally legal view another has gradually gained ground and may, in its development, itself become classic. It holds that punishment is to be determined not by the material gravity of the crime, not by the injury done, but by the nature of the criminal. It would indeed be a violation of justice if under pretext of justice useless suffering should be inflicted. The legitimate purpose of punishment is to make of the criminal an honest man if that be possible; or, if not, to deprive him of the chance of doing further harm. For the view that punishment is an infliction of injury for injury there is substituted the view that punishment is a moral instrument, a means of regeneration for the individual as well as of protection for society. Punishment has thus a social end directed to the future, while hitherto it was regarded only as the necessary consequence of a past act. It was appraised and described in terms of the crime committed without reference to future issues; and this attitude resulted in making habitual criminals.

Where formerly only the accomplished deed was considered, the purpose of punishment is now taken into account. Such purpose is not to inflict a punishment for what has been done, as if in satisfaction of a sentiment of individual or collective vengeance, but to bring about a certain result. The Germans call this aspect of punishment (in contrast to the "*Vergeltungsstrafe*," which in the classic view was a punishment by way of compensation or retribution) the

§ 3] THE STATEMENT OF THE PROBLEM 9

"*Zweckstrafe*," [1] which we can hardly render more closely than by the phrase "punishment for a purpose." Yet the term does scant justice to the important movement inspired by Ihering, and to the significance therein attached to the conception of the final purpose ("*Zweck*"), the consideration of which was to reanimate the dead bones of the law. The vital principle of every organic function is this same "*Zweck*" or final purpose ; and this is equally true of the law. The function of punishment must accordingly be directed to its social purpose and adapted to that purpose as an instrument is adapted to the operation in view. Accordingly it is the future and not the past, not the crime committed, that sets the goal and the purpose sought.

Consequently punishment for each individual case should be so adjusted to its purpose as to produce the largest possible return. It cannot be strictly and rigidly determined in advance, nor inflexibly regulated by the law. The purpose of punishment is an individual one and is to be attained through a policy appropriate to the circumstances of the case, not by the application of an abstract law, that ignores the varieties of the cases considered. Such is the "*Zweckstrafe*," a punishment characterized by its purpose, as opposed to the "*Vergeltungsstrafe*," a punishment crystallized as a mechanical and exact retribution, ineffective in regard to the past and without influence upon the future. If this conception of punishment, which looks to the future for the realization of a definite purpose, be accepted, it necessarily follows that the punishment must be adapted to the nature of the individual to whom it is applied. If the criminal is not fundamentally a pervert, the punishment should not contribute to his further perversion. It should serve

[1] For bibliography see *Von Liszt*, "Lehrbuch des Deutschen Strafrechts" (edition 1905, § 15).

for his regeneration and his rehabilitation. If the criminal is an incorrigible, the interests of society demand his punishment as a measure of protection and of radical prevention. Such adaptation of punishment to the individual is now known as the individualization of punishment. As in medicine it has been maintained that there are no diseases but only patients, so one is tempted to say that, strictly speaking, there are no crimes but only criminals.

§ 4. Practical Influences: the Jury

The movement for reform, which has now assumed a distinctively scientific character, began as a purely humanitarian reaction, prompted by a sense of popular and sentimental justice. It was the jury that first practiced such individualization and did so constantly without knowing it. It was however applied casually and inopportunely, and that is why science now attempts to regulate what is still only the issue of an empirical procedure. While the jury-system cannot be unreservedly commended, its initiative in this movement (which goes back to its first application in the French Penal Code) should, in justice, be acknowledged.

The law considers only the crime, and it ruthlessly and rigidly applies the formulated punishment, disregarding the criminal. The jurymen stand face to face with a man whose life and honor they hold in their hands; thus confronted they can hardly remain indifferent to his motives, his antecedents, and his former life. They become so wholly absorbed in the impression of the individual that, time and again, in defiance of the law, they forget the crime; and thus crimes come to be distinguished by their tendency or their failure to enlist the sympathies of the jury. There are classes of crimes in which the jury always ignores the facts and is moved by sentiment, by the sway of the instinctive and possibly irresistible passions from which the crime resulted. Such crimes have come to be called crimes of passion. For them the law prescribes punishments no differently than for other crimes and equally ignores their nature. The jury circumvents the law and brings in an acquittal, thereby favoring individualization in so far as it takes account of the individual. It often applies this policy poorly, and sometimes very unjustly. However, it reveals loyalty to a psychological impulse as well as to a principle; and it aims to place the consideration of the individual above that of the deed.

This tendency began with the introduction of juries under the Empire and the Restoration. From 1824 on, one of the first laws reforming the penal code admitted extenuating circumstances for certain crimes; not for all, but for those most likely to result in acquittals, often of a notorious nature. Extenuating circumstances are a form of individualization of punishment. Their introduction in our criminal laws was due to the influence of the jury. In 1824, in the Court of Assizes, it was the court itself, that is, the judges, who were charged with the determination of the extenuating circumstances. But juries defied judges, and continued to acquit. In 1832 the jury was empowered to determine extenuating circumstances; nevertheless, in crimes commanding sympathy, they acquitted as before. This again was individualization, but it was badly applied and purely empirical, at times somewhat emotional as were the crimes concerned.

§ 5. Types of Individualization

Neither science nor justice was thus served; and hence, under the influence of the former, there arose the problem of the individualization of punishment. It is true that science was not first in realizing the situation; but facts stronger than the law, jointly with public opinion, ever impressed by facts, forced the problem by inquiring: On what basis shall the individualization of punishment proceed? This question, in turn, implied a second, closely allied to it: By whom shall the individualization of punishment be made? Shall it be done in advance by the law? If so, it proceeds upon presumption, in ignorance of the individuals concerned, and upon the judgment of them through their actions. It groups them according to prescribed classes, and undertakes approximately to set the punishment and to adjust it to the individual criminal. This would be a system of legal individualization.

On the other hand the judge is confronted not by an abstract and nameless individual, but by an actual criminal conscious of his crime and its significance. Shall the judge then undertake the adjustment of the punishment to the measure of surviving morality still available for reform and moral reinstatement? This would be a system of judicial individualization.

Or shall we go farther still and leave the individualization to the prison authorities, on the ground that they can observe the prisoner in confinement, carefully adjust the punishment to the progress made, and in due course omit it when they consider the reform established and rehabilitation secure? For it may be found that the judge is not in a favorable position to appreciate the criminal, because he knows nothing of him but the single fact of the crime committed; and though he knows this with all its accompanying circumstances, he has not the basis for anticipating the probable effect of punishment. This would be a system of administrative individualization.

§ 6. Queries and Objections: the Schools

Such are the important issues; yet there is another, more important than any such question of application, which is beset with conscientious doubts. The classic conception sets forth an important truth, or to speak more accurately, two truths, which should be clearly grasped. The first is that in itself and independently of the personality of the criminal the evil done carries an actual injury to the community which is the victim of the crime. This injury, quite apart from an expiation in any religious or philosophical sense, requires a satisfaction demanded by the public conscience. Now if the consideration of the individual prevails above the reparation, will not the policy encourage others to continue in a criminal career? And for society, will this not produce a moral disorder which, like a contagious disease, tends to spread? An additional query or objection applies; namely, the difficulty of divesting the ordinary conception of justice from a kind of abstract mathematical equality. Accordingly, if two individuals receive different punishments for the same offense or are differently treated, it would seem as though equity had been disregarded, and that caprice had replaced justice. How shall these exacting requirements demanded by society be reconciled to the equally indispensable necessity of taking account of the individual? How shall they be reconciled to the like requirements of proportioning the punishment, not to the objective crime committed or to the material injury done, but to the inherent criminality of the criminal, to such latent or real criminality as makes him dangerous to his fellowmen? How, in brief, shall they be adjusted to the degree of morality, or, if we may say so, of normality, and to the prospects of regeneration which it holds out?

Such are the several aspects of this very large problem of the individualization of punishment.

But before considering the problem itself, it is well to guard against certain impressions that commonly arise when we classify systems, divide them into schools, and give them specific labels. We naturally emphasize the central idea in each school, and push it to the extreme. In consequence of such theoretical abstraction, we unjustly and unwisely set barriers between one school and another. It is however fortunate that the common ground of practice serves to bring the schools together. The practical solutions of the one are accepted by the other. The theoretical principles remain; but practical measures become the common property of all; and that is the essential point. The several reservations and shades of opinion should be taken at their true worth, for a name or a label or an enrollment under a different banner may be enough to prevent a mutual understanding among those pursuing the same purposes.

There are those who by reason of their belief in responsibility and freedom — and fortunately such still exist — regard themselves as forever bound by these principles to the same camp, as solemnly sworn to the same platform; and accordingly they refuse to accept any measures of social protection proposed by an opposite school. Yet there is a decided tendency for widely separated partisans to meet in agreement upon matters of practical concern — a desirable issue that should find further favor and support. Such concessions are necessary wherever there is something definite to be done. The removal of barriers and misunderstandings becomes a duty on the part of those who are in a position to facilitate such closer approach. However inadequate they may consider themselves, it devolves upon them to set to work without too much concern for the past. They should express themselves fearlessly and not be troubled by a sense of insufficient authority; nor should they set forth their personal shortcomings as an excuse for silence. We have reached a period of transition in which older conceptions are confused and traditional notions no longer satisfy; yet it is not feasible to hold back and wait until other measures shall have been tried, or newer views definitely tested and universally recognized. There is danger of waiting too long, for, while waiting, the facts demand and must receive attention. If the formulæ of other times are no longer adequate new solutions must be provisionally attempted. Through co-operative effort a more advanced position will be attained. Let each contribute his share. When the old habitation is crumbling it will not do, in false modesty, to remain under cover of a roof that threatens to fall; it is far better to build a provisional shelter. If every one, without sacrifice of individual belief, is willing to combine with the others, the structure of the future will promptly take shape and serve as a common shelter.

Instances and evidences of this commendable freedom from dogmatism could readily be cited. It is true that we pass from one inconsistency to another, but life demands such sacrifice, and history is but a striking demonstration, notably in terms of human conduct and social laws, of the persistent failure of the absolute and of the alleged principles which it embodies.

§ 7. Consistencies and Concessions of Opinion

Let us take the large question of responsibility, which for a long time was the point of dissension. Every good determinist, in order to be consistent, felt it necessary to deny the validity of the concept of responsibility; and it would appear that nowadays, his inconsistency leads him to abandon his position and to accept the postulates of the positivist Italian school. Such pardonable inconsistencies appear on all sides; and we are beginning to recognize the futility of demonstrations and syllogisms, which, however engaging as mental exercises, have never suppressed a new idea nor saved an old one. Man does not live by logic but by practical needs; yet still more he lives by conviction and personal faith.

Let us consider a few of these alleged inconsistencies. Eminent scholars and sociologists (such as M. Tarde, to mention the most distinguished) accept the strict applicability of the law of causality to the psychological order of things; yet they firmly defend, in the sociological field, the validity of the conception of responsibility.[1] Others (such as Merkel in Germany) are loyal determinists, and retain the traditional views of the classical school. In regard to the nature of punishment they hold to the notion of penalty and of reparation in the sense of rigid equity for the injury done.[2] More recently Makarewicz[3] in a masterly presentation (in Liszt's Zeitschrift) argues that the supposed antagonism between the classical and the positivist school in matters of criminal law may almost be reduced to a question of words; and that on all practical issues the two are con-

---

[1] See *M. Tarde*, "Philosophie pénale," ch. iii.

[2] See *Merkel*, "Lehrbuch des deutschen Strafrechts," § 28; and *Merkel*, "Vergeltungsidee und Zweckgedanke im Strafrecht" (Strassburg, 1892). On the same subject, consult *Mittelstädt*, "Schuld und Strafe," an essay published in the German review, *Der Gerichtssaal* (Stuttgart), Vol. XLVI, pp. 237, 387, and Vol. XLVII, p. 1; as opposed to Merkel and Mittelstädt, consult the important work of *Liszt*, "Die Deterministischen Gegner der Zweckstrafe," in the *Zeitsch. f. d. ges. Str. W.*, Vol. XIII, p. 325.

[3] *Makarewicz*, "Klassizismus und Positivismus in der Strafrechtswissenschaft" (*Zeitsch. f. d. ges. Str. W.*, 1897, Vol. XVII, p. 590).

verging, and will presently be in accord.[1] Yet the classicists, or "spiritualists," true to the conceptions of freedom and responsibility, admitted extenuating circumstances, and thereupon sponsored an extensive movement in behalf of prison reform, based upon the hope of the moral regeneration of the criminal. Ultimately they were influential in establishing in France the law of parole, which Germany, at least officially, had long resisted, and which certainly is one of the most distinctive measures in accord with the Italian school.

As a dissenting view mention should be made of the French law of 1885 on the deportation of hardened offenders, which considers them as hopeless and proposes the elimination of incorrigibles as a radical law of social defense. These two French laws, it is well to repeat, are but the application in constructive legislation of the platform which defines the position of the new school. On the one hand it proclaims the policy of aiding first offenders to re-establish themselves, and, on the other, the policy of segregating and eliminating such as are criminals by profession or delinquents by nature and psychological condition; that is, it favors liberal concessions for those momentarily led astray and ruthless severity for those fundamentally perverted. Our law of parole realizes liberal concessions for those momentarily led astray; and our law of deportation realizes ruthless severity for those fundamentally perverted. Here we find the very position of the Italian school, but find it applied by the classicists.

From this preliminary survey a very assuring conclusion emerges. In Germany there are determinists and orthodox

---

[1] See analogous views in the study of *M. Cuche*, "De la possibilité pour l'école classique d'organiser la répression pénale en dehors de libre arbitre" (*Annales de l'université de Grenoble*, Vol. IX, 1897, p. 509, *seq.*).

positivists who uphold the classic conceptions of punishment; and in France there are idealists or "spiritualists" — if not in a philosophic yet in a religious sense, as loyal to creed — who do not hesitate to go far in the direction of the proposed reforms. However it is to be interpreted, this concession serves to break down the barriers of philosophical systems, and to establish a common interest in the field alike of justice and of the needs of society.

§ 8. The Origin of the Classic School

We may now proceed to explain briefly the position of what is called the classic school, — the traditional school to which is due the French Penal Code; but before doing so it will be well to show its origins and approach it through a brief history of its teachings. How did this purely judicial conception of punishment and its application originate? By what evolution of ideas did it proceed? It has resulted in a view of the criminal act as an abstraction, — as a sort of algebraic quantity independent of the personality of the offender, — and in a view of punishment as something to be determined by the external circumstances of the act, without consideration of the nature of the personality of the human being whose fate is involved. This conception, which the rational spirit of the early nineteenth century viewed with pride, the present century is likely to regard as astounding; particularly in view of the fact that it is the rationalists who are abandoning it, and the "spiritualists" who are anxious to retain it as the motto of their philosophical faith. Let us proceed to consider the origin of this position, the historical evolution which resulted in the artificial and fictitious constructions of criminal law.[1]

---

[1] The tendency of criminal law towards the individualization of punishment has advanced since 1898. It appears in the writings of *Prins*, "Science

§ 8]   THE STATEMENT OF THE PROBLEM   19

pénale et droit positif" (1889); and in the volume of *M. Cuche*, "Traité de science et législation pénitentiaires" (1905). Attention should likewise be called to an English volume of great practical interest, which is directly inspired by the idea of individualization: "Criminals and Crime," by *Sir Robert Anderson* (London, 1907). In addition, in the proceedings of the Congrès de l'Union internationale du droit penal, see the discussions at the meeting at St. Petersburg, 1902, particularly the address of *M. Garraud*, on the "Tendances contemporaines de la science du droit pénal" (*Bulletin de l'Un. inter. de droit pénal*, Vol. 11). For legislation, see the new Norwegian Penal Code, in effect from January 1, 1904 (Paris, Rousseau, 1903); and its important preface by *M. Garçon*. It may be mentioned in this connection that a Swiss Penal Code is proposed looking toward a revision, and of date 1903 (Avant-projet de Code pénal suisse, June, 1903, Berne, Stoempflé). Since then there has been still another; but the new text has not yet been published.

An analogous reactionary movement against abstract formulæ and the purely syllogistic spirit is clearly indicated in the civil law. I refer to the newer legal interpretations, which, since the publication of *M. Gény's* "Méthode d'interprétation et Sources en droit privé positif" (1899), is making headway. For several articles inspired by the new point of view see the "Livre du centennaire du Code civil" (Vol. I). On the entire movement consult *Paul Van der Eycken*, "Méthode positive de l'interprétation juridique" (Alcan, 1907).

Of interest are several articles which appeared (1908 and 1909) in the *Revue de métaphysique et de morale*, notably two articles by *M. Mallieux*, "La méthode des juris-consultes (July, 1907); and "Le rôle de l'expérience dans les raisonnements des juris-consultes (November, 1907); also an article by *M. Meynial*, "Du rôle de la logique dans la formation scientifique du droit" (March, 1908).

I add a reference to the new *Revue de psychologie sociale*, first issued in June, 1907, and which, as the title indicates, deals with the problems of civil and criminal law in the spirit here characterized.

In regard to the contrast frequently referred to in this chapter, between "Vergeltungsstrafe" and "Zweckstrafe," see the pamphlet of *Reinhard Frank*, "Vergeltungsstrafe und Schutzstrafe"; "Die Lehre Lombrosos": zwei Vorträge (Tübingen, Mohr, 1908).

CHAPTER II

THE HISTORY OF PUNISHMENT [1]

§ 9. Introductory: Private and Communal Punishment.
§ 10. Primitive Punishment as Penalty and as Expiation: the Wergild.
§ 11. The Growth of Communal Interests and Social Consciousness: the Religious Factor.
§ 12. Early Views of Objective Crime and Subjective Criminality.
§ 13. Responsibility, Freedom of the Will, and Sin, as determining Crime.
§ 14. The Analysis of the Grounds of Punishment; Responsibility in Ecclesiastical Law.
§ 15. Consequences of the Older Position: its Contrast with the Modern View.
§ 16. Early Types of Individualization.
§ 17. The Discretionary Power of the Judge, and Individualization.
§ 18. The Protection of the Social Interests.
§ 19. The Classical and the Historical Position.

§ 9. Introductory: Private and Communal Punishment

THE history of the theory and practice of punishment has never been adequately presented; only its objective study has been undertaken. The history of ideas is elusive; some find embodiment in definite systems, and these alone attract attention. Yet systems but reflect the outer aspect of historical growth; they mark the beginning or the end of an epoch; they form a synthesis that sums up a movement, or, as in the case of Rousseau's "Social Contract," an initiative that begins one. Apart from this, systems

---

[1] In this connection see the article by *M. Durkheim*, "Deux lois de l'évolution pénale" (in the *Année sociologique*, Vol. IV, 1895–1900, p. 65, *seq.*). On the history of criminal procedure consult the classic work of *M. Esmein*, "Histoire de la procédure criminelle en France," [translated by Mr. Simpson, in the Continental Legal History Series (Boston: Little, Brown, and Co., 1912)].

§ 9]   THE HISTORY OF PUNISHMENT   21

have value only as individual statements; similarly, the history of society is shaped by popular conceptions; and these, in turn, arise from facts rather than from doctrines. They are vague, superficial, and confused; and however unconsciously maintained, they are efficient. They are at once forces in the making and in operation. It is just when their influence is most active that they are least tangible. When ready for formulation their development is often at an end. Therein lies the difficulty of writing the history of doctrines or of intellectual movements.

These explanations are necessary to excuse the inevitable shortcomings of the presentation which is to follow; and particularly to advise the reader in regard to the scope of the present task. Only a general outline, itself summary in character, is attempted, with the view of setting in relief certain conceptions which are necessary to the understanding of the modern movement. Such an historical sketch may first attempt to trace the origins of criminal law in reference to our own civilization, and the traits that have characterized it from its first appearance. It includes as well some account of current conceptions and accepted formulæ, — an account possibly subject to correction, in that the whole is foreshortened in perspective.

The statement is commonly made and accepted that criminal law began as private vengeance. That which in primitive societies took the place of what we now call public opinion was not enlisted to avenge crimes against individuals, for these did not concern the collective security of the primitive social group. Every individual had the right to defend himself and to take vengeance when attacked. Such private vengeance was conducted as warfare; the one injured took up arms against his foe. The duel is such a primitive form of penal right. The conception of penalty and censure is as absent from the primitive system of punishment as it is absent in the case of the duel as now practiced; for the duel is unaffected by the character of the aggressor or by the criminal status, either legal or social, of the act which was the cause of the affair.

There followed a period in which the conception of communal peace began gradually to emerge; and in consequence private wars came to be considered as an interference with public peace. The communal interest interposed and induced the contestants to put down their arms and agree upon a price to be paid; the proceeding was to all intents an enforced treaty of peace. As private war became less common it advanced in dignity. Instead of being the right of all free men, it became a privilege of certain special classes, such as the great barons of feudal times. But we have not yet reached this period.

At the outset such issues were in the nature of private amicable treaties; but if the contestants could not reach an understanding, the people, when they felt that they had the power, set the price which the offender was to pay to the offended, according to the nature of the offense. Such payments, which were abstract quantitative values, to be translated into the media of exchange in use at the several economic stages of history, were fixed according to the social status of the parties concerned. Later, under the influence of altered customs and contact with the Roman Empire, such payments were fixed according to what might be called the social worth of the injured party, by which was understood the position held by him; and particularly by his status in relation to the tribal chief, the "rex" or king.[1] The sum represented the worth of the man who had been killed or

---

[1] This relation is clearly set forth by *Sohm*, in his able volume: "Die Fränkische Reich- und Gerichtsverfassung."

wounded, and was accordingly called the value of a man, — Wergild.

§ 10. Primitive Punishment as Penalty and as Expiation: the Wergild

Such was criminal law at its first appearance. It was a wholly objective penal law in that the substitute for punishment, the Wergild, was a fixed sum to be paid, independently of all personal considerations. If these early instances show a first attempt at individualization, it was made in behalf of the victim and not at all of the offender. So far as either was considered, it was the person injured. According to the class to which he belonged, or, later, according to the position which he held, the price to be paid varied. The personality of the offender was not considered. So, while the evil done might vary according to the social position of the victim, the appraisal of the injury did not vary with the personality of the author of the crime. Clearly a penal law of this type was wholly objective.

But though sanctioned by law the punishment was still of a purely private character. The punishment was the private vengeance taken upon the victim. Public interest did not interfere but remained neutral. There was set in operation for the benefit of the injured party a modified application of the law of retaliation. Punishment in its public aspect had not yet appeared, but was still regulated as between individuals. Such is the accepted interpretation.

Possibly this account of private vengeance, accurate enough in outline, fails to suggest the complexity of the several points involved or to make clear the sociological and legal nature of punishment at its first historical appearance. It appears merely as an outcome of private war; its social character remains obscure. But to say that there was no public punishment would be a mistake. From the very outset, punishment had a twofold social character.[1] A point apt to be forgotten is that along with the Wergild as a private punishment, there were public expiations for acts such as treason, that threatened the security of the tribe. The most complete accounts available of the system of Wergild refer to the Germans, and date back to the sixth and seventh centuries. Tacitus, describing German customs of the second century, records public punishments pronounced in assembly of the tribe, for treason or for failure of military duty.[2] This is the first point; and the second is that the Wergild, which is ordinarily considered to have been a purely private punishment, was, if liberally construed, a social punishment. It should not be forgotten that in primitive times the conception of the State did not exist. The tribe was not considered as constituting a political bond except for purposes of war. It was the family-clan, rather than the tribe, that most closely corresponded to the social organism, and therefore to a political society.[3] In regard to its own members the clan exercised a punitive justice, similar to that later exercised within the company of vassals.[4] Thus what formerly constituted the Wergild

[1] On the social origins of punishment see *M. Durkheim*, "Division du travail social," p. 96, *seq*.

[2] *Tacitus*, "De Morib. German," XII.

[3] *Brunner*, "Deutsche Rechtsgeschichte," I, § 13; *Lippert*, "Die Geschichte der Familie," III, § 1; *Post*, "Die Geschlechtsgenossenschaft der Urzeit," chaps. i and vi; *Ibid.*, "Die Grundlagen des Rechts und die Grundzüge seiner Entwickelungsgeschichte," §§ 46 and 47; *Ibid.*, "Bausteine für eine allgemeine Rechtswissenschaft," Vol. I, chap. iv; *Bernhöft*, "Staat und Recht der römischen Königszeit," § 37, *seq*.

See also *Kovalevsky*, "Tableau des origines et de l'évolution de la famille et de la propriété"; and *Fustel de Coulanges*, "La Cité antique."

[4] On this question and the issues involved consult the study of *M. Beaudouin*, "La Recommandation et la Justice seigneuriale" (in the *Annales de l'Enseignement supérieur de Grenoble*, Vol. I, 1889), p. 35, *seq*.

§ 10   THE HISTORY OF PUNISHMENT   25

became a ransom offered by one clan to another and ceased to be the punishment of one individual for the benefit of another. It became the cost of a settlement, the price of a transaction of war between two clans.

Thus from the beginning punishment appears to have taken on a social rather than an individual aspect. It was a social reaction against forces hostile to the welfare of the communal life; it was punishment within the group, — an internal punishment. But it was at the same time a defense against the enemies without, — an external punishment, if one may so term it. When the clans united in tribes, external punishment, while retaining its character as an incident of war, was yet more organically assimilated to the conception of punishment, for the reason that the community was regarded as having recognized and legalized it under the form of Wergild.

Wherever society was organized into groups, whether of the family, the clan, or the tribe, we find these two forms of punishment, — the punishment as a protection against those outside the group, and the punishment as an expiation with reference to those within the group. When these groups, without losing their identity, formed alliances, the two aspects of punishment were combined while yet retaining their distinct functions. Protection, expulsion, expiation, — these form the three sociological functions of punishment present in every society. Individual life requires a means of self-protection, and communal life the right of expulsion.

From the beginning punishment presents a sociological aspect and takes the form of a routine legal procedure. Some authorities regard it as a necessary outcome of social interaction. It must however be recognized that primitive punishment, which we look upon as external, while yet retaining the aspect of an incident of war, is in the nature of a negotiation and is thus a contract vigorously enforced. In the punishment provided by the Germanic common law, — as, for example, in the Salic law, — the legal penalty approaches the status of a civil obligation.

It is plain that there is no sense of indignation against the offender. The sense of culpability, as it appears later, is likewise not present ; or at all events, it is not expressed as a feeling that carries an ethical implication. In a society of warriors where violence prevailed, what we characterize as crime was not considered something abhorrent or detestable, especially as applied to deeds of violence. Whoever was worsted or taken had to pay the conventional price, quite as though it were an individual affair, a matter of private law. It is not however the legal form of contract in its relation to private law that needs to be touched upon; that has been done to the neglect of other aspects.

§ 11. The Growth of Communal Interests and Social Consciousness: the Religious Factor

But even where the Wergild and external punishment prevailed, the conception of public right gained ground; and judicial procedures of a somewhat different character began to appear. For example, the sense of indignation and public condemnation, which is an early index of the sentiment of culpability, appears with reference to theft and there serves as a needed protection. This was true particularly of covert theft, accomplished by a cowardly ruse,[1] and to other situations no longer approved among primitive peoples, whose customs, however brutal, are yet compatible with a fairly developed morality. The conception of a public penalty appears wherever the prevailing system

[1] *Van Schwinderem*, "Esquisse du droit pénal actuel," Vol. II, p. 219, with references (note 3).

sanctions the division of the fine between the victim and the community. In the interests of the community the "Fredus" was a compensation for the disturbance of peace and public welfare.[1] But later these relations assume a very different aspect under the influence of Roman law, which transferred all cases of disturbance interfering with the public peace to the jurisdiction of the baron, who replaced the former provincial governor. This parallelism in Merovingian France of two forms of justice side by side is well set forth by M. Fustel de Coulanges.[2] The one was legal in form, and proceeded according to tradition and common law, and was administered democratically through courts of petty juries who awarded the Wergild according to the law; the other procedure was ignored by the law, but was almost the only one described by contemporary writers. It lay outside the administrative and legal pale, and was exercised by the authority of barons and other royal functionaries, whose decisions commonly resulted in prompt executions. But at this stage we have left the "Wergild" and are approaching the public punishment as practiced by the Romans; we are entering upon a new stage of development where new influences appear.

Yet the ensuing changes would not so readily have been accepted had they not accorded with the established practices and traditions. It seems strange that the conception of public expiation should be of Roman origin. In fact we

[1] Concerning the Fredus and the legal organization in the Frankish period, consult *Sohm*, cited above, § 6; and *Brunner*, cited above, I, § 21. Also *Esmein*, "Cours élémentaire d'histoire du droit français," 1907. — *Glasson*, "Histoire du droit et des institutions de la France," Vol. III, chaps. vii and viii; and *Viollet*, "Histoire des institutions politiques," I, p. 307.

[2] *Fustel de Coulanges*, "La Monarchie franque," chaps. xiii and xiv; also *Beaudouin*, "La participation des hommes libres au jugement dans le droit franc"; also *Esmein, Glasson*, and *Viollet*, in the works cited above.

find it in internal punishment as it affects the clan or the tribe. All that is new is the extension of this aspect of punishment, which is at once social and legal, to situations that were originally regarded as having only an individual bearing. The first encroachment upon private punishment was the "Fredus," the setting aside of the indemnity due to the State. Then the private punishment wholly disappeared in a transformed procedure in which the punishment was inflicted not after the manner of a settlement between two contesting clans, but as an indemnity imposed by the tribe acting as an internal police; it thus assumed the status of an internal punishment. From the same circumstances — the passing of the private injury and its evolution into a public offense — there resulted the dual system of punishment. Originally distinct, the two now begin to merge. The public punishment persists with the essential traits of a private punishment, and thus reflects the older, purely objective relations of clan to clan; presently it becomes nothing more than a civil indemnity added to the indemnity to the State. The treatment of punishment as internal gains ground, and carries with it a public expiation,[1] which however is as old as society itself. Doubtless primitive punishment within the group, clan, or tribe was called into play by the natural evolution of the social consciousness. Yet the community administered it according to legal forms. To condemn a traitor within the fold was a very different matter from killing an enemy in war.[2]

[1] *Tarde*, "Les transformations du droit," chap. i.
[2] The evidence points to the fact that in the primitive period (in the phase which *Gumplowicz* calls syngenetism) crimes within the fold, among members of the same social group, were extremely uncommon. In so far as these were private offenses, they aroused a feeling of astonishment and pity, rather than a communal protest. For this reason, when the protest appeared, it was likely at first to assume a religious and later a legal aspect.

The infliction of the punishment becomes a sort of religious ceremony. It is solemnized by formalities, sanctioned by law and ritual, imposing one ceremony for the verdict, and another for its execution. An assembly of the tribe is summoned for the imposition of the punishment; thereupon the execution takes place according to established rites after the manner of an expiatory sacrifice. It is in fact a sacrifice offered to the gods of the tribe; the victim is not an enemy to be put to death, but one to be immolated to satisfy the demands of the gods. The tribe does not claim the right to kill for the sake of killing; to appease the vengeance of the gods is the excuse for the immolation. It may then be stated, once for all, as a general principle of social psychology, that societies act only by virtue of natural and necessary laws. But these social needs in some way lead to actions voluntary in appearance; they come forward and reach expression as idealized feelings, at first religious, and later logical. Every social organism demands the expulsion or destruction of its internal enemies, but when society kills it has no consciousness or intent of doing so in execution of a law of its own making; its intent is to carry out an act of social or divine justice. The individual has a direct consciousness of his instinctive needs; the community has only a vague consciousness of its logical needs. What the individual feels the community reaches by reflection. The combined individual needs irresistibly compel communities to action. But practical action requires a rational justification. When men unite in a common purpose they mass their instincts, but what they present to one another are arguments; and therein lies at once the value and the danger of the individual. Conduct is due to impulse but takes cover under the sense of justice. Interest determines, but honor alone is mentioned. This social solidarity is a terrible force ; but it is also a notable tribute to the intrinsic power of the human mind.

Such is the explanation of the twofold aspect of primitive punishment. While fundamentally the expression of a direct animal impulse, it comes to consciousness as an obligation to an ideal. The culprit is appraised in terms of his crime; he is looked upon in terms of the evil that he has done, the perfidy realized. But his punishment is referred to a higher source and ascribed to an outraged divinity. He is delivered to the vengeance not of the people but of the gods ; it is they who demand an expiation, and the people offer it. Primitive punishment is thus a composite of religious observances and legal forms, and not primarily a measure of protection. It is a penalty imposed for the evil done, compensating the injury of the transgression by the punishment of the transgressor.

§ 12. **Early Views of Objective Crime and Subjective Criminality**

From its first appearance, punishment presents the inherent and persistent contrast between the conception of it as a penalty, and as a means to an end. The penalty is for the evil done; the end is that of intimidation, of preventing evil in the future. This distinction, in its present more scientific formulation, constitutes the actual antithesis between the classic and the modern school. As a social phenomenon it dates back to the beginnings of history, where it appears not as an antagonism but as a fusion of the two attitudes.[1]

[1] On the system of the Wergild and of private vengeance see in addition to authors cited above, *Kohler*, "Shakespeare vor dem Forum der Jurisprudenz," p. 119, *seq.*; *Günther*, "Die Idee der Wiedervergeltung," I, p. 162, *seq.*; *Löffler*, "Die Schuldformen des Strafrechts," §§ 1 and 2; *Thonissen*, "L'organisation judiciare, le droit pénal et la procédure pénale de la loi salique"; and *Schröder*, "Lehrbuch der deutschen Rechtsgeschichte," § 36.

In primitive times penal law was unquestionably objective; it considered only the deed done, while ignoring the personality of the agent. It was primarily the injury suffered that was to be praised. But this objective aspect of the repressive function of punishment carries a very different significance from that now attached to it. It is not alone that individualization is as yet absent, there is equally absent the conception of moral culpability. No account whatever is taken of what are now referred to as extenuating circumstances; and there is no implication that the will is to blame or that any kind of moral obliquity is involved. Consequences alone are considered. A personal or social transgression has occurred and demands reparation; a penalty must be imposed, no matter whether or not the agent is morally to blame. Material damage has been done; the perpetrator must be punished.

If the injury is a personal one, the injured party need not consider whether or not his enemy acted intentionally. The law offers him a price in requital, the Wergild, which he may properly claim. If the injury is a public one, the community seeks reparation; that is, the gods desire an expiation. The evil done requires its victim. Details of intent are not considered or analyzed. To be the material author of an act itself implies moral accountability for one's actions.

All this has been generally recognized in reference to the Wergild. The system of the Wergild may be described as one that takes no account of responsibility. It is true that certain records give the impression, in reference to public punishments, that the intention of the culprit was really considered. This may have been the case; at all events there is at present a tendency to believe that in primitive times greater importance was attached to the conception of blame and responsibility than has hitherto been allowed.

But this is not the place to enter into the details of this controversy.[1] There are certain accounts which consider the matter of the intent with an emphasis that suggests an innovation; they introduce the conception of the will in terms that show it to have been a recent advance. There is commonly cited an edict of Charlemagne that provides for the case of an unintentional crime. It provides not that the punishment is to be omitted but that it is to be diminished.[2] This would indicate that the principle previously practiced imposed the full penalty in all cases, even in unintentional crime. For there could be no more emphatic indication that liability to punishment is independent of moral culpability than by imposing it even in the absence of intent. But why the diminution of punishment? The crime, though unintentional and accidental, is not the less punishable; the lack of intent does not constitute an excuse. Even in the ecclesiastical law, which is committed to the recognition of the will and consequently of sin, there are some traces of the distinction introduced by Charlemagne, — that of a diminished punishment for an unintentional act.[3] Clearly this distinction carries some new meaning. It refers to offenses due to negligence, which are contrasted with intentional offenses; and the former do not exclude responsibility, because such lack of forethought is itself a fault of the will. The early accounts clearly show the bearing of the distinction; the advance consists in the introduction of the principle of diminishing the punishment and it is a reaction against the neglect of all distinctions, against the application of the full penalty in all cases, whether the crime was intentional or accidental. This indicates that previously the intent had

---

[1] *Brunner*, cited above, II, § 125; and *Löffler*, cited above, I, p. 118.
[2] "Capitulare missorum" (819), c. 15 (edit. Boretius, I, p. 290).
[3] *Löffler*, cited above, p. 138.

been a negligible factor. The conception of moral fault had not entered and was not made a factor of the criminal act. For the crime was determined solely by its material consequences and not by its psychological causes.

Primitive penal law had not yet developed the conception of moral sin; responsibility, in the modern sense, was foreign to its spirit. This was natural in a state of society not very different from that of wandering tribes, such as existed among our ancestors after the Germanic invasions in the sixth and seventh centuries. What we call crime carried with it no dishonor in the society of that period, least of all murder. It was a normal incident, for a state of war and pillage prevailed. To attack others and to defend oneself were among the everyday incidents of life, consequent upon unrestraint.

There was, of course, the price to be paid to the family of the victim ; and this fine was fixed in advance. The offender realized his liability. If he committed a murder, he knew in advance what he would have to pay for it. The Wergild determined the cost of the adventure; so much for murder, so much for a broken leg, or arm. This was the hazard of unrestraint.

Such objective penal law, in which responsibility has no place, becomes a penal law based upon the notion of taking one's chances. This point should be carefully noted, for whenever penal law returns to an objective attitude, this theory of taking one's chances tends to reappear ; it still prevails in the minds of professional criminals. They choose an occupation that involves risks, and they realize the risk which they incur. If they steal, they pay for it, as a debt, by so many months of imprisonment. Society appears as a creditor to whom a debt is due.

With the debt paid one may begin anew; the score is canceled.[1]

Whether this description applies to the Salic law or to the laws of our day is not an idle question. Our laws, and those who apply them, emphasize the hazard of transgression, as well as its corollary, the debt to be paid, which determines the prisoner's fate. They see to it that this is firmly fixed in the minds of the offenders; they apply it to the man who appears in court for the first time, and who feels the full force of the instrument of justice to which he is made to submit; they apply it to him who, upon his first transgression, inevitably passes from the defendant's seat to a prisoner's cell, and who, in due time, will leave it with fixed habits and the conviction that he must give an account of himself.

This conception is older than modern civilization; its revival is due to the influence of modern dogmatic tradition. In its origin it was shaped by direct contact with crude situations; it was revived as an abstract construction that proceeded independently and in neglect of the facts. It is well to note its source and its historical position. It flourished in periods of barbarism and in times of violence. The principle which it involved may be simply stated: Punishment is the hazard of unrestraint.

§ 13. Responsibility, Freedom of the Will, and Sin, as determining Crime

Such was the position of primitive law, and such will be that of punitive law wherever it emphasizes the objective side of crime. Let us now take a step in advance and consider the status of modern civilization with reference to a criminal law based upon responsibility. The question arises

[1] See the interesting observations drawn from the confessions of a noted criminal, reported by *Sir Robert Anderson*, in "Criminals and Crime" (London, 1907), p. 8.

§ 13] THE HISTORY OF PUNISHMENT 35

whether the conception of responsibility was introduced by Christianity and the ecclesiastical law, or by Roman law.[1] It seems necessary to distinguish between the popular and the scientific conception of responsibility. The notion of a deliberate transgression for which the individual is responsible forms the basis of what in Christianity becomes the origin and support of the doctrine to which it leads, the conception of sin. Though the Greek and Roman philosophers were acquainted with this conception before Christianity, it was through the latter that the conception of moral responsibility was disseminated and entered the minds of men, to spiritualize the notion of transgression. Yet the conception of responsibility thus formed had but a popular status. It spread like a notion familiarly appreciated and recognized but not as yet analyzed, clearly defined, or scientifically determined.

This conception of responsibility, which, though vague, had an active hold upon the mind, must not be confused with what the idealistic philosophy of a later day advanced as the doctrine of free will. From the beginning of Christianity the question of the freedom of the will has been a perplexing one. But the controversy was waged within the sphere not of the law but of theology and religion in struggling with the Christian dogmas of grace, divine election, and predestination. Contradictory statements may be found. The Gospels contain passages expressing views such as sociology now upholds. There is particularly the oft-cited passage declaring that a corrupt tree will produce only evil fruit, and that the good tree will ever bring forth good fruit.[2]

[1] See particularly *Günther*, cited above, I, p. 263, *seq.*; *Löffler*, cited above, p. 136, *seq.*; *Hinschius*, "Kirchenrecht," Vol. IV, p. 691, *seq.*, Vol. V, § 342, p. 916, *seq.*; *Engelmann*, "Die Schuldlehre der Postglossatoren," 1895.

[2] *St. Matthew* vii, 16; xii, 33; *St. Luke* vi, 43. Consult *Merkel*," Vergeltungsidee und Zweckgedanke im Strafrecht," p. 56.

The conduct of men is determined by the entire mental and moral character. We do not observe in each act as it presents itself the entrance of an impartial and indifferent personality choosing freely between two issues at stake. In any given situation the action that eventually ensues has its origin in the character of the man and is in a measure due to his temperament. There are indeed states of mind that are themselves the result of freedom; but it is not easy to maintain that there are free acts.

Yet modern statistical and sociological conclusions go little farther than the above citation from the Gospels. The statement of St. Paul is more positive;[1] and the position of St. Augustine in regard to the conflict between freedom and grace is familiar.[2] For what avails man, and what can he accomplish unaided? Can he effect aught without grace, can he achieve personal merit? These were the problems and the difficulties mentioned by St. Paul, and to these the efforts of theology were directed. It but added a further mystery when the antithesis was accepted of a belief in moral freedom co-ordinately with the belief that man of himself cannot achieve worth or power. The antithesis remains insoluble. It becomes a mystery which theology alone can adequately solve. However, despite the mystery and the difficulty, or even impossibility, of reconciling these views, the

[1] The *Epistle to the Romans*, vii, 19, *seq.*; all of chapter viii; ix, 14, *seq.* Consult A. *Sabatier*, "L'apôtre Paul" (second edition), pp. 178–183. In verification of certain statements, consult (on the doctrine of St. Paul) the following: *Wernle*, "Der Christ und die Sünde bei Paulus" (Freiburg, Mohr, 1897); and *Bartmann*, "S. Paulus und S. Jacobus über die Rechtfertigung" (Freiburg, Herder, 1896).

[2] A brief summary of the teachings of St. Augustine on this point are found in M. *Hatzfeld's* "Saint Augustin" (Paris, 1897), chap. i, p. 95, *seq.*

It is familiar that Luther and Calvin, and later Jansen, based their somewhat similar views of predestination upon an inadequate and too literal interpretation of certain of these passages of St. Paul and St. Augustine.

conclusion was not drawn that this effacement of human personality involved a denial of responsibility. No one doubted that man was a responsible being, — clearly not St. Paul or St. Augustine; and still less was this the attitude of the Gospels.

Thus through the ecclesiastical law the conception of responsibility began to prevail in the domain of criminal law, and with it arose the subjective attitude. While previously the law recognized only the injury to the individual or society — that is, the material crime in its direct relation — the ecclesiastical law looked to the soul of the man who had committed the crime. In its own language, its concern was the soul that had sinned, that was to be healed, purified, and regenerated through expiation and punishment.[1]

The conception of penalty persists but in a purified form, and is transformed into an expiation. Both the word and the idea are ancient and had their origin in the sacrifices offered to appease the gods. But the newer type of expiation presented other aspects. Expiation was not offered as a useless suffering to an inaccessible or implacable divinity, who might find therein a sort of cruel satisfaction. It became the sign of an effective repentance and made the repentance real.

Punishment is thus transformed and returns to its point of origin in God. Of the several theories accounting for the origin of the right to punish, none is more respectful of the dignity and freedom of man than this, unless it be its extreme opposite, the positive doctrine. For here, as elsewhere, it may truly be said that extremes meet. The right to punish belongs to God alone; it is not delegated to man. No man, except by divine delegation, has power over the liberty or the life of another; not even society has this

[1] *Pellizari*, "Il delitto e la scienza moderna" (1896), p. 441.

power. Even the positive school holds that society does not punish but only protects its own interests.[1] The same expression occurs constantly. No one man, and no human community, has sway over the human conscience or the right to judge it. Punishment is more than the exercise of control and authority of one man over another; it is an attempt to invade the human conscience, to exercise judgment upon personality, and, in virtue of this judgment of a man's conscience, to dispose of his life and liberty. In this sense man has no judge but God. So the ecclesiastical law holds; and while the positive school does not expressly say so, it implies as much, for, of all philosophical systems accounting for the right to punish, the view just set forth would alone be compatible with its conclusions. It is the only view that from the positivist position may be considered scientific. On the other hand the system that makes light of human dignity and is incompatible with individual freedom is the liberal position. There are no principles nor axioms, nothing in the doctrines of liberalism or of rationalism, that can invest society with the right to punish and legitimize the exercise thereof. In this issue philosophy is helpless; sociology by holding to realities of life has solved half the problem. It regards punishment as required by actual conditions, as a natural law, as a reflex action of the organism. To advance beyond this point the positive doctrine must find its complement in the ecclesiastical law. This, surprising as it may seem, is not impossible, because, in considering the situation as a whole and fundamentally, such fusion is not incompatible with the consideration of

---

[1] Observe the combination of these ideas in *M. Haracourt's* couplet:
"The right to punish for God alone is meant,
We dare not punish, only future woe prevent."
Revue de Paris, January 15, 1898, p. 311.

the facts, which belong to science alone, nor with that of faith, which belongs to religion alone. Ecclesiastical law had no need to make such distinctions nor to resolve such contradictions, because it was scarcely aware of them. It was satisfied with the contention that punishment belongs to society only through divine delegation.

§ 14. **The Analysis of the Grounds of Punishment; Responsibility in Ecclesiastical Law**

While punishment thus reverts to the highest possible source for its origin, at the same time it undergoes a thorough transformation. The subjective nature of the agent becomes commanding. The modern conception of a subjective criminal law is already wholly contained in the ecclesiastical law, not merely in germ but also in its application. It was applied by the officers of the ecclesiastical court, who were the justices of the church. It was introduced likewise in the practice of civil justice, and possibly with a somewhat unfortunate result.[1] It has been advanced that the admission of responsibility was but a pretext to protect the introduction of torture. Though this seems probable, it was clearly not the only consideration, for the whole matter was very complex, and other decisive factors entered. Punishment required proofs, not alone of the facts but of guilt. Accordingly witnesses were appealed to; and as ordinarily the guilty were not willing to confess, so long at least as they could plead innocence, recourse was had to torture to establish their guilt, both as to the deed and the intent.

Even before the advent of Roman law the subjective attitude was assumed, and the Scholastics applied their methods of definition and logical deduction to questions of responsibility. This does not mean that those concerned

[1] *Wahlberg,* "Das Princip der Individualisirung," pp. 3–4.

with crime, whether belonging to the clergy or to the laity, considered in detail the freedom of the will in penal questions.[1] The question of free will was considered as a theological one in its relation to grace, and it was asked: what avails the human will compared with divine grace?

In criminal law an act of volition was considered a responsible act.[2] The question was not put whether this act

[1] Engelmann, "Die Schuldlehre der Postglossatoren," p. 12, seq.

[2] To obtain the view point of the Middle Ages upon free will the important chapter devoted to it in the "Summa" of *Thomas Aquinas* should be read. Quæst. 83 (Œuvres complètes, édit. Parm., 1852, I, p. 325); also "Comment. in secund. libr. Sentent. Lombardi," 2. D. 24, quæst. 1. There the views of certain scholars, such as St. Bernard, who regard freedom as a condition of mind rather than as a motive force, are discussed and refuted in the usual scholastic fashion. This was the well-known problem of whether the free will was to be considered as a "habitus" or as a "potentia." Thomas Aquinas holds to the latter position, yet he identifies freedom with volition (see the "Summa," passage cited) and even with judgment (see the "Sententia," passage cited).

With reference to the very different question of free will and grace, the trend of the school of Thomas Aquinas is familiar, and the position taken directly opposed to that assumed by the Molinists. This question is very distinct from that of the existence and nature of free will, considered as a natural human faculty, apart from the spiritual realm and the expression of the spiritual life. It serves however to illuminate precisely, though indirectly, the notion of freedom entertained by theology, and the possibility of its acceptance of the psychological mechanism disclosed by scientific observation, without abandoning its essential postulates in the realm of faith. For theology must admit a determinism of divine origin. Such is the opinion of the majority of theologians, and especially of the Thomists. Possibly some reservation should be made in regard to the Molinists; but the difference in question pertains less to the basis of the problem than to the mode of interpreting the premises. The difficulty of reconciling a belief in freedom and responsibility with a supernatural determinism is no more serious than that involved in its reconciliation with a natural and psychological determinism. If freedom is compatible with the one, why should it not be with the other? And its compatibility may lie in the consideration of free will as the counterpart of the self, as an expression of the ego in its relation with the supernatural life, conceived as the means of adjusting the spiritual personality to the service of its physiological conditions. Freedom thus becomes a state of a free spiritual life. It may similarly be conceived, apart from the question of supernatural intervention, as a state of free spiritual

§ 14] THE HISTORY OF PUNISHMENT 41

of volition was predetermined or not, whether or not it was conditioned by a series of psychological antecedents, which left no place for the entrance of any motive unrelated to the dominant one. The position may be expressed by such an equation as that an act of will is equivalent to a free act and consequently to a responsible act.

The discussion considers the application of the formula rather than its basis and justification. Thus Thomas Aquinas takes up in detail the question of determining the purpose to which the will must have been directed in order that the deed shall be punishable.[1] For example, a person plans and wills an act which in itself is a crime, such as paying

---

activity, whereby the personality reflects its worth, and in complete independence of the inner life develops its vital initiative. This argument does not imply that scholastic theology thus clearly viewed its problems. It is intended only to set forth what would not be in marked contradiction with its position. I am well aware that the theologians have tried to reconcile the fact of divine determinism with that of human freedom, by ascribing a transcendence to the former; that is, by the avowal of an inherent mystery, which is tantamount to dispensing with all explanation. Yet they do not have recourse to the same privilege in regard to the reconciliation of freedom with a psychological determinism. Wherever psychological realities are considered, there is no mystery; for it is urged that one must hold to the one attitude or the other. But this I am not at all prepared to admit. The state of freedom, in respect of an universal determinism, is a metaphysical fact, quite as mysterious as that of predestination or divine foreknowledge; and the mystery accepted in the supernatural order is not more difficult to admit in the metaphysical order of things.

One may further consider the important passages in St. Bernard, to which reference has been made, and his peculiar view of freedom as a state of mind capable of arousing the acts to which it gives rise and so determining conduct that every action becomes an act of freedom, provided that it goes back to the initial source, which is a state of psychological freedom. He defines freedom thus: "Est enim habitus animi, liber sui." See *St. Bernard*, "De gratia et libero arbitrio tractatus," chaps. i and ii (Patrolog. Migne, v. CLXXXII, 1002). For an admirable review of the teachings of Thomas Aquinas and St. Bernard on the freedom of the will consult *M. Fonsegrive*, "Essai sur le libre arbitre" (second edition, Alcan, 1896).

[1] On these points and for the pertinent citations consult *Löffler*, as above, p. 158, *seq.*

some one for striking down his enemy. But the agent exceeds his instructions, and in the excitement of the struggle unintentionally kills his victim. Shall the instigator of the assault be responsible for the murder which he has neither planned nor desired? A similar question arises in case of drunkenness; for example, as when a man who transgresses by consenting to drink (a failing in itself), and then loses his head and commits a crime of which he had no previous intent. Such questions still arise, and have been under consideration since the days of Thomas Aquinas. Likewise other common questions of the present time are clearly anticipated, such as indirect or contingent liability.[1] We thus see how the problem of responsibility was considered. The question at issue was not to determine whether the will that initiated the act would have been capable, not in general but in this special incident, to refrain from willing and to resist the impulse or motive that inspired it; the question was solely to determine whether the forethought and intent of the act involved the consequences of the undertaking; attention was directed to the objective end and but little to its primary cause.

§ 15. Consequences of the Older Position: its Contrast with the Modern View

A further consequence of the subjective position is this: that, as will is equivalent to responsibility, so responsibility must vary with the intent, and thus directly with the objective gravity of the crime. There is no analysis of the intrinsic nature of the will considered abstractly and independently of the act; such analysis would involve an observational psychology which was hardly known to the

[1] On this question of contingent liability see the thesis of *M. Raoul Duval* (Paris, 1900).

metaphysics of the day. Every act of will, in so far as it is directed to a specified action, is of a like nature and quality; what changes is the purpose to which it is directed. The more the purpose implies an objective criminality, the greater the blame for the intent. Thus the subjective criminality of the agent is determined by the objective criminality of the deed. The one is the measure of the other, and as only that which is objective and accessible can be measured and determined, it was sufficient to gauge the criminality of the crime by the act itself. As such, it was a matter for legal statutes, for the law to determine; for the law alone is qualified to appraise the social status of conduct. The conclusion is thus easily reached that as the crime becomes objectively serious the responsibility increases. Every detail of the act is thus considered as intentional and the agent is held responsible for every circumstance aggravating his crime. It follows that in every crime committed the responsibility varies for every offender; and it varies not by reason of a difference of nature and psychological temperament but by reason of the difference of situation in every individual crime. The responsibility varies because in no two crimes are the outward circumstances precisely alike.

There is accordingly a place for the entrance of individualization in judicial practice, though clearly for a very different type of individualization from that now urged. What we of to-day propose is an individualization of punishment determined by the temperament of the agent and by the prospects of his return to a virtuous life, and most of all by the degree of his professional criminality. Such questions were not considered in the older literature. Learned scholars did not deign to consider them; they were too much occupied with theoretical principles and absolute formulæ. The science of that day left application to current practice; and it is worth noting that, as exercised by certain ecclesiastical judges — under the influence of the subjective attitude which forms the spirit of the church — the practice quite commonly took the form of a modern individualization. The ecclesiastical court exercised a disciplinary jurisdiction that made direct appeal to the conscience, and through such control aimed to produce a spiritual reform, — not, like political justice, seeking to avenge society for the wrong done and fixing its attention upon the offense without consideration of the individual. Such practical discipline, however, was not the subject matter of the writers; it was part of experience and not of law.

It is familiar that, according to the view which is as old as Scholasticism and closely associated with it, the first principle of the law is to ignore the facts of life. Apart from certain ecclesiastical or disciplinary jurisdictions in which punishment for reform was uppermost, the prevalent conception of punishment was that of setting an example; the end was not the reform of the individual but general intimidation. Hence the judge, exercising considerable freedom and untrammeled by the law, proportioned the punishment in each case to the requirements of the policy to be furthered; and the purposes of general public policy are very different from those of the sociological treatment of criminals as now attempted.

§ 16. Early Types of Individualization

Accordingly, in principle there was no subjective individualization based upon the nature of the agent and independent of the crime committed. What we find is an individualization based upon the crime but detached from the legal forms and the abstract conception of crime in order to keep close to the actual details and to reproduce their physiognomy, as it were, in the execution of the punishment. The punishment became the reaction, the recoil of the act as realized in its setting and as interpreted by the courts commissioned to avenge the body social for assaults made upon it.

Even in this attitude there may be observed two types of individualization. The one relates solely to the strength of the intent; that is, to the intrinsic qualities of the will, assuming that the will at the moment of action was more or less free to resist the temptation. It aims to appraise the state of mind of the agent; yet it does so not with reference to his true and real qualities, which form the basis of character, as in the modern conception, but according to the degree of intent of the act committed. The modern view would consider equally the examination of the abnormal state of the criminal, and thereby determine the possibilities of resistance. There would be an estimate of the degree of freedom at the moment of action in relation to the act itself; yet not an estimate of the personality as a whole, but of so much of it as participated in the act committed. There would be an attempt simply to gauge the measure of freedom inherent in the crime; and this would still be an individualization in terms of the crime committed, but considered with reference to the will of the individual. For it is clear that the greater or less strength of the intention embodied in the crime influences its gravity and the degree of emotional indignation which it arouses. It thus would become an individualization based upon the degree of responsibility. The ancient law however did not recognize it as such, at least not officially; nor is it thus found in the texts or in the commentators. Legally, every intentional act necessarily involved a like responsibility; for volition was regarded as identical with responsibility; and there was no recognition of partial responsibility.

The second type of individualization as recognized by ancient law was that derived from the material circumstances of the crime. For example, no one murder is exactly like another. There enter into consideration the fact of premeditation or the dominance of a momentary impulse ; the personal relations to the victim; the end in the pursuit of which the crime was committed; the greater or less cruelty attending it; and many other circumstances. Obviously among these circumstances some relate to the intent and others to the material setting of the crime; the former constitute an individualization based upon the degree of responsibility. This distinction and th s psychological analysis however had not yet appeared. Even when the question of the subjective circumstances was raised (such as premeditation), it was not the degree of freedom that was considered, but the manner of the execution of the crime and the greater or less degree of cruelty and unconcern which it disclosed. Attention was directed wholly to the material circumstances of the crime; and these varied with its accessory details. It was according to these details that the punishment was modified and individually adjusted. It was a purely objective individualization; though, for each individual case it was determined wholly with reference to the material setting of the crime.

Such individualization was admitted and fully practiced in ancient law.[1] The judge had full power to adjust the punishment according to the gravity of the offense, not the legal, but the actual gravity; and in the determination of the penalty he was not bound by the law. The punishment could be regulated with reference to each action and in proportion to the gravity of each particular crime. There was

[1] See *Jousse*, "Traité de la justice criminelle," first part, III (edit. Paris, 1771), p. 36, *seq.*; and *Imbert*, "Pratique judiciaire," Book III, chap. xx.

not one prescribed punishment for murder and another for theft; there were merely certain traditional punishments sanctioned by usage. From this repository of traditional punishments the judge selected the one suitable to the special case, and he was permitted (though it must be understood that this was exceptional, and rested solely with the judge), in case the list of ordinary legal punishments did not provide a punishment suitable to the crime, to impose one more fitting and better adjusted to the case, under the name of an extraordinary punishment. It is difficult to conceive a system of judicial individualization more elastic and more closely conforming to present conceptions of a true criminal economics. The system has been called that of discretionary punishment ("peines arbitraires"). And as the law did not lay down regulations instructing the judge as to his decisions, he might very well take the modern point of view, which classifies by criminals and not by crimes, and individualize the punishment accordingly. If ordinarily the individualization exercised was an objective one, it was because the subjective type did not conform to the views of the day, and, indeed, had not yet been suggested. Otherwise nothing in the law would have prevented the judge of the old régime from anticipating Lombroso and the position of the Italian school.

§ 17. The Discretionary Power of the Judge, and Individualization

In maintaining that ancient law had no legal punishments in the modern sense of the word, — that is, punishments specified by the law for designated crimes, — we follow the accepted opinion. Ancient law was unaware of our modern principle: "nulla pœna, nullum crimen sine lege." There were however certain legal texts that fixed definite punishments as a penalty for crimes of intent that carried a special criminal status; they appear in common law, and particularly in the Royal Ordinances. In this connection it is well to have in mind wherein consisted the free discretion of the judge.

Let us take an edict carrying a perfectly definite punishment for a definite crime; for example, the edict of Louis XIV with reference to poisoning. Even in such cases the judge was not bound by the letter of the law. He could mitigate the punishment, though this was rarely done, but particularly he could increase it and exceed the punishment prescribed by the law, and if the punishment in question was that of death, he could impose a more cruel torture to apportion the punishment to the gravity of the crime.

In this system of discretionary penalties, in which not alone the execution of the punishment but the determination of the penalty itself is left to the free discretion of the judge, we have, as already noted, a system of judicial individualization in the large sense of the word. It was not an arbitrary procedure, but in principle and practice was based upon an obvious fact, which may be thus stated: the law cannot anticipate the punishment best suited to each particular case; it can only set a scale of offenses indicating the status of the several crimes as they affect the social welfare, and with reference to the danger to which society is exposed through each class of crime. But the law cannot foresee the impression produced by any individual crime as committed; and so the judge alone is in a position properly to determine at once the severity and the nature of the punishment. Briefly, the law is unable to anticipate the mitigating or aggravating circumstances of the case, **and thus commits these to the charge of the judge.**

§ 18. The Protection of the Social Interests

In a system of this kind the judge stands for the protection of society. The judiciary power becomes not merely the executive of the law but the coadjutor of the law in its chief function, that of providing public security. This becomes a function of the judiciary institution rather than of legal determination. The law in itself is powerless to effect this, because the requirements of social protection vary for every crime and for every criminal. The social gravity of the offense cannot be determined in advance. The law may very well say that murder in itself is more serious than theft because the lives of citizens are more precious than their belongings; but how can it anticipate the gravity of each particular murder? In fact, all that the law can do is to set the relative scale of values of the interests protected by punishment; for punishment has no other material end. It has, however, a specific purpose, which is to prevent the repetition of crime. The penalty provides a formal protection; and this protection is directed in behalf of social values, of interests that have a social value for the individual: his life, his property, his honor. This is Liszt's theory of the "Rechtsgüter."[1] From a social and legal point of view the law serves merely to appraise the relative values of the interests protected by punishment. But to anticipate the relation of the punishment to a particular crime committed is manifestly impossible. The law can only indicate that life should be more strongly protected than property. But to conclude in the abstract and as a psychological conclusion that a murderer is more criminal than a thief and is so in all cases, is an assumption that may readily prove

[1] *Liszt*, "Lehrbuch des deutschen Strafrechts" (edit. 1905), § 12; see *Ihering*, "Der Zweck im Recht," Vol. I (second edit.), p. 492; *Binding*, "Die Normen" (edit. 1890), § 50, p. 338.

to be absurd. In ancient law the judge had the authority to punish a murderer no differently than a thief; and especially could he apply to theft punishments ordinarily reserved for murder. Such was the province of justice.

If, in a measure, punishment is the protest of public sentiment and the expression of social reproof, it is not possible to anticipate the emotion and the feeling of indignation aroused, and to take account thereof in the application of punishment in each particular crime. If the judge is to become the interpreter of communal justice, he alone can judge the social disturbance occasioned by one crime or another. The judge becomes, in fact, the trustee of public security, and in ancient law he played the part according to his lights. It is hardly necessary to recall the spirit in which he undertook the task and applied the individualization of punishment with which he was charged. Bailiffs, wardens, courts of final jurisdiction, and appellate courts rivalled one another in the zeal and in the severity — not to use a stronger expression — of the choice of punishments and their application. The policy of a judicial individualization entrusted the social defense to the body of judges; it placed it in good hands. The France of those good old days did not have the problem of the habitual criminal; and this is hardly surprising, when one remembers that in those days criminals were hanged for their first theft. Such severity, not to say barbarity, of practice may profitably be recalled in order to understand the spirit of the penal system that had its origin in the Revolution and in the codification made during the Empire; or, more correctly expressed, that was due to the classic spirit which they reflected, the psychology of which Taine has recorded in his memorable pages.[1]

[1] *Taine*, "L'ancien régime," Book III.

§ 19. The Classical and the Historical Position

It has been agreed to call this purely objective penal system the classic theory, — not in the traditional sense, but in conformity with the spirit of abstract and logical generalization, characteristic of intellectual activity in France for at least two centuries. Against such classicism a reaction has appeared, affecting all realms of thought; to it the works of Taine and of the historical school have influentially contributed. But in fairness it should be pointed out how far the origins of the classic theory form its justification. It arose at a time when history had not yet become, as it is now, a scientific study, but was looked upon as an unalterable record, despotic and austere. The present historical school is wholly opposed to any such view. It favors evolution and progress, and rejects the conception of history as the crystallization of facts. The classic position in turn was the issue of a protest against the subjective system, which made it possible for the judge to wreak personal vengeance for the slightest transgression.[1]

As is true of political parties, the pendulum swings from one policy to another. Accordingly let us be careful not to substitute for the classic system, which has had its day, a "subjectivism" that would make it possible for a judge to sentence to the gallows for slight offenses, or to secure immunity or confinement in an asylum for capital crimes. History gives no support to a rigid fatalism. It is a living determinism in which we form the decisive factors. It is for us to direct the course of history towards the welfare of the social life and the progress of humanity.

[1] *A. Esmein*, "Précis élémentaire de l'Histoire du droit français de 1789 à 1814" (Paris, 1908), p. 250, *seq.*

CHAPTER III

THE CLASSIC SCHOOL

§ 20. The Eighteenth Century Philosophy of Crime.
§ 21. Modifications and Concessions of Later Codes.
§ 22. Advantages and Defects of the Classic System.
§ 23. The Reaction and the Neo-Classic Transition.

§ 20. The Eighteenth Century Philosophy of Crime

THE preceding historical survey prepares the way for a review of the classic doctrine. If we are justified in taking a harsh view of this system, it is by reason of its present consequences and not by any lack of justification in the past. What is conventionally known as the classic system of punishment is the direct issue of the philosophical school and of the principles of Rousseau's "Social Contract." Its most distinguished representatives are Beccaria in Italy, Bentham in England, and Feuerbach in Germany. It was inevitable that the general intellectual movement of the eighteenth century should include a consideration of penal law, and of the arbitrary and cruel practices that then characterized it. The immediate and urgent need was to abolish the arbitrary power of the judge and to mitigate the severity of punishments. In spirit and expression ancient law favored severe and arbitrary punishments along with all the abuses to which they led. Accordingly the first measures of reform were directed in a practical spirit against the prevalent system of punishments. Yet the school of eighteenth century thinkers was primarily one of doctrinaires and theorists.

They could not conceive of practical reform unrelated to a philosophical basis.

However, before abolishing arbitrary forms of punishment, the philosophers of the eighteenth century stopped to inquire as to the nature of punishment and the origin of the right to punish. The latter problem, simply disposed of by history and sociology as an inherent right of society, was in reality a perplexing philosophical issue; and particularly for those who withdrew from the individualistic position of Rousseau [1] and the Encyclopedists. To claim the right of vengeance for society is to return to savagery and places society on a par with the victor who puts his prisoners to death; to base the right on the ground of an expiation through punishment is to assume the position of religious dogmatism. The only other ground for justification of punishment is its deterrent effect — to make the punishment of the guilty serve to intimidate those tempted to imitate their example, — a general or collective prevention, as the Germans say.

By what right does society bring to bear upon the offender such collective prevention as proceeds by depriving him of liberty or of life? In a system founded upon inalienable personal rights, shall the State have authority over life and liberty? Rousseau would reply that this could not be done unless a citizen had forfeited his right to liberty, or even to life, by reason of an attempt against the welfare of the community, — a position involving the theory of the "social compact." The right to punish comes to society by way of a contract, and may be exercised only within the limits of such presumed contract. Such limits prescribe punish-

---

[1] For Rousseau's political theories and their connection with criminology, see *Liepmann*, "Die Rechtsphilosophie des Jean-Jacques Rousseau" (Berlin, 1898), especially chap. iii.

ments on the basis of equal rights. Any one may be called upon to forfeit his right to liberty, but upon the condition that others do the same. Punishment is thus an enforced exercise of the general will; this, as described by Rousseau, indicates the combined concessions made by individual citizens and thus becomes the expression of law.

Let us return to the primitive theory as embodied in the Salic law. There punishment becomes a right of the individual guaranteed by the law. The right pertains to the injured party, which, in this case, is society. But it is likewise a personal right of the offender, who has the vested right of paying no more than another and of paying the precise rating of the injury, whether by fine or by imprisonment is immaterial. The price becomes a prescribed and invariable forfeit: so much for such and such a crime or transgression.

This system of criminal law obtained at the time of the Revolution. In 1791 the French code, however imperfect in itself, admirably reflected the spirit of the times. Punishments were fixed by law which permitted the judge no discretion to fit them to the crime. Punishments were set in accordance with the code of 1810, but, with the obvious exception of life sentences, presented a maximum and minimum limit, between which the judge might vary and adjust the punishment to the particular circumstances of each offense. In contrast to what obtained in ancient law, the judge's power of sentence could be exercised only between the two set limits. In the system of the penal code of 1791 these limits did not appear. In it punishment was absolutely fixed, as in the Salic law. It was a fixed tariff; for such a grade of theft, so many years in prison or at penal servitude, — in principle, not a day more or less. No account was taken of the circumstances of the deed, nor of the possible provocation, nor of the antecedent situation. All who had committed the same kind of theft were placed upon the same footing. They were regarded as equally responsible. The punishment imposed was the same for all. The judge was no more than a mechanical instrument to administer the punishment; he was the automatic wheel of fate that dealt the punishment as the law prescribed; his sole function was to confirm the evidence of the facts.

This system of penal law was accordingly objective, as was the Salic law. There was however much of the spirit of the penal law of the sixth century that could not be revived. For civilization had progressed and there was a background of Christian conceptions that could not be set aside. The objective equity of the Salic law may be appropriately represented as a system of indemnities to be paid, as a penal law that ignored responsibility. But the Christian spiritual conception of freedom as a personal and psychological possession had never been more exalted. Society had no power to punish by the deprivation of liberty except when such liberty had been voluntarily jeopardized. Punishment could be directed only against a free act. The judge had merely to examine to what extent the agent may have been morally free in his actions.

It was presumed that those guilty of the same crime (theft, murder, etc.) must have been equally free agents and consequently equally responsible. Each crime was assumed to involve a like moral freedom, and to imply a like responsibility. All this corresponded substantially to the conception of the freedom of the will in the traditional philosophy. If freedom is to be considered as the power to decide in each situation by a controlling choice with no intrusion of any other inner impulse, then there can be no such thing as partial freedom. The status of every man in resolving upon the same act is parallel. He has the choice of two courses: to act or to refrain. The responsibility varies not with the measure of freedom but with the gravity of the act in question. It is not the place of the law to consider anything but the social and material seriousness of the crime. All guilty of the same crime present the same responsibility. Hence there is no pertinence in taking into account the agent, no advantage in considering the personality. Ignoring such considerations the deed alone is to be dealt with. That the same responsibility merits the same punishment thus becomes the conclusion of a supposedly spiritual theory of the freedom of the will.

By the exercise of practical reasoning analogous to that expressed in primitive law, the criminals themselves reached about the same position. To them the legal punishment, definitely set by the law, stood as the risk incurred, as the price of the crime. As von Liszt remarks, the penal code becomes the true Magna Charta of the criminal. It is his written constitution; he knows just how far he may venture within the law; and if he brings the arm of the law down upon him, he knows precisely the risk he incurs. The main point is to be a good sport and a good loser, and consider the many successes as against the occasional failure. We are now beginning to recognize that in a situation of this kind the odds of the game do not favor society.

§ 21. Modifications and Concessions of Later Codes

Though the severity of this objective classic theory of the Revolution was tempered in the penal code of 1810, its essential principles underwent no change. But the system of set and invariable punishments was modified. There were introduced, as above noted, variable punishments between the two set limits fixed by the law. But this implied no change of attitude in the classic theory of responsibility. The judge acquired some discretion in setting the punishment, which in appearance suggested the power of individualization; yet this did not imply that the subjective circumstances in terms of responsibility were deemed adequate to modify the punishment for a given crime. Responsibility was determined, as before, by the freedom of the will; and a free will implied the power to choose equally between two courses, which in turn depended upon the motives between which the choice was to be made. But the issue is not predetermined nor definitely conditioned by the motives; it is not regarded as the necessary consequence of a predetermined subjective state, or otherwise than as a supreme act of freedom. The free choice is like an act of sovereign creation, by which the ego in the choice of conduct decides as would an absolute master, unaffected by any imposed pressure. The creative act partakes of the absolute; for the same situation it inevitably remains the same for all. If the will were subject to an extraneous influence it would no longer be free. As soon as any measure of influence by circumstances is admitted, the door is opened for all possible influences, and inevitably admits the extreme supposition of an absolute determinism. There is no middle ground. A partial freedom equally involves determinism.

The variable factor affects only the outward conditions of responsibility, that is, the material circumstances of the act. For even an objective view of crime, as in ancient law, recognized that crimes were never alike; such objective variations the law could not anticipate but committed to the jurisdiction of the judge.

Consequently the penal code of 1810 established not a judicial discretion but a certain elasticity of punishment, by introducing sentences variable between two fixed limits.

It is well to remember that in theory the code of 1810 did not admit extenuating circumstances for crime. The judge had no authority to lower the punishment below the legal limit, or to substitute one punishment for another. In cases in which the law imposed penal servitude for stated periods, the judge could impose from five to twenty years; he could not substitute solitary confinement. Whatever the circumstantial details of the crime may have been, the crime, in terms of its class, and especially of its social gravity, remained the same. If, for example, it was a case of burglary, then the offender had to undergo the punishment for that offense; and in case of murder, this system reached the almost inconceivable conclusion that all murderers were to be subjected to the same degree of punishment. Murder, whatever the circumstances, was liable to penal servitude for life; and, as no extenuating circumstances were considered, all murderers without distinction were given life sentences.

It is evident that the position of the code of 1810 was fundamentally that of 1791 and was purely objective, placing all guilty of the same crime on the same footing. Quite after the manner of the theorists of 1789 who constructed their political system upon the basis of an abstract conception of humanity — a type that had no real existence — the legislators of 1810 established their penal code in terms of the abstract criminal, — an anonymous individual found guilty of a specified crime.

§ 22. Advantages and Defects of the Classic System

This penal system had the great merit of treating all alike and the still more indisputable merit of forming an adequate check against arbitrary sentences. But the equality thus realized may well be considered most unfair in that it treated all men as mere digits. As applied to criminals, this equality in terms of punishment commonly ran the risk of introducing a cruel and intolerable injustice, in that it brought together in perilous promiscuous association those guilty of the same crime, whether they happened to be first offenders, habitual criminals, men blinded by the sudden passion of the moment, thorough degenerates, those unaffected in character by their crime, or those whom the system had thoroughly contaminated and who became the means of corrupting their associates. For all, the punishment was similar or nearly so, and upon this feature the system prided itself. But the equality was only in name, and in its popular appeal; for the equality that justice demands is an equality of treatment for the same established degree of criminality. But how can one establish any comparison between the insensitiveness of the recidivist, hardened to prison life, a total stranger to the exciting emotions of a first sentence, and the keen impressionability of the first offender upon contact with his cruel and humiliating fate; or between a vagrant, whose self-esteem is unaffected by punishment save in the small measure of character that he may have saved from the general wreck and ruin of his career, and a man of social station whose position is involved in proportion to the consideration he enjoyed; or, once more, between one accustomed to the amenities of life, for whom the prison routine must be intolerable, and the poor fellow without food and shelter who has come to look upon jails and even the penitentiaries as dispensers of hospitality, offering an assured living and a shelter for the unemployed.

The sole virtue of the system — and though it has no other it may be conceded that it accomplishes this perfectly, — lies in its elimination of arbitrary sentences. In every case for the same crime punishment is prescribed by the law. The judge has no power to alter it; he has no occasion to probe the consciences nor examine the hearts of those whom he sentences. The mental condition at the moment of the crime is not considered. A crime has been committed; there is an injury to be made good towards society and the law. The reparation is fixed by the law ; it must be paid in the same terms for all cases, and regulated not by the hardship which the punishment imposes upon the individual but by the measure of injury which the crime has inflicted upon society. The injury to an individual or to society remains the same, independently of the agent. The punishment is an indemnity and the criminal charge approaches the status of a civil injury. Both are based upon the idea of damage, and both result in a reparation corresponding to the injury done, without involving the consideration of the personality of the doer. The careless man, who, in passing, breaks a show-window must pay its full value whatever may be his resources. This is a trifle to the man of wealth, while it considerably embarrasses a poor man, dependent upon a small income. The same principle is applied to criminal offenses that give evidence of a vicious disposition. When the vicious refuse to meet the demands of social life, they pay like anybody else; only they pay in the coin of imprisonment. But the nature of the debt is not determined by that of the debtor. Whether the latter feels the injury to his honor or to his future, and in what degree, society does not consider. The theory is notably false, inhuman, and supremely unjust, but obviously simple and easy to apply. Here is an injury to be repaired, and there a punishment that will make it good. It resolves itself into a question of penalty and reparation, a question of the proportionality between the ill which the offender has caused and the ill he is to undergo. This proportionality expresses the summary and harsh conception of punishment and the undeveloped conception of justice which it reflects. It is at once barbaric and crude, to say nothing of its being the most dangerous theory for society; and it is so, because, though it attempts to make criminals pay for their debts, it does not succeed in preventing them from contracting new and equally irresponsible ones.

§ 23. The Reaction and the Neo-Classic Transition

However this may be, such was the system; and it may be summarized in this formula: the punishment for the same crime should be the same, because the responsibility is the same. As a system recognizing responsibility in its objective aspects alone, it considers only the material injury inflicted and in no measure the state of mind of the transgressor.

At every point this artificial and abstract construction runs counter to the facts of life. It sets up abstractions and constructions of a wholly logical and ideal type, while in practice criminal law must deal with concrete realities. Ultimately, practice must make or mar every system. As a consequence a neo-classic theory is coming to the front, which, without abandoning the classic position and while taking its stand upon the same data, is yet proposing to transform and revolutionize the legal structure of the penal code. It is developing apart from the law and even in opposition to it. It is proceeding under the influence of the facts primarily, but also under the inspiration of a new school, properly called the eclectic school. In a measure it reflects the accredited traditional position; yet it contributes a new insight growing out of the increased emphasis of the subjective aspects of the problem of crime, and contributes as well to the complementary problem of social protection. A similar emphasis is placed upon conditions and their investigation, which in turn is a creditable characteristic of the French school. It proceeds directly to conclusions without succumbing to the attraction of theories, and keeps to its practical task without the minute discussions of the purpose of punishment, which appear in the German writers.

The movement presents a distinct revival of interest. But the neo-classic theory is as yet only an abstract in outline of a future construction; the detailed features have still to be brought together and shaped to a system. This must be borne in mind in considering, as is next to be done, this newer doctrine. It presents a position sufficiently definite and clear-cut in its larger features, yet it is quite variously developed according to the personally favored views of its several loyal adherents, each of whom seems to bring forward a new and different shade of opinion. Indeed, if attention were to be confined to these several dissensions and reservations, the movement [1] would seem to dissolve into a fictitious unity without any practical reality. What follows may serve to correct such impression.

[1] Its most distinguished representative is Rossi. Its adherents include distinguished university professors, such as M. Ortolan. The school is further represented by such brilliant exponents as *M. Garraud* (see his Précis du droit criminel, Paris, 1906), whose able writings are deservedly popular. The perspective of the data and conclusions is well set forth in the works of *M. Joly*. It is the inspiration of the work of the *Société générale des prisons*. It is also finding its way into academic instruction, such as the courses given in Paris by *M. Leveillé;* and is represented by the contributions of the representatives of the higher education, — *M. Le Poittevin, M. Garçon,* and *M. Garraud.* See also the account of the new modern judicial school — as it calls itself — in the study of *Ugo Conti,* "Il delinquente nel diritto criminale," in the *Archivio giuridico,* Vol. LII (1894). p. 266, *seq.*

CHAPTER IV

The Neo-Classic School and Individualization based upon Responsibility

§ 24. The Assumption of Free Will: the Fallacy involved.
§ 25. Empirical Conditions of Freedom: Premeditation.
§ 26. Potential and Actual Freedom: Applications.
§ 27. The Social Regulation of Conduct.
§ 28. Responsibility proportioned to the Degree of Freedom; Irresponsibility and its Establishment.
§ 29. The Basis of Mitigation and of Exemption from Punishment.
§ 30. The Individualization thus resulting; Practical and Theoretical Objections.
§ 31. Remote and Immediate Responsibility.
§ 32. The Social Responsibility for Crime.
§ 33. Motives and the Impressionism of Juries.
§ 34. Individualization resulting from the Variable Attitude of Juries.

§ 24. The Assumption of Free Will: the Fallacy involved

In common with developing systems the new movement in penology presents two aspects; the one mainly destructive, and the other constructive. It is likewise natural in the evolution of a doctrine that it should proceed upon the criticism of existing institutions.

Let us consider the critical side. The classic system, though apparently simple, as soon as it enters the field of application, finds itself directly in conflict with two irresistible forces, public opinion and science. It is in conflict with the former because the classic penal system inexorably places every one upon the same footing, treating alike those who may claim attention and sympathy, and those who excite aversion. It is in conflict with science because it is based on a supposition at variance with established truth,— the supposition that every man in the same situation enjoys a like freedom of action. In this issue popular justice, which judges the man in preference to his act, is in full accord with the justice of equity; for the summary justice that disregards distinctions and allows no concessions violates the common instincts of humanity and charity. Men of science, philosophers, physicians, and jurists alike refuse to accept this antiquated view. They are almost unanimous in refusing to admit that a like freedom of action obtains under like conditions, or that a crime is to be considered only in terms of its outward character and the gravity of the offense, and not in terms of the degree of inner conflict which had first to be overcome. A distinct change is observable in the conception of responsibility and an approach is made to an individualization based thereupon; it appears as well in theory as in practice, in the exposition of principles and in the attitude of juries.

A new epoch is approaching, marking a development or rather a disintegration of the older classic position. This disintegration is significant and is demanded by the logic of events. The older classic school rested upon a fiction which consisted in believing that in regard to the same act every man had a like freedom of action; the newer view replaces it by a truth. The older position was based on two assumptions: the first, the belief that every one who realized the nature of his acts was necessarily free, for every willed action was regarded as a free act; the second, the belief that freedom existed to a like extent for all men with reference to the same act. If such were really the case, if for all persons there were operative identical factors of equal value and degree, there would be no need to consider the individual. He might as well be eliminated from the penal equation, — just as in an algebraic equation, equal quantities on the two sides may be cancelled.

But can the freedom of the will be so simply conceived? Let us consider the first assumption, that every willed act is a free act. The formula may be accepted in the sense in which the "spiritualists" maintain that every voluntary act emanates from a being capable of exercising freedom. But this statement must not be confused with the classic formula of the French penal law which held that every voluntary act was a free act. Volition and freedom are not to be made identical. To posit these as the two terms of an equation is wholly false.

The fallacy enters because a possible state of affairs is confused with the situation that actually is realized. As a possibility the deed accomplished may be considered as on a par with the alternative of restraint. A man fires a gun at another; we know that to fire or not to fire are like possibilities. We conclude that the murderer was well able to realize the alternatives, to act or to refrain. If we believe thereby to have proven that he was as free to act in the one way as in the other, and thus to have established the freedom of his will, we are relying upon an argument that clearly is fallacious. The fallacy consists in substituting a general and abstract situation for a special and concrete one. It is true that man abstractly considered enjoys the potential power to realize an act or to refrain therefrom. But does this prove that a particular man at a particular juncture of his career enjoyed the moral freedom to determine his conduct? This we cannot know. It is as though one were to say that a horse when unrestrained may go forward or backward; he has the same control, the same possibility of either movement. If he goes forward, does it follow that he has chosen one alternative rather than the other? Does it follow that, as a free moral agent, he has made a free choice? The situation may really have been like that of Buridan's ass placed between two bundles of hay. The creature exhibits little if any hesitation. Hunger decides; and a physiological instinct determines the reaction. He begins with either of the two bundles that happens to be the more convenient, or, it may be, with the one that he happened to see when a strong impulse urged him to feed; and all without a moment's hesitation. The human situation is commonly solved in like manner.

There arises the ready and cogent objection that the animal has no consciousness of his acts, and accordingly that there can be no question of freedom when the idea of choice does not enter the mind. Freedom involves the power to anticipate one course or another, and the power to represent possible alternatives; but in particular it involves the consciousness of one's freedom. Now this is precisely the human prerogative; man foresees, mentally reflects upon his intention, has the consciousness of freedom, of the power to choose one course or another. The consciousness of self-determination involves the power to act, as is preferred, in one direction or in its opposite.[1] Moreover, if in accord with the determinist position and the results of physiological experiment, the mechanical impulse to action depends upon the cerebral intensity of the thought, then the presence of the ability to realize the future, to have in mind appropriate images and ideas, is adequate to establish the presence of freedom. It becomes the power to distinguish between right and wrong.[2]

[1] *Fonsegrive*, cited above, p. 93, *seq.*, p. 113.
[2] The equivalence of the two was assumed by the code of 1810. It appears, or is suggested so long ago as in the "Sententiæ" of *Peter Lombard*, and in the "Commentaries" of *Thomas Aquinas*. See also above, p. 40, note 2.

In this argument there is at once a subtle confusion to disentangle and a distinction to be drawn. Is freedom as realized an intellectual process? If so, then the intensity of the thought determines the freedom. This would be a deterministic position, provided that it be established that the will is effective in the realm of ideas rather than in that of action. But it is just this that may be questioned. May it not be, on the contrary (approaching the thesis of M. Fouillée in his "Determinism" and in his "Insistent Ideas"), that the knowledge of our freedom makes us masters of our will, and free agents? But this, in turn, is but one aspect of a psychological determinism in that it makes freedom at once the cause and the effect of the idea of freedom. With this reservation we turn to the statement that freedom of the will consists in the idea of being free; it is man's consciousness of his own freedom. To have the consciousness of being a free agent is all that is necessary to realize one's freedom. This ideal aspect of freedom acts upon the will as an independent motive, and is summarized in the expression: It is my will because I wish it so. The thought of setting the will to act itself determines the will; and, likewise, the consciousness of possessing freedom exempts us from dependence upon merely instinctive impulses or physiological forces.

Approaching the question from this direction, and admitting the philosophical validity thereof and admitting likewise that the consciousness which we have of our own freedom is an effective force which in a measure makes real the freedom itself, does it follow, when the question is shifted to the practical field of penal law — which alone is here to be considered — that every one in relation to a given act has experienced such adequate consciousness of his freedom?

§ 25. Empirical Conditions of Freedom ; Premeditation

That every man in a general and abstract way feels himself free is a simple and undeniable fact of consciousness; but it is far from clear that in the presence of a particular situation this consciousness is aroused strongly and clearly enough and with sufficient vividness to induce reflection and hesitation. There are certain spontaneous and instinctive situations, as well as acts of impulse and habits that take place automatically; there are manifestations of the intimate self that reach expression not only without arousing a consciousness of the freedom to act otherwise but even without the thought of a different action entering at all. Shall we speak of freedom when the idea of choice has not been present, when of two possible issues only one is inherent in our nature, and, indeed, is imposed upon it, without the possibility of its opposite coming to mind? And is not this the case with all excitable, intense, and sympathetic natures, commonly described as emotional but more properly called passionate?

The question for the moment does not concern those inner conflicts and hesitations that are weighed one against the other; such belong to the state of doubt. There are persons so spontaneous in action, so impulsive in feeling, with ready convictions on all subjects, that they do not experience such hesitations. Indeed, in regard to acts performed instinctively, in which there is not the least suggestion of a possibility of acting otherwise, this applies to all of us. Let us consider the hypothesis, which is both probable and often realized, that there are actions — and this refers to other than spontaneous and instinctive acts— that we have duly willed, which are alone present to consciousness, and in which the state of mind does not entertain the contrary issue. This then may be said to have been the serious mistake of our classic penal law, — the acceptance of a premeditated and deliberate act as a distinctively free act, — for thus, as affecting certain crimes such as murder, premeditation became in its penal aspect an aggravating circumstance of the crime. Premeditation implied that the agent had prepared, considered, reflected, devised, and confirmed the decision of the will. Take the case of a man possessed by a fixed idea, who is moving toward the type of crime which we call crimes of passion. The more irresistible, blind, absorbing and all-pervading the obsession becomes, the more the will becomes cold, calculating, patient, and contemplative. There is nothing more calm, more premeditated, and more deliberate than the obsession of suicide or than the passionate obsession of certain murderers, but at the same time there is nothing less free, if we understand by freedom the ability to withdraw from the fixed idea, — the consciousness of control and of the obligation to act otherwise. Premeditation is a sign neither of freedom nor of moral responsibility; it is more commonly a sign of obsession, or of innate perversion, and therefore a sign of temperamental taint. It may also be a symptom of the formidability (*la temibilità* in the Italian phrase) of the individual. Possibly the penal code of 1810 anticipated the applications of the Italian school; if so, it may be credited with having done so unintentionally. It is not proper to conclude that premeditation is a fair criterion of responsibility as based upon the presence of freedom. In speaking of actions that do not involve the conscious presence of the idea of freedom we should have in mind premeditated, possibly even enforced acts, and not mainly spontaneous actions.[1]

[1] On the question of premeditation see the excellent work of *Alimena*, "La Premeditazione," especially the second part relating to the psychology of premeditation, p. 79 and p. 116, *seq.* Also consult the thesis of *M. Legrand*, "De la Préméditation (Paris, 1898), p. 35, *seq.*

§ 26. Potential and Actual Freedom; Applications

The conclusion that emerges from this discussion — that freedom is a potential quality of our nature — is a conviction capable of logical defense. The illusion, or better, the indefensible fiction, consists in supposing that such freedom is realized in each actual situation as a profound and intimate motive force that serves as an intermediary between the will and the external world. It is undeniable, even for the most normal and well-regulated mind, that in regard to many actions, including crimes, this potential freedom (which is not questioned) does not exist as a real and available motive, acting independently and contributing the decisive impulse. This of itself demonstrates that the fundamental assumption of our classic penal law that every willed act is a free act, or, at least, an act committed in a state of freedom, is false, artificial, and fictitious.

Turning to the second assumption that serves as the foundation of the classic theory, we may examine the position that, inasmuch as freedom is a spontaneous force, unaffected by extraneous influences, every act involves the same measure of freedom. Under this view there is no question of greater or less — one is either free or not. The traditional conception of the freedom of the will inevitably reaches the surprising result that there is no partial freedom, no state of semi-liberty.

Considering freedom as something intelligible, and neglecting the metaphysical obscurity attaching to the concept, it can be nothing else than the inherent ability to resist. As applied to a criminal act, freedom is the power to resist the evil impulse; and this, in turn, is the strength of character that may be appealed to, to oppose the inherent instincts and passions. If this is true, how can it be maintained that the power to resist evil remains the same for every one, or for each individual at all times and for all situations? To put the question is to answer it. It is a fact of consciousness, a common experience, that an act, above the purely automatic and instinctive stage, is often the issue of an apparent hesitation, of a choice implying antagonistic influences and at times fierce conflicts. And these occur precisely and particularly where the consciousness of freedom, and accordingly the sense of duty, is actively present. There come to consciousness the force of impulses and the push of instincts, and opposed thereto, rational considerations. The conflict grows, and the impulses succeed in obscuring the outlook, in suppressing the sense of duty and the sense of freedom; and in the end they overcome the surviving power of resistance, dissipate it into a vague and inert idea, and deprive it of value as a counteracting motive.

This cumulative power of the will depends upon many familiar conditions. It depends upon the state of health or the presence of a pathological factor, quite apart from the question of true mental disorder. To use the accredited expression, there may be a real disorder of the will involving an almost physical incapacity to will. Such aboulia is a common sign of neurasthenia. The status of the will depends upon habit, in short, upon character; and this varies for each individual and for each of the several possible aspects of his personality. It is unnecessary to enlarge upon what is established by common experience.

The revisers of the penal code took account of this relation by introducing punishments variable between fixed limits, and thus adjusting the punishment to the degree of freedom as well as to the objective status of the act. For like reason they attached importance to premeditation;

and in so doing, as above noted, they committed a serious error and followed a false clue. To take premeditation as a basis for the individualization of punishment implies a belief that the measure and degree of intent embodied in an act corresponds to the degree of freedom in the act as realized. This is far from being the case. It really corresponds to the degree of determination that induced the act. It becomes an indication that the act sprang from a powerful resolve that had completely overpowered the agent. The deeper, the more compelling, the more absorbing the resolution, the less it gives way to other influences, the less it yields to advances from without, to any external impressions from the environment. As it proceeds, it grows by what it feeds upon and becomes ever more compelling. It is, or presently becomes, the tyranny of a fixed idea, and constitutes the very reverse of a state of freedom. Nine times out of ten the more an act is premeditated the less will it be free. If the degree of punishment is to be based upon the measure of freedom, then premeditation is the worst of criteria. But whether or not it is a fitting criterion, it is significant of a certain tendency. It proves that the supposition of a like measure of freedom for every identical act, and consequently the supposition of a like responsibility, is quite untenable.

The view that seems likely to prevail substitutes a reality for a fiction; and inasmuch as it must deal with responsibility and hold to some belief in freedom, it builds upon a true responsibility in place of an assumed responsibility. It aims to substitute the realities of experience for purely judicial abstractions; to give fact a place above law, the spirit of observation a place above the legal spirit. We may now proceed to the results developed from these commendable purposes.

§ 27. The Social Regulation of Conduct

But before presenting them it may be well to set in relief the contrast of the two systems. The penal code of 1810 may be said to have been a legal construction in the extreme sense of the word; it was the work of jurists. The chief characteristic of legal constructions is the prominence of straight lines, of abstract regulations, and, consequently, of fictions and formulæ to which living realities are forcibly made to conform.

The law is primarily a social discipline and the foundation of the social order. Now social regulation requires the formulation of certain general limitations to which individuals must submit. From this assumption it necessarily follows that every regulation made for a group of similar cases must be strictly applicable to each of the cases in detail. This, however, is but an assumption, though a necessary one to introduce some measure of order and uniformity in the control of individual freedom. It is an assumption of the same kind as obtains in politics and in constitutional matters; as the right to liberty, the right to equality, and such other rights as the principles of written constitutions provide. These can be applied to particular cases only by way of legal fictions; which means that commonly the application is most imperfect. The classic penal law, following the spirit of social regulation, was a legal construction based wholly upon assumptions and fictions.

It is, however, the case that penal law is of all social sciences the least amenable to a system of fictions and assumptions. Any such system opposes the living realities which protest against the rigidity of formulæ and against their imperfect adjustability to the facts; or rather, against the difficulty of shaping the formulæ to the requirements of individual justice. The same is doubtless more or less true of other departments of the law. Yet elsewhere the system of legal assumption readily yields in special cases to slight personal concessions, which it accepts in the interests of order and the social welfare. It is the cost of the social protection, indeed, of efficient regulation; and such regulation is accepted as a necessary limitation to which all must submit.

Penology no longer concerns itself with enforcing payment for social protection. The question as it affects the individual is very different and vital, — that of determining whether he shall continue to participate in the social life; whether he shall remain in the class of active free citizens, enjoying social rights under the protection of the State; or whether he shall be permanently or temporarily debarred from social privilege. The issue concerns not an incidental disability justified by the interests of society, but the very right to a share in the social life. The issue appears as the choice of one of three possibilities, singly or in combination. There may be a deprivation of life, of liberty, of honor. Such a serious deprivation cannot be demanded in obedience to a mere assumption, cannot be imposed by virtue of a legal fiction. If such punishment is based upon the conception of responsibility, it cannot be applied upon a mere assumption of responsibility; there must be a concrete and definite proof thereof. Accordingly, the personal issues involved in a criminal case differ wholly from the forfeitures or sacrifices at stake in other types of legal issues.

The system of assumptions and fictions should long ago have been recognized as untenable. It is time to replace it by a concrete examination of the facts of the case. The penal code of 1810 was based upon a system of assumed responsibility. The criminal practice that is to be substituted for this legal theory looks to a system of true responsibility, — a responsibility that shall be concretely and individually applied, with due reference to the personality of the offender and the details of the case. It is to replace a general fictitious and abstract responsibility, assumed for one and all by the warrant of the same legal formula. The contrast between the two systems is pronounced: in the written law, responsibility is assumed and fictitious; in the law as applied, it is real and concrete.

§ 28. Responsibility proportioned to the Degree of Freedom; Irresponsibility and its Establishment

Let us now turn to the formulated conclusions. They appeared as a first attempt towards the individualization of punishment based upon the degree of responsibility. The responsibility, in turn, was based upon the conception of freedom; justice required that the punishment should be proportioned to the degree of freedom; and, finally, justice required that the punishment should be entirely omitted where there was no freedom of action. Such is the logical and just position of the neo-classic school. The first application thereof was made by the jury. The latter naturally would not submit to the subtleties of legal assumptions. They might be informed that every man accused of the same crime had a like responsibility and consequently should be given a like punishment. But they were brought face to face with the defendant as he disclosed the details of his life, the impulses to which he was subject, the delusions that distorted his outlook; and the jury recognized that, quite apart from the question of insanity, there may be degrees of freedom, and consequently degrees of responsibility. But having no power to grade the responsibility, since the law made no such provision, they simply found for acquittal. In 1824 with some limitations, and in 1832 in a more general provision, there was introduced a concession to this tendency of juries to recognize extenuating circumstances. The term indicates the purpose in mind. It was not to adjust the punishment to the degree of perversion of the individual, but to the degree of responsibility; that is, to the precise moral status of the act in question. It was an individualization based upon and measured by responsibility.

The penal code considered in the first instance the case of minors. It made the distinction as an individual one and not as the result of a presumption. The exemption of minors was not in deference to a period of presumed irresponsibility in regard to crime, but to a legal incapacity to commit crime, as the phrase goes. Any minor of whatever age, even a young child, may be liable to criminal prosecution. But the question of the presence of normal discretion must be raised, and thereby the question of responsibility becomes an individual one. Modern practice proposes to introduce and apply an analogous procedure in regard to adults.

In the introduction of extenuating circumstances the law entered upon a new and approved path. Recent legislation endorses the position of the neo-classic school. It is not merely that modern codes assign a large place to extenuating circumstances, but that recent tendencies as exhibited in foreign criminal legislation of a later period than the French have introduced conceptions ignored by the older penal codes.

The first of the important innovations affects the status of responsibility. The French penal code assumed that in every adult man of sound mind and normal condition responsibility was the rule. It was assumed to be present in every voluntary act. To this general assumption the only exception was made in behalf of a condition of mental disorder, clearly defined, incompatible with normality and leaving no doubt of the subject's irresponsibility. Accordingly the French penal code admitted no irresponsibility apart from true dementia; and likewise, although this is not definitely stated, apart from such pathological conditions as idiocy or similar mental defects. So long as insanity was not present, the defendant could not plead irresponsibility. As a point of law the plea was not admitted that the defendant, while in possession of his intellectual faculties, had not the exercise of his free will, or that he did not possess sufficient freedom to resist the crime. The assumption of responsibility was suspended only in the presence of a proof of a pathological condition of irresponsibility. One assumption was substituted for another; and the second, like the first, was determined by a pathological test. The point at issue was not to be determined by a psychological opinion but by expert medical testimony; it was a question of the evidence of a pathological mental defect or a state of clearly marked insanity medically attested. Given such a condidition, the assumption of irresponsibility necessarily followed. Inasmuch as a state of abnormality had replaced the normal condition, the one assumption had to give way to the other. From these clear, definite, simple, and direct premises the following conclusions result: every man not insane is responsible; to establish irresponsibility insanity must be proven; there is no middle ground, no intermediate condition. For the French penal code responsibility and irresponsibility are alike states of mind or, if one may say so, potential states of mind. When the pathological condition is once established it determines the psychological status. There is no need of determining it in its bearing upon every special act.

The neo-classic school and the legislation associated therewith abandoned any such simple and legally exact system. They made irresponsibility dependent not alone on the evidence of a state of dementia but upon the evidence of a lack of freedom. The proof of an antecedent pathological state is in itself not sufficient. It is but the preliminary requirement to warrant an examination and a psychological inquiry.[1] Some of the resulting legislative proposals logically, if radically, contended for a psychological criterion alone, requiring unconditionally the evidence of a lack of moral freedom. The consequences of this position were disastrous. It permitted the accused in all cases to plead irresponsibility. There were indeed few cases of crime in which the defendant could not allege a moment of distraction depriving him of true freedom of action. To remedy this defect a twofold or composite criterion was introduced; the further evidence of a pathological state was required to permit the plea of the absence of moral freedom. But it is self-evident that the pathological criterion is not considered sufficient in itself to establish irresponsibility, unless, as in true dementia, the case unmistakably involves a condition that eliminates responsibility. But would a simple brain disorder, provided that it was present before and not merely during the crime, be sufficient to establish irresponsibility? Would it be easy to decide? Obviously the presence to any degree of a pathological disturbance however slight, and yet more obviously, of any neurosis not to say nervousness, should warrant the privilege of an investigation and the possibility of establishing the absence of freedom. But in actual practice this composite principle, despite the assurances which it seems to offer, amounts to a dependence upon

[1] See the scholarly work of *Gretener* on the Preliminary Draft for the Swiss Penal Code; *Gretener*, "Die Zurechnungsfähigkeit als Gesetzgebungsfrage" (Berlin, 1897), § 2, p. 17, *seq*. As germane to Gretener's treatment, and to offset the partisanship which it expresses, it will be well to read the review published by *Zurcher* in the *Revue pénale suisse* (1898), p. 51.

a psychological proof with the abuses and dangers attaching thereto. The physician is really appealed to for an opinion not upon the existence of a mental disorder, which is his proper field, but upon a psychological question, — the compatibility of the abnormal condition with the presence or the degree of legal responsibility. Or again, take the common case in which the physician renders an opinion upon the question of responsibility. The judge invested with superior authority, may in turn review the opinion of the physician. He may thus revise and determine upon other considerations what is fundamentally a psychological issue, depending, however, upon a state of abnormality. Hence there results general confusion of their respective functions.

§ 29. The Basis of Mitigation and of Exemption from Punishment

But what other procedure is available? The question may be consistently answered. If responsibility is based upon freedom, it should necessarily end where freedom of the will ends. Every defendant should have the right to establish that the deed of which he is accused was not a free act. Unquestionably the absence of free will may be proven apart from the existence of true insanity. Hence a concession allowed by many modern legislatures is the admission that the establishment of irresponsibility is an evidence of a lack of free will, and that such evidence is possible apart from cases of true insanity. In dealing with this problem modern legislation was called upon to take a position upon the metaphysical question of free will.

On this issue the French penal code reaches a remarkable conclusion. It assumes free will but does not mention it; it assumes that every adult is responsible for his actions. To suspend this assumption requires the evidence of dementia or of a similar pathological condition. The word "freedom" is not mentioned. The evidence to be furnished relates to matters of medical diagnosis that involve no philosophical or religious convictions. So far the position is clear. The medico-legal expert has to pronounce solely upon the presence or absence of insanity. This lies within his competence. He is not called upon to pronounce upon the freedom of the will; and if he does not believe in free will, no sacrifice of his conviction is involved.

The question of moral freedom is raised in the German penal code, in the laws of the majority of the Swiss cantons, in the draft of the Austrian penal code, and in the Italian penal code. To prove irresponsibility requires the establishment of the absence of freedom. The evidence bears directly upon a psychological question; and the medico-legal expert, summoned to pronounce upon the mental state of the defendant, finds himself, in fact, called upon to solve a question in moral psychology and to decide a philosophical issue. If he does not believe in the freedom of the will, may he not be tempted to decide against responsibility? Following upon the opinion of the physician, the same problem is put to the judge or to the jury; namely, the general problem of the existence of free will and of its special application to the case in question. Under these circumstances the inconsistency of the verdicts of juries is not surprising.

However, such is the result of the new position. The legal evidence no longer turns upon a medical diagnosis, — a relatively simple matter to be established by medical evidence; but it turns upon a question of moral psychology. It presupposes a metaphysical problem, — the question of determining whether the particular act was executed in a condition of moral freedom. The second result of the neoclassic doctrine is the legislative sanction of individualization based upon the degree of responsibility. This is termed the theory of partial or limited responsibility. In view of the treatment of the problem in a later connection, it is sufficient to give a brief summary thereof.[1]

If there are degrees of responsibility it follows that the punishment should vary with the degrees of this subjective factor. If the power to resist evil fluctuates with the psychological condition of the individual, and particularly with that of the brain and the general health, the punishment should reflect the precise status of this subjective condition; the measure of punishment should be regulated according to the degree of responsibility. The principle is clear. The French system relies upon the very considerable elasticity of practice which the recognition of extenuating circumstances permits. A more developed view, more considerate of fine distinctions, points out that the extenuating circumstances cannot be anticipated in the law, and must be left entirely to the discretion of the judge. They refer directly to the incidental circumstances of the crime; to whatever contributed to the issue, — the nature of the act, its motive, and the occasion which provoked it and possibly justified it. All these circumstances are variable and cannot be anticipated; they have no reference to previously existing or acquired traits.

At this point a further distinction enters. There are states of the mind or brain or health that are not accidents of condition and should not be confused with them. Indeed, they are permanent conditions and in themselves restrict and lower the energy of the will and thereby its power to resist evil, without completely suppressing it. Such are the vari-

[1] See the study of *M. Sumien*, "Essai sur la théorie de la responsabilité atténuée de certains criminels," in the *Revue critique de législation et de jurisprudence*, 1897, p. 451, *seq*.

ous forms of neurasthenia, degenerative taint, or cerebral excitement bordering upon monomania in the medical sense of the word. All such conditions lower, in some measure, the capacity to act as a free and responsible agent. They weaken, in some measure, the legal assumption of responsibility. Accordingly the law can and should recognize them as grounds for a legal reduction of punishment. Just as irresponsibility is a legal ground for exemption from punishment, so should semi-responsibility be a legal ground for concession; it should not be merged with the indefinite group of extenuating circumstances. It is a special condition which the law can and should recognize. It should not be confused with the objective extenuating circumstances; indeed, it may occur along with them. The abnormal condition may so combine with the circumstances of the crime as to become a partial provocation, which in itself reduces the objective gravity of the offense. As a part of the variable conditions it should be considered along with the extenuating circumstances. But before applying this ground of extenuation there should in justice be considered a more fundamental factor; namely, the condition of the will, the state of the defendant's mind. He may in that case present two cumulative grounds for indulgence; consequently, he may be entitled to two degrees of extenuation, the one superimposed upon the other. To admit but one, as is the rule in France, is decidedly unjust.

Accordingly, in recent legislations these different types of partial responsibility are recognized as grounds of mitigation by the law, apart from the extenuating circumstances. In practice, as already noted, this amounts to conceding to the jury the right to apply two successive grounds for the mitigation of the punishment: the one by reason of the partial responsibility of the criminal, and the other, if the jury so finds, by reason of the extenuating circumstances. Thus the punishment might be reduced to nothing; and the question arises whether it would not be better to omit the punishment in the first place. A defect in our punitive system is the abuse of short sentences. Punishment should be long enough to act as a reformative measure; otherwise the complete remission of punishment is preferable. Short sentences are long enough to degrade and contaminate, but not long enough to offset the moral evil which the prison breeds. The modern view regards the criminal as even more of a menace than the man suffering from disease or from tendencies to insanity. It would appear that the more dangerous he is, the more promptly is he restored to society.[1] And yet this result seems to follow from an individualization based upon responsibility.

§ 30. The Individualization thus resulting; Practical and Theoretical Objections

The consequences of the new conception of responsibility are clear. If you start from the concrete question of the freedom of the will and determine to what degree a criminal act has been committed in full freedom, you necessarily reach two conclusions: the first, to exempt from punishment when it is established pathologically or psychologically that freedom of the will was absent; and the second, to reduce and lower the punishment when it is established that the defendant exercised only a partial freedom. Though these positions are ignored by the French penal code they have been more or less completely recognized in modern legis-

[1] See the report of *Professor D. von Speyr* at the Swiss Congress of Medical Alienists at Coire, in 1893: "Wie ist die Zurechnungsfähigkeit in einem schweizerischen Strafgesetzbuche zu bestimmen?" published in the *Revue pénale suisse*, 1894, p. 183, *seq.*; and also *Liszt* in the *Zeitsch. f. d. ges. Str. W.*, Vol. XVII, p. 77, *seq.*

lation. Such recognition has been generally regarded as an advance in consistency as well as in justice.

The new system may very properly be termed the neo-classic system. It appears at once as a result and as an application of the earlier classic theories, and again as a reaction against the unyielding rigidity of the classic view. It appears as a natural logical development, because, if responsibility is based upon freedom, it seems absolutely just to gauge the responsibility for an action by the degree of freedom exercised by the one who committed it. But this is a violent reaction from the original severity of the penal code; for there it was assumed that freedom remained ever the same, and required approximately the same punishment for all who committed the same crime. It is against this fiction that the neo-classic school protested; and it should be given the credit for this first attempt scientifically to apply the subjective position to criminology. The neo-classic position is avowedly subjective, advocating the consideration of the individual, taking account of the state of the will at the moment of the crime, and estimating the degree of the culpability of the offender. It marks the recent introduction of the subjective point of view in penology. To find an equally liberal humanitarian justice and one equally solicitous of moral values, we would have to go back to the ecclesiastical law. We are withdrawing from a justice of conformity to the letter of the law to return to a justice of discipline, less controlled by legal formulæ and more considerate of the individual. The crime no longer stands alone; the criminal becomes the chief consideration.

However, this first attempt in subjective criminology will be found quite inadequate. It is open to two serious criticisms in that it involves a practical difficulty and a scientific error.

§ 30]   THE NEO-CLASSIC SCHOOL   85

The practical difficulty is obvious;[1] it is the absence of a criterion to determine the degree of freedom. Every one, even the extreme upholders of the freedom of the will in its traditional form, recognizes that freedom is not the same as the will. An act of volition is different from an act of free election. The will is a mechanical expression of the moral nature shared by all who reason and act; it exists in the insane as in the rest of mankind. The insane man exercises a will, and a reasonable one. He desires and he reasons. What he lacks is fundamental; he objectifies his ideas and builds his reasonings and desires upon a foundation devoid of reality. But apart from this his mental mechanism functions as in any one else. His acts of will are activities similar to those carried out by others; and yet he is not regarded as free. Freedom is not the same as will. The mistake consists in believing that it is possible to determine and measure the will. But if freedom is to be distinguished from will, how shall we find a general standard of freedom?

Freedom is not open to scientific demonstration and proof. How then shall it be graded, even approximately? We may possibly measure the degree of intelligence and the strength of the will; but this is not freedom. Science and observation discover only causes and effects; but the freedom of the will consists in breaking away from the principle of causality. It is a force produced apart from the field of experience. This does not imply that it has no existence. The findings and methods of science set forth that science cannot determine, or discover, or observe freedom; it escapes every device of scientific analysis. Accordingly, the jury in its practical function of gauging this question of freedom and responsibility has no other resource than to follow the example of the law; it holds to the criterion of premeditation,

[1] See the very interesting chapter in "La question de la liberté et la conduite humaine," by *M. Paul Moriaud* (Paris, F. Alcan, 1897), p. 185, *seq.*

and quite generally confuses premeditation with freedom. Far from being the same, the two are commonly opposed.

Yet the argument likely to carry conviction is this:[1] if freedom is the power to resist evil and the ability to act by virtue of such resistive power, it follows that the more a man is perverted and corrupt the less is he free and accountable. If the degree of freedom is to be measured by the power to resist evil, then the criterion can be applied only to the crimes of first offenders, for they alone show the necessary hesitations and conflicts. In such cases it is evident that the agent could really have resisted. Thus the man convicted for the first time becomes the really responsible criminal. If punishment is to be gauged by the degree of freedom, he is the one to be punished mercilessly; for commonly, except under stress of passion, his crime will appear as a free act.

Is it to be supposed, when the hardened and habitual criminal is bent upon theft or even murder, that any thought of the moral significance of his crime enters his mind? The power to resist implies the thought of resistance. But the thought of such resistance is not even present. It has been deadened by habit and lost in the growing degeneracy of the man. The more perverted and hardened a man becomes, the less is any freedom of action perceptible in what he does; and hence he becomes less and less free and accountable. Accordingly he should be exempt from punishment, if the test of real and concrete freedom, the test of the actual proof of a free will, is to be accepted. It is in his behalf that parole, according to the law of Bérenger, was provided. If, however, this reasoning offends common-sense, one may withdraw from the position that punishment should be inflicted because of a respon-

[1] *Wahlberg*, "Grundzüge der Strafrechtlichen Zurechnungslehre" (in the *Gesammelte kleinere Schriften*, Vol. I, p. 1, especially pp. 33, 35).

sible state, and uphold punishment for the reason of the criminal's menace to society. Under this view it is not a punishment that is applied but a precautionary measure. This brings one back to Liszt's view that such criminals are in his sense no longer responsible. As a rigid determinist Liszt regards the conception of responsibility as distinct from the conception of moral freedom; and he is thus led to deny that such incorrigible offenders exercise responsibility, and to ask in their behalf precautionary measures which are not in accord with the classic conception of punishment. Yet this is the modern position, and appears as well in Stooss, who, however, does not abandon the classic conception of responsibility. He finds it objectionable to speak of punishment for those who have become insensitive to punishment. He regards such men as he regards minors, though in a very different sense, as exempt from punishment.[1] Responsibility is no longer identified with a liability to a criminal charge. But this conclusion is based upon the modern conception of individualization considered in terms other than those of responsibility. This solution the neo-classic school cannot consistently accept in view of its recognition of responsibility as universally present, and of its acceptance as the sole factor in the determination of punishment. It should thus agree with Liszt that professional criminals are irresponsible, but should add that therefore society has no occasion to take vengeance on them.

§ 31. Remote and Immediate Responsibility

If we may still speak of freedom of the will and responsibility in connection with such debased individuals, it is not

[1] See the lecture of *Stooss* at the opening of his course on penal law at the University of Vienna: "Der Geist der modernen Strafgesetzgebung," in the *Revue pénale suisse*, 1896, p. 269, *seq.*

at the moment of committing the crime that they apply; that is the very moment when there is no freedom. One must go far into the past to find the precise moment, the very instant perhaps, when the sense of wrong-doing was present to their conscience and when they passed beyond its influence, crossing for all time the fatal boundary and entering upon the path of what is now called chronic criminality. At certain solemn, possibly infrequent moments of our existence, we certainly have the consciousness of committing ourselves and our moral future, a consciousness of a critical period, at which it lies with us to set our course in a definite direction. We are conscious of a freely acting power, though doubtless the decision is reached through some motive which itself creates the decisive resolve, or at least gives it the headway that determines its dominance and so impresses the cerebral equilibrium as to result in the action taken. Possibly many criminals have had such moments.[1] But how shall it be possible always to find such a precise moment in the turn of affairs, and, if found, how shall it serve to determine the proper measure of punishment? The punishment warranted by law, which alone the judge has the right to impose, is that which the law provides for the crime, and which, accordingly, relates only to the crime committed. It has no relation whatever to that remote situation when the irrevocable decision was taken, of which the present crime is the distant issue. The punishment, which the judge can and must impose, refers to a crime for which there was no freedom of action; and on the other hand, the action which seems to be free has probably no criminal status and carries with it no punish-

---

[1] George Eliot presents an admirable psychological analysis of the truly decisive effects of this first step in the path of compromise with conscience. See *George Eliot*, "Romola," end of chap. ix, "A Man's Ransom."

ment. Hence the criminal should not be punished at all, neither on the one account nor on the other: not on the latter, because it was not a criminal offense, or, if one, because it is ruled out; not on the former, for though it constituted an infraction of criminal law it does not involve a free act.

To reach a different decision it would be necessary to abandon the theory of responsibility and return to the conception of the social risk. There is no real responsibility for an act committed in a condition that is not free; there is only the initial responsibility dating back to a former action which was executed in a state of freedom and of which, by an inevitable sequence, the present crime has become the issue. The first and responsible action carries with it the series of consequences. For an act committed in a state of freedom the agent accepts the full responsibility, not alone morally but socially and in all its consequences, however remote. The act becomes related to the social interest. To commit a crime involves the acceptance of every responsibility which it entails, both with reference to society and to all further contingencies. The agent incurs the risk of becoming dangerous to the community; hence he is responsible for his further conduct, and society punishes the resulting criminality. For every crime that ensues society has the right to exact payment. It may be that the issue was unintended, but it is the issue of conduct adopted in a former state of freedom. This view may be acceptable, but clearly it is no longer the principle of punishment based upon moral responsibility. It is the principle of social responsibility so well described by Ferri and the Italian school. According to them one is not responsible for a crime unless it was premeditated in a state of freedom; at any rate, one is but socially responsible, because the danger and injury to society which the action might cause, should have been taken into account. Or if one holds to the principle of moral responsibility the crime must be considered as a misdemeanor due to negligence. The act itself was not a free act, but was the issue of a previous action committed in freedom. Such was the position of the classic school relative to offenses committed in a state of intoxication, when the crime was not premeditated but was the issue of indiscretion. The crime thus committed refers back to the responsibility for the first error — that of indulgence in excessive drink — and becomes a misdemeanor. Under the theory of responsibility a man so fuddled by his vices and his passions as to have lost the consciousness of freedom for his acts is like an intoxicated man who acts blindly and who is responsible only for his intoxication. Yet, is it quite certain that the criminal is always really responsible for his intoxicated state? Is it so certain that one can find a precise and decisive moment which warrants, so far as any ordinary appearance goes, the inference that it is freely determined and itself determines the future? May it be maintained that everyone experiences such critical and impressive moments, when the decision taken fixes the responsibility for the rest of life?

§ 32. The Social Responsibility for Crime

In the Middle Ages this issue between freedom and responsibility was dramatically expressed. A man vowed himself to God or to the Devil, and the vow once taken there was to be no complaint of the final reckoning. But can it be supposed that the story of Faust is repeated in the life of every criminal? The ordinary criminal is from infancy reared in crime and misery, with no other education than that of vice, with no other trade than that of theft. Is it possible to specify a moment in such a career in which there occurred the free and critical act which justifies the application of punishment? The most responsible factor in such cases is poverty; and for this society possibly is responsible in that it imposes upon these unfortunates hard conditions of economic life, with an inadequate education and without the steadying support of religion. The fault lies in the environment with its deprivations and its irregular relations. It is a life without outlook and without opportunity, and makes these lowly unprivileged classes feel that they belong to another race, and that, after all, to steal is their profession just as for the upper classes, whose luxury they resent, the privileged life is the life of pleasure.

In the old-time ballads the humble were told that their lot in life was the best possible. The simple life was depicted as a beautiful life, as furthering the mystic longings of the soul, as secure in the promise of the life to come. Such ballads endowed these lowly and simple folk with the privileges of the spiritual life, and awoke in them a correspondingly deep feeling of morality, for they felt that being called to future reward they must be more worthy. It was they who formed the upright and virtuous portion of the people; and the miracle was realized that the least fortunate class in the world preserved their morality intact, maintained a higher and stricter responsibility, and through such means became, in truth, the most fortunate. Such ideal days no longer exist. We have entered upon a period of disillusioning realism, which reveals the conflict of classes and the feeling of unconquerable antagonism among the various strata of society. We are not in a position to understand what may be the psychological conception of responsibility on the part of the submerged, who have nothing to lose by crime or by the penalties of the law. They probably experience states of mind from which we are exempt and which we can but feebly appreciate. Unquestionably there are conditions of innate perversion, of hereditary degeneracy, which the environment but fixes and develops. Some individuals do not seem to have at any moment of their careers an active consciousness of a moral distinction thoroughly and intimately felt, such as the penal code requires as evidence of responsibility. It is not possible in their cases to establish a real and specific responsibility; neither for their most recent crimes for which they are held to account, nor for the first petty theft, which, itself undetected, may have been the starting-point for all the rest. But does it follow that these criminals should be permitted to live on in peace, and be free to continue their exploits as they choose?

The first and chief objection to which the policy of individualization is exposed is that it encounters insurmountable difficulties in establishing a proper basis of application. Instead of finding freedom of action everywhere, the newer view is inclined to find it nowhere, and to recognize only irresponsibility. All men at times entertain more or less unworthy or perverse motives, more or less fierce or passionate impulses; and these, when developed to the extreme, darken the mind and blind the reason, and thus contribute to the immediate causes of crime, and like increasing shadows obscure the waning freedom of action. Shall they be regarded as a sufficient excuse, or even as a justification, for acquittal? And though this supposition seems an anomaly, to the discredit of juries let it be noted that their verdicts have frequently made it a reality. When we come upon quite inexplicable acquittals, and most unexpected claims of extenuating circumstances, we suspect and find that in fact there was an underlying belief that the defendant lacked moral freedom. And since it is never possible to tell whether moral freedom was present, there enters an uncertainty that affects the entire position; and verdicts in criminal as in other cases are commonly decided by such impressions.

§ 33. Motives and the Impressionism of Juries

Such is the first charge against the neo-classic school: that in practice it encounters a difficulty, and that its principles lead to untenable results. As a second objection, it may be advanced that it is based upon a scientific error. As M. Tarde has well demonstrated in his "Philosophie pénale," responsibility is universally recognized as a conception of social origin. Therefore it must not be converted into an abstract and preconceived notion, into something quite visionary without any corresponding reality. It must be taken as it is actually found in the general consciousness of the people, as it is currently accepted by the average mind.

It is the jury that best represents such average opinion. Every legal or judicial application of responsibility that runs counter to common opinion may be considered as a scientific mistake of the first order; for it opposes the findings of history. Though the principle is but vaguely expressed, there is found underlying the social aspect of responsibility an inherent faith in the doctrine of freedom. But it is noteworthy that, in practice, freedom is not relied upon to determine the degree of responsibility in concrete cases. Freedom is regarded as everywhere present, and accordingly is never mentioned; as similarly it was not mentioned in the code of 1810. Freedom is a negligible factor because it is assumed to be everywhere present. Attention is centered upon the perversity of motives and upon the circumstances that condone the crime, such as the antecedents of the defendant, his environment, his education, and his general morality. The majority of astonishing acquittals are not due to the jury's belief that there was no freedom of action. On the contrary, in such cases there is usually established a deliberate intention and premeditation, and of this the jury is thoroughly convinced. But the circumstances of the crime, and particularly the motives that incited it, are such as do not arouse general indignation. They are motives that accord with the normal public opinion. The criminal, far from appearing to the members of the jury who must pass judgment upon him, as abnormal through the perversity of his feelings, as deviating from their own social standards, or as unattached or ill-adjusted, appears as a fellow-man whose thoughts and desires and passions are aroused as are theirs. The feeling that led to the crime is such as is universally approved, and, on occasion, is acknowledged by every one. The emotion is possibly more violent than usual, but that is only a question of degree. The man is not a being of another type, offensive to the body social; his crime is regarded as an accident, and not as the manifestation of a dangerous personality to be scorned and repudiated. Accordingly, while well aware that he is the material agent of the crime, juries acquit him; they pronounce him unaccountable, and therefore morally irresponsible. Their decision is reached not on the basis of a mental defect but as a general psychological impression. It is this complex yet definite group of sentiments that accounts for the majority of surprising acquittals. The juries base their verdict not upon the greater or less degree of freedom involved in the crime but upon the nature and motives of the feelings that incite, control, and characterize it.

And indeed to detach a human fact from the series of its antecedent factors is wholly unwarranted and unscientific. To make responsibility depend solely upon the evidence of freedom is to separate the human action from everything that contributes thereto, to look upon it abstractly as an expression of pure will. Such a procedure leaves out of account the motives, the fundamental impulses, and all that leads up to and accounts for the act. What could be more anomalous than that the criminal judge regards such matters as indifferent, as unworthy of his consideration! Furthermore he detaches from its setting the act of the will which contributes the decisive impulse, as though it were an isolated action, independent of circumstances and antecedents. The circumstances are considered only in their bearing upon a judgment of the degree of will and of freedom that the crime implies. Such procedure is like dividing the human act in two and judging it by the latter half alone. This is the least evidential and convincing if its moral status is to be judged independently, instead of being judged as a whole and in its inherent complexity, as an expression of the morality or immorality of a human individual whose future interests have a right to a hearing.

§ 34. Individualization Resulting from the Variable Attitude of Juries

Furthermore, juries will not assent to the legal paradox that requires responsibility to be determined solely by the degree of freedom. Hence, under the influence of public opinion, the jury introduces a twofold measure of individualization. To begin with, the jury is thus instructed: "You have not to consider the degree to which freedom was present when the act was committed. From the point of view of the law this is always the same. You have only to decide whether the accused was of sound mind, and whether he was the material agent of the crime; the question of freedom does not concern you." But the jury, when charged with the question of accountability, decides the issue upon this same conception of freedom, and considers that its function and duty is to estimate and appraise the degree of freedom.[1] This is the first step in the individualization of punishment; but once launched, it is forced to go farther in the consideration of the individual; and thus the second step in individualization is reached. To determine the degree of freedom is futile and impossible. The psychological judgment observes and confirms not the freedom of the action, for this is always elusive, but the motives, the contributory causes as a whole, which, various and complex, have incited the action. The responsibility, as judged and considered by the jury, is a responsibility based upon the aggregate complexity of the moral causes that account for the commission of the crime, and this is the principle that must be followed, because it is the principle of all human estimates and judgments. Responsibility as ordinarily applied is a conception based upon a preconceived conception of freedom; but it is determined in fact and in its application by a strictly empirical standard. The question of freedom remains the underlying issue; but a deterministic principle furnishes the means of application

[1] See the proposal submitted (on the 20th of March) to the Chambre des députés, by *M. Briand*, "having for its object to confer upon criminal juries the power to consider the application of punishment." This proposal is designed to place the law in complete agreement with the facts (Journal officiel documents parlementaires, Chambre des députés, No. 1605). Consult the excellent study of *M. Corentin Guyho*, "Les Jurés 'maitres de la peine'" (Paris, A. Pedone, 1908). Also consult on the subject of the Briand proposal an interesting letter of *M. de Seigneux*, the former president of the "Cour de cassation" of Geneva, who sets forth in suggestive manner the results of the reform at Geneva. *Temps*, April 4, 1908.

and remains the sole possible criterion of judgment. This we observe universally in human judgments, and it equally directs the deliberations of juries.

From this source arise, in practice, the wholly inconsistent verdicts of juries, the injustice of which is well-nigh scandalous; for there is no rule, no uniform standard of judgment. At times the jury's attitude is derived from the consideration of freedom and intent alone, and accordingly it is the degree of premeditation that is considered. In other instances freedom, will, and premeditation are disregarded, and the crime is recognized as a freely willed action; and then it is the motives and the determining circumstances of the crime that are taken into account. There is likewise a tendency to penetrate more and more deeply into the analysis of the nature and character of the defendant, utilizing the consideration of motives and contributory causes for this purpose. All this leads to capricious and variable decisions. Each jury has its own standards of judgment, and each juryman individually has his. It is almost a justice of chance, which is the worst and most disconcerting of all.

But all this belongs more to the past than to the present. We have reviewed the history of these doctrines, and what has preceded may be considered as belonging to former stages of penology. The state of affairs about to be considered belongs to the present, to the actual status of criminal justice. It applies not alone to France but wherever justice is subject through juries to the reflex influence of popular sentiment and public opinion. We have thus reached an alternative from which there is no escape. We must either return to the purely abstract and objective justice of the penal code or find, as best we may, other measures of individualization, based not upon an empirical procedure but upon a truly scientific criterion.[1]

[1] The theory of diminished responsibility, involving as its sole consequence the mitigation of the punishment, which is the essential principle of the neo-classic school, has been the subject of active controversy since 1898. In chronological order may be mentioned, first, the discussion upon "The problem of the limited responsibility of offenders," in the ninth session of the German division of the International Union of Penal Law, held in June, 1903, at Dresden (*Bulletin de l'Union internationale de droit pénal*, Vol. 11, p. 625, *seq*.). The same problem was considered in the discussions before the Société générale des prisons in 1905, in the report of *M. Leredu*, relative to the "Traitement à appliquer aux délinquants à responsabilité limitée" (*Revue pénitentiaire*, 1905, p. 43, *seq.*, p. 187, *seq.*, p. 313, *seq.*, p. 474, *seq.*). The question was reconsidered September, 1905, by *von Liszt* (*Revue pénitentiaire*, 1905, p. 1008). In the same year a discussion on this subject was entered upon at the Congress at Budapesth (*Revue pénitentiaire*, 1905, p. 1183).

The work of *Dr. Legrain*, including an important preface by *M. Garcon*, should likewise be mentioned, "Eléments de médicine mentale appliqués a l'étude du droit" (Paris, 1906); and also the scholarly work of *Dr. Grasset*, "Demi-fous et Demi-responsables" (Paris, 1907). Note particularly the chapter on the "Demi-fous devant la justice," p. 218, *seq*. A critical review of this book appears in the *Revue scientifique* of February 2, 1907, p. 143, *seq*. "La responsabilité des criminels (Paris, 1908) was written as an outcome of the important Congress of Alienists and Neurologists held at Geneva, August, 1907. It reports the discussion at the Congress, and the controversies that followed. As opposed to the views of Dr. Grasset, the important report to the Congress at Geneva by *Dr. Gilbert Ballet* may be read: "L'expertise médico-légale et la question de responsabilité," Geneva, 1907. Also by the same author, "La responsabilité des criminels" (an answer to Dr. Grasset), in the *Journal de psychologie normale et pathologique* (January–February, 1908). [English translation of Grasset, 1909.]

Lastly, on the same subject, may be consulted the thesis by *M. A. Néret*, "La Responsabilité attenuée," particularly chap. ii, p. 59, *seq*. Attention should be directed to the very interesting discussion on this same question that took place at the Société française de philosophie, on January 30, 1908, "Des Responsabilités attenuées en matière pénale," and to the able report of *M. A. le Poittevin*, professor in the Faculty of Law at Paris (*Bulletin de la Société française de philosophie*, March, 1908, p. 71, *seq*.).

Consult on these points articles 16 and 17 of the "Avant-projet du code pénal suisse" (the text of 1903); and on "Zurechnungsfähigkeit," § 51 of the German penal code, apart from the Lehrbuch of *von Liszt*, see *Reinhard Frank*, "Das Strafgesetzbuch für das deutsche Reich (Tübingen, Mohr, p. 107, *seq*.).

CHAPTER V

THE ITALIAN SCHOOL AND INDIVIDUALIZATION BASED UPON FORMIDABILITY

§ 35. Historical Review of the Italian Movement in Penology.
§ 36. Practical Situations and Reforms: the making of the Recidivist.
§ 37. The Solution proposes the personal Consideration of the Offender and his Social Reinstatement.
§ 38. Gradation by Presumptive Morality and Good Conduct of Offenders: Protest against Promiscuous Association.
§ 39. Criticism of the Position: its Basis in Law and Public Opinion.
§ 40. Purpose and Effect of Punishment: Consequent Status of Crime.
§ 41. The Types of Criminals and their Individualized Treatment.
§ 42. Difficulties attaching to the Position of Lombroso.
§ 43. A Third Italian School.
§ 44. The Physical Recognition of the Criminal: Innate and Acquired Degenerate Traits.
§ 45. Other Phases of Italian Penology: Judicial Diagnosis.
§ 46. What Italian Penology has accomplished.

§ 35. Historical Review of the Italian Movement in Penology

THE several shades and grades of position of the classic school have been passed in review, and their inadequacy duly set forth. Let us consider the proposals offered in place thereof. Shall we find the desired principles of individualization in the contributions of the anti-classic modern schools? That remains to be seen. It is familiar that the modern school, which it has been agreed to call the Italian school, is deliberately and radically opposed to the classic legal system. No complete exposition of this school will here be attempted. It will suffice to present a survey of its teachings in so far as they pertain to the problem of individualization.

It may be well to begin by removing a slight misunderstanding on the part of those unacquainted with the meaning of the term "Italian school" in current penological theory. It must not be supposed that under this generic term are included all modern Italian criminologists. On the contrary, it should be borne in mind that in Italy there always have been and still are many distinguished criminologists, such as Carrara (to mention only the most eminent), who belong to a notable classic school, nor should it be forgotten that Rossi was of Italian origin. But since Beccaria, Italy seems to have been constantly at the head of the scientific movement in the field of criminal law, and, indeed, may be said to have been ever in advance of the age. Beccaria and his followers rejected the abstract and objective foundations of the classic school, and this at a time when the abuses of the discretionary power of the judge seemed to show that there was no alternative other than the provision of a general and uniform application of a legal principle. Later, at the time of Rossi, the Italian school, with the support of the men who brought fame to its universities, became the promoter of the great movement of individualization with reference to responsibility, which may be considered as the characteristic of the neo-classic school. For thirty years, as is well known, this school has promulgated a new and most radical reform.

Finally it should be noted that the classic Italian school was the sole source and inspiration of the new Italian penal code of 1889. This code is the most developed embodiment of the neo-classic school. As a work legal in essence and in form, it is a most remarkable achievement; it presents an unexampled nicety of distinction and detail; it enters into a discerning analysis of the facts; it considers the minutest details; and it anticipates every contingency. In it the law takes the place of the judge; it aims to foresee and provide for all possible cases of individualization, and to point out the proper treatment. It is a catalogue of individual cases. The judge has only to refer to his code to find the special case applicable to the situation confronting him, and when the case is found, the solution is at hand; he has but to read and apply. The code is an admirable scientific production, but unfortunately it serves as the epitome of a completed stage, and not as the introduction to a further advance; and for this reason it is unsuited as a basis of legislation. To delay codification until a system is scientifically complete is to run the risk of making it merely an historical record, the registry of a movement that admirably summarizes the work of the past but is no longer in conformity with the new conceptions in process of formation. Codes of law, even at the risk of omissions and imperfections, should be framed when a system is beginning to enter public consciousness. They should direct the application and the formulation of the doctrines based upon them. If they appear when the system they represent is far along in development, and, indeed, close to its decline, they are no longer in sympathetic contact with life; and for legislation this is a serious evil. This misfortune is perhaps threatening both the new Italian penal code and the proposed revision of the French penal code, unless, indeed, prompt measures for fundamental reconstruction of the latter be taken. The abuses involved in the abstract character of the Italian classic school have given rise to another school which is known simply as the Italian school without further qualification.

An extremely important scientific movement began in Italy about 1875.[1] In general the movement was the culmination of several positivist systems, but was inspired more

[1] The first edition of *Lombroso's* "The Criminal" appeared in 1876.

particularly by the growth of two sciences of relatively recent origin, anthropology and sociology. Thus this new Italian school has variously been called the positivist, or the anthropological, or the sociological school. To include its several aspects without committing oneself to any one in particular, it has been called more generally and with sufficient definiteness the Italian school.

This school, whose most distinguished representatives are Lombroso, Ferri, Garofalo, Sighele, arose as a direct reaction against the principle of the freedom of the will as understood in the classic sense, which made crime the issue of a free act. The Italian school looks upon crime as a natural product, as a result of purely natural factors that leave no place for freedom. For Lombroso these factors are almost wholly anthropological; for Ferri they are more particularly sociological; but this distinction is not important.[1] Whether crime is the issue of hereditary conditions or of factors purely social, it is, in either case, the necessary consequence of a group of natural conditions in which the conception of freedom has no place. The significant social factors include the momentous influences of the environment, the economic conditions of life, the limitations of poverty, or rather, in M. Tarde's phrase, the reflex influence of increasing luxury and of the corruption which its example spreads through all stages of society.

The divergences in the position of Ferri and Lombroso are of slight consequence, at least so far as they concern the intrinsic character of crime; for both, crime is a purely natural product. As it affects the masses, it has a social function analogous to that attaching to war; it serves the same function of elimination in its relation to individuals. As is also

[1] *Ferri*, "Sociologie criminelle"; see also *Vaccaro*, "Genesi e funzioni delle leggi penali."

true of war, crime seeks only to transform and not to destroy; and in so far there is a common psychological or sociological inspiration.[1] It is however important to distinguish between the point of view of Lombroso and that of Ferri in so far as relates to the practical consequences of their views and the reforms which each proposes to introduce in criminology.

§ 36. Practical Situations and Reforms: the Making of the Recidivist

Although on the positive side the Italian school appears primarily as the consequence of a series of philosophic and scientific considerations, it presents as well a negative side, which is based upon a criticism of the results attributed to the prevalent system. Yet this dominant school, if judged by its results, may be said to have gone bankrupt, as the popular expression goes.

The level of a movement is never higher than its source. Under the influence of the leading idealists (Rossi), criminal law became humanized, ennobled, and in a measure spiritualized. The conception of freedom remained its starting point; yet equally the analytic study of each offender was undertaken. The conception of penalty as a satisfaction due to the sense of justice was retained; and equally, in a happy eclecticism, punishment began to be looked upon as an instrument of social defense. The practical interests were combined with those of abstract justice, and jointly there emerged the conception of a social justice, — an appropriate expression that meets the requirements of principle and of society alike. It seemed that in this advance criminal law had reached its highest development. Reflecting the popular acceptance of natural law in human affairs, criminal law seemed to have found its true principle as part thereof. This

[1] See *Lombroso*, "La Funzione sociale del delitto," Palermo, 1896.

however did not affect the practical results, for crime had never been more prevalent. The tide of crime arose with each successive statistical inquiry, and the more severely justice was administered, the more crime increased and spread. One seemed justified in believing that punishment was the chief concern of criminology, and that criminal laws favored the growth of crime.

In truth the increase of crime was largely due to the recidivists; or to be more exact, to young offenders and recidivists jointly. But perhaps the two are, in origin, one. The criminality of the young leads to their technical acquittal with detention in reformatories; when they are again sentenced at adult age they are put down as first offenders in the official statistics, and in law they are such. In reality they are habitual offenders, graduating from a state colony, who give evidence of the effect of the penitentiary system. They illustrate its results and its value. It may be urged that from the days of their adolescence these youthful offenders are already so thoroughly contaminated that no penitentiary discipline, no educational system, can serve to redeem them. Very possibly the defect lies in them, in their character, and not in the remedial measures. Lombroso and Ferri hold that they are either born criminals or by nature incorrigible. This is not the view of those who believe in responsibility and freedom, and consequently in the possibility of reform through moral appeal. The Italian school takes its stand squarely on the other side of this issue. Yet the school, together with the legal practices which it upholds, is in every respect losing ground.

Moreover, apart from the persistence in crime of young offenders, as above noted, statistics establish a considerable increase of crime among habitual adult offenders, that is, of those whose first sentence occurred after they had reached majority. In so far as this is true either of minors or of adults, and whether we consider penal colonies or jails, in general it may be said that prison life breeds the prison habit. When the increase of crime occurs particularly among first offenders, the social conditions are primarily unwholesome and public morality low; and this at present is the case. But when the growth of crime reaches its highest point among recidivists, it is the punishment that is at fault, since in place of preventing crime, it encourages it. Instead of eliminating the latent and potential criminality of offenders, it furthers it; and it does so by weakening the sense of honor and personal worth, which is among the surest safeguards of morality, and, for the majority of men, the most enduring.[1]

If a system is to be judged by its results, the classic school may be pronounced a failure. To this it may be replied that the fault lies not in the system of punishment as determined by the law or the judge, but in its administrative application, and that a theoretical school is responsible only for the code and for its influence upon the judiciary but does not control the administration of punishment. Therefore it is not the penal code that is at fault, and still less the judge or the jury, but it is the administration of the punishment. It is the promiscuous association within the prison, the contamination of its communal life, and the

[1] In addition to the striking article published by *M. Fouillée* in the *Revue des Deux Mondes*, January 15, 1897, see the chapters by *M. Henry Joly* in "La France criminelle," p. 164, *seq.*, p. 179, *seq.* (also an article by *M. Fouillée* in *La Revue Bleue*, October 30, 1897). Also *Joly*, "Le Combat contre le crime," p. 156, *seq.*, p. 182, p. 203, *seq.*; and the lecture delivered by the latter at the Young Men's Christian Association on January 22, 1898, on the "Criminalité de la jeunesse," published in the *Réforme sociale*, 1898, p. 433. See *Eugène Rostand*, "Pourquoi la criminalité monte en France et baisse en Angleterre," in the *Réforme sociale*, pp. 345, 531, 585, and a supplement in the same review, p. 850.

exposure to the vices of humanity, that make the habitual criminal. A first offender introduced to this environment becomes the companion and partner of the most corrupt among the corrupt, and inevitably loses the last remaining vestige of honor. To maintain the emotions actively efficient requires the support of an environment; they live their life in a world without, as well as within, and require an external influence, either of social intercourse or of unworldly communion as provided by religious faith. Direct personal contact is essential. The man who shares his life with degenerates inevitably assimilates his character to theirs. Moreover, the safeguard of morality, especially where its survival is somewhat uncertain, is the sense of personal honor and esteem, and this, in turn, depends upon influences of social origin. It consists in feeling oneself a member of a larger or smaller group, of a human community, accepted by it, esteemed by it, and not excluded therefrom; it is the feeling of forming a part of an organism and reflecting a collective consciousness; in default thereof, one drifts to the outcasts. Punishment, through its discrediting stigma, withdraws the criminal from the group of the honest and sends him over to the criminal community. It makes him a man dishonored and branded, an exile from the reputable social life. Even though he is not corrupt and has withstood contamination within the walls, the prison removes him from the class of the honest. The only social life that prison affords him is that incorporated in a community which is under the social ban, though it likewise has its social organization. He belongs to them and there is every chance that he will remain one of them; and thus is the recidivist accounted for. The fault is not with the legal system of the penal code; and the classic school is not responsible for it. The fault lies in the administration of punishment and especially in the promiscuous association of prison life.

§ 37. The Solution proposes the Personal Consideration of the Offender and his Social Reinstatement

To remedy this defect is the commendable purpose of the penitentiary school. Its most distinguished representatives, if not its most successful results, are to be found in France. Its adherents are many and especially among the representatives of the bench. Indeed, the interest and the generous humanitarian spirit displayed by the French judiciary in the problems of punishment and in proposed reforms has not been sufficiently recognized. The eager and earnest desire for improvement that is finding universal support cannot be too cordially acknowledged. Through the influence of this movement there have been inaugurated prison congresses of international scope, and these serve as the great centers of interest, which in turn stimulate desirable reforms. To it also is due the French "Société générale des prisons," which, in its field, serves as a permanent congress, devoted to the study of problems as they arise, and to furthering the improvement of punitive treatment. The publication of its "Bulletin" is a means of recording and popularizing its conclusions. By broad discussion and analysis it seeks an insight into problems and prepares the way for legislative enactments. Its services extend beyond France to all countries where penology is considered. There is hardly a recent European criminal law which is not under obligation, for its form as well as for its data, to the "Revue pénitentiare française." The reforms sought by this large penological school may be reduced to two: the first, the segregation of the condemned during the term of punishment with a view to prevent their contamination by associates and to facilitate their reform; and the second, the social reinstatement of those who have served their term, their return to the group of honest men from which they have been excluded, with the purpose to secure their readjustment to, and their participation in, an environment of work and an honest and regular life.

We thus reach the conclusion that it is not the legal but the administrative side of penal legislation that is in need of reform. The penal code, and yet more clearly the criminal law, need not be disturbed; it is the manner of administering punishment that requires modification. Yet an administrative reform is not adequate to bring about a proper administration of punishment, for the law prescribes the mode of administering punishments. Accordingly, in this respect, the penal code must be reformed. Possibly it will be sufficient to revise some of its articles; possibly the fundamental principles on which the system of the penal code itself is based must be modified. This is to be determined by the penological movement itself. For sooner or later the principle advanced by this school must bring about a reform, not alone of the administration of punishment but of the legal system of its individualization.

This does not imply that the penological school has accepted the principle of the Italian school. Such is not the case, and it would be unjust so to regard it. But in a certain measure the two are in accord; unintentionally the one has prepared the way for the other. It may be interesting to examine the common ground and set forth the points of agreement of the two systems which, superficially, seem inconsistent.

Obviously the basis of the theories of the penological school is the consideration of the individual temperament of the condemned. When sentence has been passed he must at once be treated according to his merits rather than according to the crime. The crime must be ignored in order the better to see the man, for thus only is reform possible, and the purpose of the penological school is the reform of the criminal. Now all reform comprises two functions: the negative one of preservation, consisting in this case in withdrawing the man from contaminating influences, and the positive one of reformation, which is directed to the remoulding of the moral character. Accordingly, since no education is possible without a suitable adaptation of the means to the nature and character of those concerned, the punishment must be adapted to the temperament of the individual.

It must not be inferred, however, that the penitentiary policy is to be confused with what may be called the policy of solitary confinement. The fact of prolonged segregation is indeed the most radical and the most primitive method of reformation, but it is also the least adequate means of education. If education through punishment is to consist in fitting the prisoner to resist the temptations of environment and associates, it must be conceded that it is an illogical measure to shield him from every temptation and to withdraw him wholly from social life. If it is functioning that develops or, at all events, affects the organ, it is a strange procedure that in order to prepare the organ for service one should deprive it of opportunity to function. Accordingly many criminologists, particularly the English, believe that solitary confinement for long-term punishments has only a provisional value, that of getting the prisoner to realize his situation by leaving him for a time to his own reflections. But the practice must not be abused. To effect the reform of a developing character, it is well to encourage initiative. A communal life is not to be feared provided that it is properly safeguarded. A new apprenticeship of life must be undertaken, and particularly in the moral sphere. There should be no hesitation in guaranteeing a properly limited initiative such as a penal régime permits. Yet there remain the difficulties of proper safeguards. These, one believes or hopes to find in a system of successive grades of privilege. According to the behavior of the prisoner and the progress made, he passes from one stage to another, and by a system of gradual reinstatement he reaches his freedom, — that is, a conditional freedom whenever reform seems assured. The progress is thus tested at each stage.[1] The principle involved has been applied in the Australian system of deportation. It was devised by Walter Crofton, and was first applied in Ireland. It has become the English penitentiary régime under the name of the "progressive system." This system of progressive promotion may be recommended and in part applied, particularly to such countries as ours in which solitary confinement for long-term sentences is not in vogue. For example, it would be readily adaptable to our system of deportation. The basis of the system of our law of 1854 (on the administration of penal servitude in the Colonies) is the progressive English system. Thus a first attempt, although a crude one, must here be recognized in the adjustment of punishment to the progressive improvement of the individual.

The present demand is for the perfection and extension of the practice now crudely and indiscriminately applied to sentences of penal servitude. It has been urged that the system be extended to the penitentiaries; and M. Leveillé has urged its application to the military company

[1] For details see *Aschrott*, "Strafensystem und Gefängniswesen in England," p. 50, seq., p. 70, seq., and particularly p. 181, seq., and 195, seq. Also *Krohne*, "Lehrbuch der Gefängniskunde," § 10.

§ 38] THE ITALIAN SCHOOL 111

known as the African Battalions, to which are sent, at the time of their enlistment, young recruits who have already undergone certain special sentences. In its detail the plan presents some difficulties of application, but the principle is clear.[1] It is the principle of classification or gradation according to the presumptive degree of morality. Unquestionably the practice involves a considerable inequality in the administration of punishment, yet an inequality that is beneficent and strictly humane and just. Moreover it is an inequality, as explained above, in which is considered not the crime committed and its social gravity, but the moral status of the individual and the prospects of reinstatement of which he gives promise.

§ 38. Gradation by Presumptive Morality and Good Conduct of Offenders: Protest against Promiscuous Association

Admittedly this seems to distort and confuse the issues. The kind of individualization just mentioned is to be applied only in the administration of the punishment and in conformity with the progressive improvement of the condemned. A premium is placed upon the good conduct of the prisoner, and he is encouraged to exert himself, and accordingly to further his own moral advancement. Such individualization is not determined by the judicial sentence at the time of condemnation, when an attempt is made to select a punishment in terms of the individual and not of the crime. It is not an initial decision made at the outset and before the administration of the punishment has revealed the nature of the individual committed to its charge;

[1] See the report of *M. Leveillé* to the Société générale des prisons (*Revue pénitentiaire*, 1896), p. 1007, *seq.*, p. 1199; and the plan of *M. Leveillé* in the same review, p. 1217, and in the *Revue pénitentiaire*, 1897, p. 519. Also the proposal of *M. Pierre Richard* at the meeting on December 2, 1897 (*Revue pénitentiaire*, 1898, p. 145).

it is a re-classification made after the sentence, and during the execution of the punishment, and based upon the progressive improvement of the prisoner. It thus bears but indirectly upon the principle of uniformity and equality of punishments; for since it puts a premium upon good conduct, all may merit and attain it. It is made a part of a generally applicable discipline. The principle of equality before the law remains secure, and this is one of the most inalienable principles of our criminal law. The individualization made after the sentence and in course of punishment and under the form of progressive promotion by reason of the good conduct of the condemned does not constitute an exception thereto.

But the penological school is not content with this belated individualization reached in course of punishment but permitting an initial promiscuous association of all condemned to the same discipline. For this period may permanently contaminate, or at least expose to the worst influences, such of its unfortunate victims as retain a vestige of virtue, who, though guilty of an isolated infraction, have not lost the sense of right and wrong. By the logic of its principles the penological school opposes such conditions. In the absence of solitary confinement, and at all events as a subsidiary measure, it urges a preliminary segregation of prisoners. It proposes, for example, instead of a separation in different quarters within the same reformatory institution, — a separation which is never complete, — a definite assignment of different groups of offenders to different reformatory institutions. In this way the offender, from the beginning of his punishment and according to the character which he presents, would be sent to an appropriate institution and placed in an appropriate group with his equals, that is, with persons of an approxminately similar morality.

The French law of 1875, on the partial application of solitary confinement as applied to those committed for more than a year to penitentiaries with their promiscuous associations, grants a possible conversion of the punishment, in response to a request for a change of discipline. Such prisoners are allowed upon request, even from the beginning of their sentence, to serve their time in solitary confinement; and M. Leveillé, whose scheme of reorganization of the African Battalions has already been referred to, asks the like privilege for certain types of convicts, so that instead of serving their time in jail they may be permitted to serve a double or even a triple period in the colonial military service, and thereby earn their reinstatement and pay their debt to society.[1] This amounts to a method of individualization from the very outset of the punishment, — an initial segregation into different groups of the condemned, applied administratively in place of judicially.

A provision of this type appears in the application of the law of 1885 on the deportation of recidivists. Our colonial arrangements provide two forms of deportation: the one involving a true penitentiary discipline in the colony, and the other assigning a discipline in freedom or in partial freedom. Upon the rendering of the sentence an administrative commission in Paris passes upon the classification of the deported into one or the other of the two forms of deportation; and it does so without considering the crime committed.

Such provisions indicate a tendency to make the individualization an initial one in terms of the individual, and not a progressive adjustment according to his behavior during the course of punishment. By such a procedure the worth of the individual may be considered at the outset,

[1] See *Revue pénitentiaire*, 1897, p. 513, *seq.*

even at the moment when sentence is passed; according to his character, his environment, and his antecedents, a suitable régime of punishment may be arranged.[1]

Such measures are at present carried out through the channels of administration, without legal or judiciary warrant. Is there any reason for not assigning to the judge the duty of making this first individualization, when it may be determined under the influence of the facts given in the evidence, the impression produced upon the hearers, and the important guarantee of publicity? The individualization is thus determined openly rather than through the variable influences to which administrative procedures are subject.

§ 39. Criticism of the Position: its Basis in Law and in Public Opinion

The principle of the penological school has as its necessary consequence the substitution of the consideration of the criminal for the exclusive consideration of the crime. The Italian school makes the same demand; the form of its demands and their acceptability remain to be examined.

Before taking up this point let us review the conclusions reached. In the first place it appears that the classic school is condemned by its practical results. Yet in justice some reservation of this verdict must be made and certain objections met. The criticisms set forth that the fault lies in the administration of punishment and not in the judiciary system; the principle of legal and judicial equality of punishment remains secure. Admittedly if there is anything

---

[1] This argument applies with greater force to the system of parole, or, properly speaking, of pardon, which is a matter presently to be considered in our penal legislation, under the name of the law of pardon. On this subject see *M. Octave Aubry*, "L'indulgence et la loi" (Paris, Libraire générale de droit et de jurisprudence, 1908).

awry in penology it is the mode of administration of punishment, and it is here that the remedy is to applied. We have come to realize that the remedy can be effective only by abandoning the initial, that is, the judicial equality of punishment, by adapting the punishment through the judiciary procedure to the individual rather than to the crime. The idea that for the same crime there must be imposed a punishment alike in nature and equal in duration is indeed no longer tenable. To recognize that existing conditions can be remedied only by beginning at this point, is to admit that the whole system, or much of it, must be reformed, that its foundations must be reconsidered. Indeed the basis of the classic system is most uncertain.[1] Such is the state of the problem. It is in presence of this situation and of results unfavorable to the dominant school that the Italian school has come forward. Let us see what it proposes to accomplish.

The position of the Italian school may be reduced to a very simple formula; it proposes a system of applied sociology based upon determinism and accepting it as its guiding principle. Whatever in this position does not come directly from sociology is but a slightly disguised deduction therefrom. Sociology primarily observes and determines facts, accepts principles established by historical experience, which in turn form the basis of the laws of social psychology. Now among these principles, which lie at the base of public sentiment, there are some that remain secure despite the passing of philosophies and the disappearance of creeds;

---

[1] Moreover, whenever the advocates of the classic school agree and are disposed to record their opinion on the subject of the operation of the actual system, they testify that it is disastrous and leads to unfortunate consequences. See, in reference thereto, an especially instructive discussion at the Société générale des prisons, on the "Suppression of Vagabondage," March 16, 1898. *Revue pénitentiaire*, April, 1898.

such is the belief in responsibility, and, however vague, the conception of moral freedom. It is upon them that the universal distinction is made between the repressive measures applied to criminals and the purely preventive measures taken against the insane. The criminologist, especially if he is also a sociologist, must take account of these sentiments and of their reaction upon criminology. A system of punishment that disregards them would so conflict with popular sentiment as to be thoroughly impracticable. To construct a criminology as an abstract system, without considering the popular collective consciousness, would be to follow the plan of Sieyès in his construction of political constitutions. Such philosophical dogmatism has had its day.

§ 40. Purpose and Effect of Punishment: Consequent Status of Crime

Now let us consider the proposals of the Italian school and the necessary logical conclusions to which it is committed. Man cannot control the direction of his impulses or of his moral propensities. According to Lombroso crime is the inevitable issue of a pathological temperament, and according to Ferri it is a result of the social environment and economic conditions governing human existence. Hence punishment can have no social status either as a penalty or as disapproval. Atonement can be exacted only for a wrong which one was free to avoid, and reproof can be demanded only for evil issuing from an act of free will. Punishment is only a means of public defense and security, analogous to the preventive measures taken against dangerous animals or insane men. Moreover there are no repressive measures; there are only measures of prevention to check the repetition and dissemination of crime. What is dangerous in the criminal and makes him a menace to society is not the crime once committed but the criminal himself : his personality, his temperament, ever leading him to further crime ; the latent fundamental impulses which, when acted upon by circumstance, may break out into murder, theft, or offenses against morality. How is society affected by the punishment of the crime or the failure to punish it? The evil done belongs to the past. Nothing remains but to repair the injury inflicted if this be possible. The greater concern is to prevent crime in the future; and for this the criminal instinct in the criminal must be checked or suppressed, or if, as is most commonly the case, such a prospect seems unrealizable, it is the criminal himself who must be disposed of, as would be done in the case of a plague or a dangerous animal. It is with reference to his evil potentiality, to the dread that he arouses (which the Italians call *La temibilità*, the formidability of the offender) that prospective measures must be framed. They must be directed to reform in so far as any measure of improvement yet remains possible, or, if none is possible, to elimination. Such, approximately, is the logical position of the Italian school.

In this view the crime committed has an altogether different status from that assigned to it by the classic school. It is no longer the fixation point of punishment; it ceases to be the punishable factor. The older view recalls the primitive theory of the right of vengeance; as though one turned against the author of the injury to make him expiate it by subjection to punishment. Crime has no status except as a symptom of the criminal instinct of the agent, as an indication of his dangerous character. There are no punishable actions, only individuals to be placed beyond the range of doing harm; and crime serves to identify them.

Crime has a purely symptomatic value. The record and the appearance of the criminal, to speak in the spirit of the system, are to be substituted for that legal entity known as crime. The catalogue of crimes is to be replaced by a classification of criminals. Instead of adjusting the punishment to the presumed gravity of the offense, it must be adjusted to the nature of the criminal. It is not of crime but of criminality that we are to speak; and the one is by no means the evidence of the other. The one is a fact, and the other a psychological factor. The two conceptions are not necessarily identical. Criminality always breeds crime, but crime is not always the issue of criminality. The legal system is wrong in associating the two. Every truly scientific system must clearly distinguish between them.

§ 41. The Types of Criminals and their Individualized Treatment

Henceforth criminals must be separated into two mutually exclusive groups: those amenable to improvement, and those who are not. The latter, the refractory to punishment, the incorrigible, form the group that cannot be assimilated and made part of the social life. There is nothing to be done but to place them beyond the possibility of doing harm, to suppress, or to eliminate them. The former are to be carefully studied and assigned to appropriate groups, for though presumably amenable to regeneration, they may not be responsive to the same measures. If, as Lombroso holds, crime is primarily a pathological phenomenon, punishment, or what will still bear the name, must be adjusted to the type of disorder or criminal disease which is to be cured; and this brings us to the theory of penal individualization in the true and proper sense of the word. Such individualization will no longer consider the crime committed; it will even disregard the degree of responsibility, for responsibility bears upon the accountability towards a particular action, which is not here pertinent. Such individualization will consider the true nature of the individual, his latent and potential criminality, and will seek to adjust the punishment to the requirements of moral improvement which each criminal presents. Such is the new individualization proposed by the Italian school.

Surely this type of individualization has great merit; and further progress must be directed to its practical extension. Yet what may almost be called deterrent in the Italian school is its formal reasoning, its radical and insistent logical position; here, as elsewhere in the field of law, there is a natural recoil from the rigid logical attitude. It needs no further insistence that logic may perhaps produce revolutions, for it may express the simple conviction of the masses and the psychology of the crowd; yet unquestionably society in a normal condition does not proceed by logic but by something quite different. It lives upon realities which are complex, and the complexity of the friction of diverse interests and their final issue is something decidedly opposed to the straight lines and regular contours of logic. Reality disturbs the outline. It is the spirit of abstraction, of dogma, or of radicalism (which amounts to the same thing), that attempts to mould a structure as a whole and to hold it inviolable.

The logical principles of the Italian school lead to two conclusions: first, to hold exempt from punishment many guilty of crime; and secondly, its converse, to punish in advance some who have not as yet committed crime. This makes two new classes of criminals: the one, the not-to-be-punished criminal, or the group of pseudo-criminals; and the other, those to be punished without having become criminals, or the group of suspects.

Let us consider the first group, the pseudo-criminals,— and fortunately for mankind they are still very numerous. It includes first offenders whose crime was but an irregular incident, who have been tempted to abuse the confidence placed in them, or even to commit a serious crime, under conditions in which their true nature did not prevail. Such crimes might indicate that they did not as yet possess the criminal impulse ; but that imprisonment might develop it. Their character is not yet involved. Punishment is altogether unnecessary as a preventive for further misdeed and may prove a menace. There is no abnormality to be cured, no disposition to be reformed; at most there is needed a break from the old habits or a change of environment. What good will punishment do? What we call punishment has no longer the function of chastisement, that is, in reference to the evil committed, but its function is to prevent evil in the future by cure of elimination, and that is not here relevant. There is nothing to be cured and still less to be eliminated. Punishment would be useless and therefore unjust. Such are the characteristics of the pseudo-criminals or of the fictitious criminals who are not to be punished. It is thus made clear that a distinction must carefully be drawn between the external appearance of criminality and that which alone is significant, an inherent criminality. The former is a superficial phenomenon; it is revealed in an external act in which it is embodied and made manifest. Shall it be regarded as an index of the true criminality that discloses the intimate character? The reply cannot be determined in advance. The crime may be an acute crisis, quite incidental and transitory, without likelihood of a disastrous return. The true criminality against which measures must be taken is chronic criminality, the issue of fundamental character which at any time may express itself in criminal action. Hence we should put in a group by themselves criminals who lack such inherent criminality; they show the phenomenon of criminality but no natural criminal tendency. They are criminals only in the eyes of the law.

The second group forms a serious problem. Here belong cases of natural criminality not yet expressed in legal criminality, — an inherent and demonstrated criminal tendency that has not as yet issued in crime. The group includes such as should be liable to punishment without having become criminals; in other words, those who are the objects of suspicion. If society is to be defended against future crime, then, obviously, society must take possession of the criminal before he commits his crime. When a house threatens to fall and is a menace to passers-by, one does not delay its repair until an accident has occurred. Similarly in dealing with the insane who threaten to become dangerous, — they are confined before they cause disaster. When an animal is suspected of having an affection that may prove a source of danger to others, it is confined or killed, even before the contagion breaks out. Why hesitate to segregate the instinctive criminal, born and reared in vice, and incapable of assimilation? He was not made for a social life, and social life was not made for him. Why delay self-protection until the career of misdeed has begun? Such might be the only available procedure if crime were the sole expression of the criminal, but it is sufficiently obvious that there are many other symptoms of the criminal temperament. A man becomes a member of a gang; he is a vicious fellow, destitute of all moral sense; he pursues most suspicious ways; he has no scruples of conscience; the very idea of a moral conscience is foreign to him ; his past, his education, his environment answer for the future. From the pathological point of view he has all the signs of the criminal. He is, to all intents, a thief who has not yet picked a pocket; or a murderer, by impulse violent, brutal, and cruel, who, on slight provocation, will inevitably go to the extreme. Why not anticipate the execution of a possible crime? If punishment itself is not to be resorted to, there are at all events protective measures to be pursued and definite steps to be taken. It is not wise to wait passively until a victim is found. When once a crime is committed, punishment becomes a means of defense to prevent the repetition of the crime; so much the more should it be a measure of prevention of the first crime.

To the two groups composing the preliminary classification of criminals, two others are thus to be added: the class of criminals in advance of the crime or criminals by suspicion, and the class of pseudo-criminals. In the former there is a criminal but no crime; in the latter, a crime but no criminal. To reach a precise individualization in accord with the principles of the system, four varieties must be recognized: — the criminals by suspicion who have given proof of their criminality without committing a crime; the criminals lacking criminality, perpetrators of crime who are however not criminal in nature; the criminals combining crime and criminality, but incorrigible; and lastly, the entire class of criminals (with the considerable variety of sub-classes, which it includes) who have shown at once their participation in crime and in criminality but are susceptible to treatment.

§ 42. **Difficulties attaching to the Position of Lombroso**

The serious point in the system of individualization in precise conformity with the principles of the Italian school is the admission of the first two groups, the criminals by suspicion and the fictitious criminals, the former being guilty only of criminality but not of crime, and the latter guilty of crime but not of criminality. That the two conceptions have a different range of application cannot be questioned.

Preventive measures that shall place the criminal under the power of the law before the commission of the crime involve the detection and treatment of suspects. Yet, however solicitous one may be for the social safety, it is far better to run the risk of having thefts or other crimes committed, than to condemn any and every man on the basis of his features — merely because nature has given him a jaw, a lip, or a skull that corresponds to one of Lombroso's criminal types. In the life of society, as elsewhere, there are always risks to be run; one must learn how to accept them and to find wherein lies the least social risk. If through fear of crime men are deprived of liberty, where is the advantage? Society must guarantee not alone life and property but also the means of enjoying them. If to secure life and property the chance is incurred of losing the possibility of enjoying them freely, the social risk incurred is quite as serious as that of the dangers that threaten us individually. Against the latter one may with proper caution come to protect himself; against the danger of an arbitrary authority in the hands of the State or the police, one is helpless. Such policy is followed by individuals without initiative or courage, and by decadent peoples. Therefore let us beware of introducing a system based upon suspicion, which, in its endeavors to provide complete security, constantly exposes men to the serious danger of an accusation upon appearance alone.

But no less serious is the alternative that no punishment should be imposed if the author of the crime happens to be an ordinary individual, whom nature has neglected to brand with the pathological marks that reveal the criminal. Even though there were an infallible means of recognizing the criminal by accident, — the man at bottom honest but momentarily led astray or taken unawares, who is not at all liable to a further relapse in the future, — the interests of public morality will hardly sanction the example of such patent of immunity in cases of grave offenses that do violence to public sentiment; for the public conscience would thus lose the right to condemn, because the justice by which it is represented considers that it ought not to interfere. Shall murders, thefts, violations of trust, and other serious crimes be regarded as in themselves of slight significance and as morally of no different status than any other act expressive of an individual's true character? In that event a suspicious appearance would be more indicative of criminality than the actual brutal assault upon a victim. The indignation of the people and their stern disapproval of criminal actions would be out of place. It is cowardly and stupid fear that makes one believe that he is threatened, and makes one turn against a suspected enemy, for who knows where the enemy is to be found? Is it the man who plans murder, or the one who seeks vengeance against the murderer? The public cannot decide, and necessarily turns to doctors and specialists who must detect the criminal by pathological symptoms, and then place him under surveillance. The realization of crime becomes only the most terrifying but not the most convincing symptom of crime. The indignation aroused by the crime is an unworthy sentiment due to fear or ignorance. Such appears to be the logical consequence of this position. If it should ever be adopted, which is hardly likely, it would destroy the last safeguard of human nature and of common manhood.

§ 43. A Third Italian School

In view of these serious consequences there has arisen an intermediate position, which presents the same point of departure and follows a like determinism, but has as its chief purpose to restore to punishment its traditional character and classic function. This composite school likewise finds its principal contributors in Italy, and has been given the name of "La Terza Scuola" (the Third School).[1] Its position is centered about the psychological effect of punishment; it aims to justify the retention of its traditional function, that of intimidation and of the prevention of crime by its effect upon others. Thus, in punishing a pseudo-criminal as soon as a crime has been committed, it intervenes to teach a lesson to such as might be tempted to follow his example, were immunity from punishment assured. This is the principle of intimidation and example. Alimena, a leading exponent of this school, emphasizes this function as the essential and distinctive characteristic of punishment, by which it differs from the preventive measures taken against the insane. It may perhaps be doubted whether it is possible to influence the future conduct of an insane man by holding up an example. It is evident that the psychological effect of punishment does not react upon other insane persons. They are immune to such intimidation by example. In this respect punishment, in so far as its psychological effects are concerned, whether upon individuals or upon groups, is essentially different from

---

[1] Principally Carnevale and Alimena. See *E. Carnevale*, "Della pena nella scuola classica e nella criminologia positiva e del suo fondamento razionale"; and *B. Alimena*, "Naturalismo critico e diritto penale" (1892); this is reproduced in "I limiti e i modificatori dell' imputabilita" (Vol. I, 1894, in the Introduction). See *Vargha*, "Die Abschaffung der Strafknechtschaft" (Graz, 1896), I, p. 216.

the precautionary measures exercised with reference to the insane.

But this school upholds not alone the restoration of the psychological function of punishment as an example but its popular function in accord with public opinion. In this respect it is most appropriately called the historical school rather than by its preferred name of the critical school.[1] For what is distinctive of an historical school is its allegiance to the evolution of thought, yet not uncritically but in a spirit of thorough conformity to equity as embodied in the law and also to the sense of justice as embodied in the public conscience. It is, then, wholly unwarranted to neglect the popular sentiment that attaches a public disapproval to crime, a sentiment that may be quite unjust if crime is really the inevitable result of an all-conditioning determinism, but a sentiment which the criminal law, even in that event, must formally recognize. If this were not the case public morality would be endangered, — a very serious matter for social security. This does not imply the impossibility of conceiving a social morality independently of the conception of freedom, which is the traditional basis of penalty, but such a conception is confined to a small coterie of astute philosophers, such as Guyau, with a nice and discerning sense of analysis and a distinctive nobility of sentiment. Yet it may be admitted that this conception might be popularized and enter into the consciousness of the masses, if it could be freed from the purely philosophical status that men like Guyau give it, or the too exclusively sociological position defended by scholars like M. Tarde. In that event there would appear a new development in the character of punishment. Until then, if the law breaks too brusquely with traditional sentiment, it will endanger

[1] *Carnevale*, "La questione della Pena di morte," chap. iii.

morality by shattering the foundations upon which it rests before sufficiently establishing the principles to serve as its future basis. Accordingly this conception of the social sanction, in so far as it is the expression of the popular idea of justice, must be retained. Yet this is admittedly a temporary consideration that will eventually give way under changing views. For the present, the maintenance of a proper public conscience remains a second distinctive trait of punishment. Such in rough outline are the principles of this intermediate school.

§ 44. The Physical Recognition of the Criminal; Innate and Acquired Degenerate Traits

It thus becomes evident how far from acceptance are the extreme consequences of the logic of the Italian school, even by the most confirmed determinists. But the problem turns upon the possibility of an exact scientific criterion of distinction between the true and the false criminal. If we are to make arrests before crimes are committed, there must be positive assurance that we are dealing with a criminal prepared to commit crime; otherwise the liberty of all is threatened. Conversely, if a patent of honesty is granted to a man who may be a thief or a murderer there must be positive assurance that there is no mistake. A characteristic index of honesty as infallible as the criterion of criminality must be available. If such a criterion exists, practically any system will work; if not, the whole system is nearly or quite worthless.

Hence Lombroso's criminal type becomes an important factor of his system. The advocates of the Italian school maintain that the varied and increasing discredit of such a type does not affect the fundamental ideas and conclusions that proceed from their principles. This may be the case in theory, but practically the entire system in general becomes impracticable. Granted the pathological criminal type, all is simple and easy; given such a cranial contour, such a facial angle, and related characteristics, and the classification follows. The diagnosis becomes as unmistakable as that of tuberculosis. Under such conditions suspects might be arrested and put under restraint, or their cure attempted before they had committed their first crime. Likewise, when a crime had been committed by a person with normal features he would be confidently held exempt from punishment; he would be pronounced a pseudo-criminal. The true criminal would be recognized and differentiated from the pseudo-criminal, the fictitious criminal, chargeable with crime but not with criminality ; and, likewise, an incorrigible would be differentiated from one amenable to reform. Every variety of criminal would be recognizable by his pathological features. There would be a type of the assassin, and another of the thief; a type of the political criminal, and so on. Even the different varieties of assassins would be thus disclosed. Such a discovery would indeed be marvelous. A few measurements would be sufficient to determine the nature of the case. Penal justice in the future would be free from the possibility of judicial error. Even if there were an error in the evidence and the circumstances of the crime and an innocent man were to be condemned, it would not matter; for the fact of having committed a crime would become but an incident. The chief consideration would be to have spotted an individual of a well-defined criminal type. It would be his skull that would make him guilty and not his crime.

That justice thus administered, however confident of itself, invites other difficulties, is obvious, and is admitted by Lombroso. For if criminality is a chronic pathological expression due to temperament or to an hereditary taint, it is a natural defect; and there is no hope of cure. The temperament as a part of the congenital individual constitution is not subject to reform. This appears in Lombroso's analysis, which regards criminality as a congenital phenomenon of reversion, a survival or reappearance in modern social conditions of the ancestral primitive man, thus making of the criminal a separate variety. Likewise, those unfortunates who display the somatic symptoms of crime have no possible hope of reform. The only policy is mercilessly to eliminate them. They are anti-social; they are diseased elements that cannot be assimilated by the body social. Why not dispose of them as was done with the unfortunate American Indians? This conception of Lombroso's school suggests mediæval justice, — the gallows for the very first theft, at all events for thieves by temperament. The theories of the Italian school were in some measure put into practice in the punitive justice of the fifteenth century; and to introduce them now would be but a return to the insecurity and the despotism of those days.

It is well to recognize that the criminal type, which forms the sole reliance of this system, does not exist; or if it does, it is not as yet determinable by any exact method.[1] Unquestionably no one can deny that pathological abnormal-

---

[1] For the bibliography see *Liszt*, "Lehrbuch," ed. 1905, § 14, note 2, p. 69; and the authors cited in the following note. In the *Revue pénitentiaire* there will be found some interesting views on one of the editions of "L'Uomo delinquente," Turin, 1897, by *M. Granier* (*Revue pénitentiaire*, 1897, p. 1410). Consult also *Frassati*, "Lo sperimentalismo nel diritto penale," Turin, 1892. In refutation of the theories of the Italian school, among other books published or translated into French, see *Lucchini*, "Le droit pénal et les nouvelles théories"; *Albert Desjardins*, "La méthode expérimentale appliquée au droit criminel en Italie" (Paris, 1892); and *Vidal*, "Principes fondamentaux de la pénalité" (1890).

ities are found among the majority of criminals. Marks of degeneracy, in part hereditary, in part acquired, are almost always present. But it is not possible to interpret such symptoms as a characteristic sign, infallibly, universally, and necessarily indicative of criminality; and still less is it possible thus to determine particular varieties of criminals. There are born criminals who are thorough perverts, who lack every moral sense and have lost all feeling of compassion and uprightness, and who yet bear the normal features of honest men ; and on the other hand there are persons who conform to the degenerate type, who present all the Lombrosian abnormalities, who may be, and probably are, neuropathic and ineffective, but who have not committed crimes and are not likely to do so, and many of whom, if given a favorable environment or a saving moral support, will keep to regular ways and steer an honest course through life. If they reach a third, or even a half, of the normal period of life without having committed a crime, shall they be objects of suspicion solely by reason of their features?

Moreover such abnormalities are quite as commonly acquired as hereditary or congenital. They are due to habitual vice, and in the confirmed criminal they are due to habitual crime; they bear the indelible mark of their professional type.[1] Such stigmata may also be due to the prison-habit, and bear witness to the influence of the environment. As a consequence of like routine and occupation, of like habits

[1] See *Baer*, "Der Verbrecher in anthropologischen Beziehung" (Leipzig, 1893). Consult also *Tarde*, "Criminalité comparée," the chapter on Le type criminel; *Puybaraud*, "Les malfaiteurs de profession," passim; *Dostoievsky*, "Souvenirs de la maison des morts" (third edition), p. 13, *seq.*; *Morrison*, "Crime and its Causes" (London, 1891), chap. vii. Consult *L. Ferriani*, "Delinquenti, scaltri e fortunati" (Como, 1897); and also the excellent chapter by M. Joly on the organization of criminals: *Henry Joly*, "Le crime," p. 277, *seq.*

and manners if not of like thoughts, the physical type tends to become the same for all members of the same profession. This is observable in all callings; and crime for certain individuals, sadly enough, is a calling. It thus becomes most difficult to distinguish among pathological marks those that are congenital from those acquired and artificial.

However, criminality acquired through contagion has not the same pathological standing as innate criminality. In one respect it is more serious, in another less so. In so far as innate criminality remains latent and inactive, there is hope of its elimination; while that which is due to habit or environment may appear with all the violence of an acute crisis. But, on the other hand, this same acquired criminality may often yield to a cure less drastic than does the hereditary form; and even in the case of the latter its origin is not a matter of indifference. Is it a racial survival, or a degeneracy of a more immediate source? In the former case it is the outcrop of a primitive racial trait that reappears in all its original force; in the latter it is a new racial trait taking the place of the old. Or is the latter hypothesis but a forlorn hope that the regeneration thus affected may bring to light not the primitive man but his remote ancestor as he was before the fall? But if for all these phases of individual criminality the pathological marks are the same, how can we distinguish, at first blush, the type of individual with which we have to deal? How can we avoid confusing all types, — the born criminal in whom criminality has not yet shown itself even in the form of moral perversity, and the criminal by practice; or again, the hereditary criminal, and the criminal by contagion. Where shall we find the decisive marks for such discrimination? Indeed they do not exist. The danger lies not in the lack of criminal somatic symptoms, but in their partial presence. For this reason, if one follows Lombroso and ascribes to them an absolute and exclusive status, the application of punishment becomes a matter of chance, for this type of relation is inherently variable. The relations between the moral and physical are not subject to exact scientific laws, at least not with the instruments and the methods at our disposal. Hence this position is untenable.[1]

§ 45. Other Phases of Italian Penology; Judicial Diagnosis

But what is there left of the Italian school if deprived of Lombroso's theory of the criminal type? What remains may be formulated in the following four propositions. First, punishment is but a simple measure of prevention in no way different from the precautionary measures taken with reference to the insane. Second, punishment is not the sole measure of prevention to be taken against criminals, for in place thereof use may be made of a whole series of measures, in part economic or social rather than purely individual, all designed to suppress or to cure latent criminality. Third, punishment is not a penalty but a sort of individual treatment, which must not be fixed in advance by law in terms of an abstract crime considered solely as to its objective character. In the practice of medicine it cannot be determined in advance just how long the treatment of a given disease must be followed; that depends upon the patient. Just so in criminology. It is absurd to fix in advance, without knowledge of the individual, the nature and the period of his punishment. The legal assumption that the law alone shall determine the maximum period of punishment has no justification. Fourth, crime retains its purely symptomatic value. Doubtless, if Lombroso's criminal type falls away, there is no occasion to guard against alleged criminals who have not

[1] See *Colajanni*, "Sociologia criminale"; and a very interesting lecture by *M. Prins*, "La criminalité et l'état social" (Brussels, 1890).

committed crimes. But the commission of a crime has no other status than legally to confirm the prognosis disclosed by various symptoms by which are made manifest the organic criminality of the individual. If this is the case, it is absurd to suppose that the list of crimes may be prescribed by law in definite terms. There may be many other abnormal actions, many other expressions of criminality than those legally recognized. The judge, well informed in the progress of science, must shape the conception of crime. The intervention of the law in determining the social gravity of crime is intelligible but not justifiable. The crime enters only as one factor in the judicial diagnosis. Accordingly, the judge, who is charged with the diagnosis, should have the right to treat as criminal symptoms such abnormal facts and actions as have a comparable status and may serve as evidence of criminality. If the criminal type falls away, it is but an additional reason for substituting for it the aggregate evidence and the symptomatic marks that constitute the judicial diagnosis of criminality. The position tends to abolish yet another principle legally upheld; namely, that there shall be no punishment and no violation unless there be a clause of the law that specifies the offense and prescribes the punishment. In the theory under consideration this amounts to saying that there shall be no penal law, that the penal code may as well be abrogated.

These several conclusions may be reduced to the following two principles: that crime in itself has only a symptomatic value and serves but to reveal the presence of criminality and the special degree of criminality of the offender; and that punishment is not the penalty of the crime, but a preventive measure to be taken against individual criminality, — a curative measure if a cure is possible, a measure of definite elimination if there is no chance for improvement. We are thus brought back to the classification of criminals and the measures of individualization.

We thus reach an individualization of punishment, which, once and for all, replaces the entire punitive procedure prescribed by the law according to the outer character of the crime, — an individualization adjusted not to the crime but to the organic, latent, or manifest criminality of the individual. This point alone persists; the conception of responsibility disappears, and individualization takes its place; and we reach the order of ideas and the sphere of action of the Italian school. Their definition of individualization becomes merely the utilization of repressive measures to attain the essential end, which is the elimination of criminality either by the moral reform of the criminal, or, if not amenable to reform, by his segregation; and in either case the adaptation of the punishment to the psychological character of the criminal.[1]

§ 46. What Italian Penology has accomplished

We should be very grateful to the Italian school for having called attention to this new aspect of the individualization of punishment, and for having thus substituted the individualization based upon the character of the agent for the neo-classic conception of individualization based upon responsibility. Doubtless it should not be forgotten that Wahlberg in 1869, at the same time that he introduced the word "individualization," had already established, with a mass of detail that still retains its importance, the essential relation between the psychological character of the individual and the determination of the punishment.[2] But nevertheless it should be recognized that to give the new principle its full scope, and

[1] See an important chapter of *Vargha's* "Die Abschaffung der Strafknechtschaft," Vol. II, p. 119, *seq.*, and p. 504.

[2] *Wahlberg*, "Das Princip der Individualisirung in der Strafrechtspflege," Vienna, 1869. Note particularly chap. vi, p. 144, *seq.*, and p. 160.

still more its setting and its definite basis, there was needed the solid logical construction of the Italian school.

This school deserves recognition on still other counts: for having indicated by its inexorable logic where the consequences of an absolute determinism lead; and for having thus clearly set forth the nature of the penal law of the future, if ever this practical philosophy shall take the place of the popular and traditional conception of responsibility. One must also be grateful to it for its extension of the conception of the judicial function in penology — for having made it clear that a judge is not an automatic distributor of legal punishment but has a distinct part to play in criminal economics, and that punishment in itself is of no avail but must always be supplemented by the introduction of educative and preventive measures, which in turn must be under the jurisdiction of the judge.

Finally one should be grateful to this school for the several problems which it has proposed and the several queries which it has raised, and, particularly, for having produced such works as Garofalo's "Criminology," which, for jurists as well as for sociologists, is a most characteristic and suggestive production of the penological literature of our times, — a work of original scope, and a most useful contribution to the needed reform of our criminal laws.

We may now take up this new group of conceptions and examine what portions thereof are to be considered false, and what, in the present stage of development, may be retained as sound.[1]

[1] To understand the logical position of the Italian school it is well to become acquainted with the work of the International Congresses of Criminal Anthropology, organized by followers of this school, the detailed reports of which will be found in the "Archives de l'anthropologie criminelle et des sciences pénales," published under the direction of Dr. Lacassagne, at the Congress at Rome, 1885 (Archives, 1886); at Paris, 1889 (Archives, 1889);

at Brussels, 1892 (Archives, 1892); at Geneva, 1896 (Archives, 1896); at Amsterdam, 1901 (Archives, 1901); at Turin, 1906 (Archives, 1908). The seventh took place in October, 1911, at Cologne. It appears from these several Congresses, particularly that of Amsterdam, that the anthropological point of view which is looked upon, though incorrectly, as the characteristic point of view of Lombroso, at least in its origins, is tending to lose ground even within the Italian school, and to give an ever-increasing place under the influence of Ferri, to the social causes of crime. On this point consult the important account given by *Ferri* at the Congress at Amsterdam: The Fifth Congress of Criminal Anthropology (*Revue Scientifique*, 1902, p. 331). Likewise at the same Congress a very interesting report was given by *M. Gauckler* to the section of Prisons, followed by a general discussion, and by critical remarks by *M. Tarde* (*Revue pénitentiaire*, 1901, p. 1458).

But the Italian school, despite criticism, is unwilling to give up entirely the conception of the born criminal. On this point see an article by *M. Cuche*, "L'Eclectisme en droit pénal" (*Revue pénitentiaire*, 1907, p. 944, *seq.*).

In regard to the classification of criminals and its most recent literature consult the bibliography in the last editions of the text-book of penal law (Lehrbuch) of *von Liszt;* and equally the last editions of the standard representatives of the Italian school. Consult also the excellent work of *Sir Robert Anderson*, "Criminals and Crime," London, 1907, principally chap. vii, p. 102, *seq.*; and in regard to Anderson's book, a most important article by *Sir Alfred Wills*, "Criminals and Crime," in the *Nineteenth Century and After* (December, 1907), p. 879, but principally pp. 884–894. In answer to this remarkable essay there will be found in the same review (January, 1908, p. 80, *seq.*), and under the same title (Criminals and Crime), some personal observations of a former prisoner — *H. J. B. Montgomery* — in which he expresses somewhat less favorable opinion of the system of indeterminate sentences, and an estimate, which seems very just, of the deterrent effect of long-term sentences. He presents, side by side with these opinions, certain views which seem less correct, at least so far as they touch upon professional offenders. This last point has been answered in a decisive reply by *Sir Robert Anderson*, in the following number of the *Nineteenth Century* (February, 1908, p. 199), again under the title of "Criminals and Crime." See also an interesting attempt at classification by the administration itself, and as applied to prison government, a most suggestive report of *M. Antoine Ballvé*, director of the Penitentiary at Buenos Ayres (Le Pénitencier national de Buenos-Ayres), in the *Archivos de Psiquiatria y criminologia* by *Dr. José Ingegnieros*, professor at the University of Buenos Ayres (May, June, 1907, p. 264, *seq.*); and finally by *Professor Jose Ingegnieros*, "Nuova classificazione dei delinquenti," second edition, appearing in the *Biblioteca di Scienze Politiche e Sociali* (Remo Sandron, Milan).

See also the second study of *Reinhard Frank*, "Vergeltungsstrafe und Schutzstrafe "; "Die Lehre Lombrosos" (Zwei Vorträge), Tübingen, Mohr, 1908.

CHAPTER VI

The Doctrine of Responsibility

§ 47. The Moral Issues in Punishment.
§ 48. The Criterion of Normality; Crime and Insanity; Mental and Moral Maturity.
§ 49. Preventive Punishments for the Irresponsible.
§ 50. True Punishments for True Criminals.
§ 51. A Mediating View.
§ 52. The Popular and Social Bases of Responsibility; Social Solidarity.
§ 53. The Subconscious Basis in Feeling and its Logical Justification.
§ 54. Criminality and Motives; Responsibility and the Moral Nature.
§ 55. General and Specific Freedom of Action.
§ 56. Responsibility, Freedom, and the Will.
§ 57. Freedom and the Principle of Causality.
§ 58. The Human Will as a First Cause.
§ 59. Determinism and the Environment.
§ 60. Freedom Essential to Punishment.

§ 47. The Moral Issues in Punishment

THE position of the Italian school, however consistent and thorough in construction, yet as a whole, with due consideration of its practical consequences, must be rejected. However, a selective analysis thereof will disclose many desirable factors; for it will not do to judge a system wholly by its practical consequences. Such eclectic procedure has been followed by some criminologists to the disadvantage of their position and the discredit of their views. Even Liszt is open to this charge. He declines to accept Lombroso's determination of an anthropological criminal type and rejects as well some of the practical applications that seem to follow from the premises of the Italian school, but he accepts others that involve the same assumptions.[1] This indicates a bias, along with a catholic scientific spirit, in the general trend of his position; but the contour lines of his system seem somewhat wavering. It is not that the conclusions lack clearness or precision; indeed, many of them, as will duly appear, are wholly commendable. But the foundation of this compromising system seems uncertain; it lacks a positive and definite criterion of procedure.

The two principal points at issue may be thus set forth. With the discrediting of Lombroso's criminal type the possibility of a preventive criminology that shall legally recognize the criminal in advance of his committing a crime falls to the ground, for any such procedure would bring about a wholly undesirable and impracticable régime of suspicion. Liszt likewise discards a second practical conclusion, namely, the complete abolition of penal legislation. This would involve the doing away with all legally prescribed offenses, and consequently with the principle that there shall be recognized no punishment and no crime except by authority of statute. Liszt constantly insists that this principle is a bulwark of individual liberty. To allow the judge at his pleasure to introduce new charges is to open the door to caprice and to the privileges of authority, and thus to political influence. This is equally indefensible.[2]

In other respects Liszt accepts the position of the Italian school.[3] He is a confirmed determinist, though many criminologists holding this view remain loyal to the classic school.

[1] *Liszt*, "Lehrbuch des deutschen Strafrechts," 1905, p. 72, note 5.

[2] *Liszt*, "Die deterministischen Gegner der Zweckstrafe," § 5, *Zeits. f. d. ges. Str. W.*, Vol. XIII, p. 354, seq.

[3] *Birkmeyer*, "Die Strafgesetzgebung der Gegenwart in rechtsvergleichender Darstellung," an interesting article in the Review above cited. This should be read with caution since it presents a biased view.

§ 47] DOCTRINE OF RESPONSIBILITY 139

Liszt [1] long ago showed that any such compromise is untenable. It can no longer be questioned that in the absence of freedom there should be no penalty ; for punishment, while something more than a penalty for moral transgression, is nevertheless a social measure, very different from the police regulations which society employs in regard to the insane. Although a normal individual cannot be charged with a thorough-going criminality, yet his crime gives evidence of conduct which discredits, offends, and arouses a strong aversion on the part of others, and is thus looked upon as evidence of moral obliquity. A man who shows himself equal to the boldest crimes is more than a potential criminal; he is an actual criminal. He proves his moral abnormality. If it is his purpose to steal he will commit murder to accomplish it. He is socially antagonistic. Yet this anti-social and abnormal being exercises the same intellectual functions as the rest of mankind. His brain functions normally; he understands, he reasons correctly, but his conscience is wholly abnormal. It is impossible to refer this anomaly of conscience to a physical or morbid disorder. It is a psychological abnormality, inherent in his personal character. If one may speak of his having a soul, using the word in an acceptable symbolic sense, one might say that his soul alone is at once the source of his criminality and the point affected. In this he differs from the maniac, who is blindly and unconsciously a social menace, in consequence of a physiological disorder that makes him not only abnormal but alien to our moral nature. Hence, if the entire inherent difference between the insane and the

[1] See *Liszt*, principally in the article cited above, "Die deterministischen Gegner der Zweckstrafe." Consult also *G. Fulliquet*, "Essai sur l'obligation morale," Paris, F. Alcan, 1898, p. 160, *seq.*; and the report of *M. Garraud* to the Congress of the International Union of Penal Law: "De la notion de la responsabilité morale et pénale" (*Bulletin de l'Union intern. de dr. pen.*, Vol. VI, 1897, p. 330).

criminal is to be referred to the status of the conscience, let us appreciate how different should be the measures employed by society towards the two. The clue to the difference of attitude lies in responsibility.

But apart from these considerations which are psychological because the source of criminality is psychological, punishment is yet further to be differentiated from the preventive regulations concerning the insane. The two differ necessarily and materially as well as in their psychological purpose, as Alimena has pointed out. Even if we disregard the difference in legal status between the measures of protection against the insane and the measures of repression for criminals, the two will ever differ in their effects, and hence in their practical regulation. The measures adopted to cure the insane will never serve to intimidate or to reform criminals.

§ 48. The Criterion of Normality; Crime and Insanity; Mental and Moral Maturity

We must now proceed to define responsibility apart from its usual reference to free will. Such responsibility is social or sociological in character; it must also be given a legal recognition which is to serve as the requisite criterion between the insane and the criminal, alike in preventive, curative, and protective aspects. In this connection there seems to emerge a generally acceptable principle. After much discussion upon the power to distinguish between right and wrong it became evident that this criterion constitutes one but not the sole factor of the moral nature; that, in addition, the strength of the will and of the entire moral personality had to be considered. There was thus reached the conception of normality. A normal being is one capable of exercising responsibility. Such normality is especially

§ 48] DOCTRINE OF RESPONSIBILITY 141

related to the will ; and since the will is determined and conditioned by the motives that make it effective, the normality in question may be referred to the human faculty of determining conduct through motives. Hence the normality ultimately becomes related to the motives themselves. The normality of a human being consists in his being subject as are other men to the influences of the ordinary motives that regulate conduct and human actions, such as those derived from religion, ethics, and conventions. Not to be subject to such influences, to remain unimpressed by what impresses others, leads at first to an insensibility to these motives, then to a gradual failure to understand them, and finally to a withdrawal from a normal condition. Eventually ordinary and normal motives tend to arouse almost reflexly an antagonistic reaction, in all aspects contrary to that experienced by other men. The conduct appears — though this is but an appearance even in the insane — to be reached without motive. In the extreme such conduct approaches complete abnormality and constitutes mental alienation. The intermediate degrees form the transition from responsibility to irresponsibility.[1] This position is set forth definitely and confidently.

But the whole position may be questioned. Liszt himself may be credited with its refutal in an illuminating document.[2] If one may judge by the replies which his manifesto (for such it truly may be called) has aroused, and by Liszt's supplementary article in rejoinder, his strictures seem to

[1] *Liszt*, "Die strafrechtliche Zurechnungsfähigkeit" (*Zeit. f. d. ges. Str. W.*, Vol. XVII, p. 75, *seq.*). An abstract of *Liszt's* important report will be found in an article by *M. Roux*, in the *Revue pénitentiaire*, 1897, p. 970.

[2] See the well-known report of *Liszt* to the Third International Congress of Psychology, 1896, republished by him in his Review under the title of "Die strafrechtliche Zurechnungsfähigkeit" (*Zeit. f. d. g. Str. W.*, Vol. XVII, p. 70).

have made a profound impression.[1] What indeed is normality in terms of the power of determining conduct by motives? Are the conditions to be found only by pathological tests? If so, one must make sure that alienists are agreed upon the definition of insanity. But this can rarely be determined in cases of chronic insanity leading to crime. The question is whether insanity — even where there is a pathological basis, such as is revealed in crime and coexistent with it, or indeed culminating or made manifest in a criminal action — answers to the formula of a chronic state of insanity as traditionally diagnosed. While crime represents an acute and perhaps a wholly transitory crisis, it is no less a pathological crisis. How can the evidence of insanity be found at the time of the criminal action apart from the psychic factors through which the abnormality of the conduct in relation to its psychological motives and impulses is revealed, and especially how can it be ascertained when insanity — as in cases of moral insanity — does not appear until after the decisive action, yet is preceded by a period of incubation during which the brain functions normally, while the moral normality is gradually lost?

Moreover such cases are not likely to be referred exclusively to alienists, nor will purely medical diagnosis be accepted as satisfactory. There are many cases of morbid disturbance giving rise to what may be called partial responsibility, in which, so far as responsibility for crime is concerned, there is no way to determine the degree of cerebral or mental abnormality except by the degree of

[1] *Liszt*, "Die strafrechtliche Zurechnungsfähigkeit" (*Zeit. f. d. ges. Str. W.*, Vol. XVIII, 1898, p. 229, *seq.*). The important study on *Liszt's* report by *Stooss*, "Von Liszt's Angriffe auf die Zurechnungsfähigkeit" in the *Revue pénale suisse*, Vol. IX, 1896, p. 417, *seq.*, may be read with benefit.

§ 48] DOCTRINE OF RESPONSIBILITY 143

abnormality of the will in relation to its determining motives.[1]

It must not be forgotten that along with such deviations from normality in the adult there is likewise a normal psychological and organic development; and standards of normality must likewise be determined with reference to adolescence. This does not involve a question of a pathological condition or disease. To determine whether a minor may be considered responsible, he need not be referred to alienists or physicians. The older laws accepted as such a criterion the capacity for distinguishing between right and wrong. This is now regarded as unsatisfactory, for such distinction is a purely intellectual aspect of responsibility, while account should be taken of the behavior of the will and the general character. Accordingly the proposed laws, like those of the Swiss revision, speak both of intellectual and of moral maturity, which is not by way of definition but of referring specifically to the stage of acquisition of psychological normality. It thus appears in general and in particular that psychopathic examinations are warranted in cases of crime only to establish psychological abnormalities, and that the latter alone definitely constitute the fundamental criterion of responsibility or irresponsibility. Moreover this psychological normality is not an original and wholly spontaneous condition, but a slow and progressive one; when once acquired it may in turn disappear and be lost, and this state of lapse, devi-

[1] On these points useful and pertinent information is found in *Gretener*, "Die Zurechnungsfähigkeit als Gesetzgebungsfrage," 1897. It is difficult to accept the general position of this work. Its criticism of the proposed system in Switzerland, modelled upon the French system, of a purely pathological criterion of responsibility, is interesting, but hardly warranted. The standard work, however, is *Maudsley*, "Responsibility in Mental Diseases," chaps. v and vi; and his "Pathology of Mind," chaps. vii and viii.

ation, or of complete perversion, has corresponding to it a similar variation in the relation existing between responsibility and irresponsibility. Thus there can be no doubt, in case of the hardened, the professional, or the incorrigible criminal, that moral reactions fail to occur, or rather that they take an abnormal form. If the normal behavior of the will is the criterion of responsibility, it is obvious that such normality is less closely approximated in the criminal of the ordinary detached, unassimilated type, than in the minor, or even in the child approaching adolescence. Yet the law declares the latter totally irresponsible, while yet his conscience is awakening and shaping by contact with the morality of his surroundings. The chasm that separates the adolescent from the adult is less deep than that which separates the hardened criminal from the normal man, in that in the criminal the normal development of morality is replaced by a definite condition of constitutional lack of morality. The criminal by natural constitution is clearly irresponsible. This was the conclusion reached above from the point of view of freedom and of responsibility based upon freedom of the will. If we disregard the conception of free will and hold to the purely pathological and psychological conception of normality, we inevitably reach the same conclusion, — as Liszt's logical insight recognized. Without intending to introduce a summary or exact reproduction of the development of his position, we may yet derive from this general impression and suggestion of his clear and vivid exposition, the corroboration of his conclusion that the true criminal, the criminal by nature and by psychological condition, is not a responsible being.[1]

[1] See the important discussion at the Congress at Lisbon, especially the discourse of *M. van Hamel*, in the *Bulletin de L'Union intern. de dr. pén.*, Vol. VI, 1897, p. 468, *seq.*, p. 472.

§ 49. Preventive Punishments for the Irresponsible

It must be concluded that the measures to be applied to this class, which we may call punishments for security or elimination, will no longer be punishments in the legal sense of the word but will now become true measures of preventive regulation, analogous to those taken in regard to the insane. Others have recognized this similarity; the psychological effects of punishment and the psychological reactions that normally follow upon the application of preventive measures have much the same specific character as punishment itself. Stooss, for example, emphasized this point. It is indeed plain that punishment, properly so called, produces no effect upon perverted natures; for persons of this type cannot be reached by such measures.[1] They require something quite different from the ordinary normal punishment, which is intended to be an instrument of moral and psychological influence. For certain criminals by birth there is no hope on the moral or psychological side; there is nothing to be done but to eliminate them as one would eliminate a dangerous and uncontrollable creature. Their susceptibility to punishment is gone. Children are not amenable to punishment although they are really quite responsible; the constitutional criminal lacks the susceptibility because he has psychologically lost it. He has become immune to the punitive point of view.[2]

But this immunity to the action of punishment is not necessarily irresponsibility. Stooss is content to say — or

---

[1] Possibly the same is true in regard to the depressing effect of long term punishments. See the article, above cited, of *Montgomery*, "Criminals and Crime," in the *Nineteenth Century*, 1908, p. 86.

[2] Compare *Stooss* in the article cited in the *Revue pénale suisse*, IX, p. 417, *seq.*, and see his able lecture at the beginning of his course on criminal law at the University of Vienna: "Der Geist der modernen Strafgesetzgebung," and published in the *Revue pénale suisse* (1896), IX, p. 269, *seq.*

at least this seems to be his thought — that the repressive measures to be taken against this class have lost their specific character as punishments. For them something else must be adopted, namely, elimination and segregation. But this is not necessarily equivalent to an admission of irresponsibility. The question is one of the definition of punishment; if it is defined by its psychological effects, Stooss is right. Punishments for purposes of protection are not punishments in the ordinary sense of the word ; they must be differently administered since they look to a different end, and their effects are no longer the same. But if punishment is defined by its legal character and its psychological basis rather than by effects, and if this basis of punishment is to be found in the idea of responsibility, one may say that every measure, whatever may be its outward form, that is applied to a responsible person by virtue of his responsibility, is a punishment.

The proposed plan of Stooss admits responsibility for adolescents so far as they have attained the age of responsibility, and applies to them either a simple reprimand or educative measures.[1] On the other hand it admits as treatment for the incorrigible no other possibility than that of elimination. But they are held to account for being thus intractable; they are responsible for what they are. Accordingly, even these measures, different as they are from ordinary punishments, are still imposed upon them under the name of punishment. In this sense it is that society confines them, as it would a dangerous being whose restoration to a normal condition is despaired of, and through

[1] Art. 7 of the first draft. See *Stooss*, "Exposé des motifs de l'avant-projet de Code pénal suisse " (1893), p. 18; and the discussions on this point before the commission of experts. " Verhandlungen der . . . Expertenkommission über den Vorentwurf zu einem schweizerischen Strafgesetzbuch " (Berne), Vol. I, p. 49, *seq*. See also the second revised draft, 1903, art. 14.

such measure is expressed the social condemnation which, in turn, appeals to the criminal's innate morality, or to so much of it as he retains in common with the inalienable basis of human conscience. It is true that in terms of their external character and their practical administration these measures of protection are not punishments; but they are such in their legal and social status. They thus differ from the measures taken in regard to the insane. According to Liszt's present position they are not different; they are merely applied to criminals who are no longer responsible.

As applied to the majority of criminals, the attempt is made to retain in appearance this criterion of responsibility, and so far as possible, to save the conception thereof.[1] But can this be done? Is the conception of normality, which in essence ever remains the practical basis of responsibility for crime, compatible with the conception of criminality? Assuredly it is so for those accidental offenders whose nature is not affected, in whom there was no real criminality before the crime, and who have acquired none even through the effect of the degradation which objectively is inherent in the crime they have committed. But punishments of pure intimidation are provided especially for this group. Their purpose is to act as deterrent influences, and in so far they likewise become psychologically a modified order of punishment; since those subjected thereto are not supposed to be morally benefited, standing, as they do, in no need of moral reform. Moreover, the measures applicable to the incorrigible class are not reformatory. If such psychological purpose is the characteristic of punishment, these repressive measures are not punishments, since they are only measures

[1] *Liszt* presented this view to the Congress at Lisbon. *Bulletin de l'Union intern. de dr. pén.*, VI, p. 471. His answer to the criticisms against his report of 1896 is found in *Zeit. f. d. g. Str. W.*, 1898, Vol. XVIII, 229, *seq.*

of protection aimed at another group of persons. Here also, since the idea of penalty no longer applies, one should speak neither of punishment nor of responsibility. The class concerned are fully normal individuals. The elimination of criminality is not involved.

§ 50. True Punishments for True Criminals

There is still to be considered the intermediate group of criminals, presenting a natural criminality which is to be eradicated and is amenable to treatment. Punishment is designed for them. But the term "criminality" refers to an initial foundation of abnormality. Moreover, this acquired and chronic insensibility of the moral conscience, which constitutes the abnormality of the incorrigible, is almost always found as a temporary state and as a more intense and acute condition at the moment of committing the crime,— it may be, the one and only crime. Whether or not this is true can be ascertained only by examination of each case as it arises.

With reference to crimes that degrade and dishonor, — assuming that they do not imply at the moment of action an antecedent state of abnormality, — it is clear that in some manner they create such a condition by the very consciousness of being abnormal. This comes to the author of the crime as a revelation and remains with him as an obsession, as a feeling of his moral lapse and his social exclusion.[1] Before the crime, the obsession of the deed in contemplation dominates the criminal; he lives in it, he cannot get away from it. After the crime, it is the obsession of memory, the haunting vision of the act committed, and along with it the feeling that through it he has ostracized himself from the

[1] The point is well covered in an admirable address by M. Tarde before the School of Political Sciences, Thursday, January 20, 1898.

§ 50] DOCTRINE OF RESPONSIBILITY 149

social group of honest persons, that he belongs to another class, that the criminal world alone is open to him, and that he has fallen to its level. At once the dividing line of dishonor and wrongdoing created by the crime blocks his path, and brings him close to abnormality. Even a single lapse may fundamentally pervert. The habit of crime is not always a requisite for the making of an incorrigible; often a single crime may suffice. It may be that the extreme infamy of which the individual is capable rises to the surface and overwhelms him; under the shock thus produced his previous morality and the social ties that stood by him as a support are swept away. If, accordingly, in order to apply the appropriate treatment, it is not the act itself that is to be the object of the penalty but the establishment of a state of normality or abnormality, it is clear how readily the idea of constitutional criminality may be extended. It may even be suddenly acquired, but that is of little consequence; and the related conception of abnormality may apply by a like accident — all this apart from the conception of punishment or responsibility. It is this parallelism of measures of protection in regard to the insane and measures of punishment in regard to criminals that is being more generally recognized; and this brings us back to the demands and the proposals of the Italian school. In returning to this position it becomes clear that in the realm of moral and psychological normality as of that of free will, as was observed in the neo-classic school, responsibility is denied, if not as a theoretical conception, at least in the individual and concrete form. We are dealing only with the abnormal classes, and these will soon be recognized as the irresponsible classes. It is true that the neo-classic school favored an exemption from punishment, which was a serious matter, while now the conclusion drawn is a treatment by way of penal individualization, and the social danger is thus avoided. Yet the view offends the popular conscience, and the traditional ideas of morality and justice are likely to suffer. Far from this being a lesser danger, some believe that the menace to society is thereby increased.

§ 51. A Mediating View

It would thus seem that between the extreme solutions of the classic and the Italian schools there is hardly place for an intermediate system resting on a solid foundation and presenting a real unity of doctrine. There are certain tendencies, and based thereon, somewhat fragmentary and empirical conclusions, determined by such different interests as those of society and of constituted authority. The construction of a legal system requires something different from this. Clear ideas are needed and a comprehensive system that may serve as a guide for the judge's attitude. Such legal construction seems lacking; and for this reason Liszt and his followers do not favor a purely classic system. Yet they do not, and never will endorse certain positions of the Italian school. They hold it as a duty to science, as well as to society, to attempt a statement of these current and irresistible tendencies. The reconstruction of penal law requires co-operation. The older era had as its point of departure the notion of the "criminal risk," and the era now reaching its completion that of responsibility; the era approaching is that of *témebilité* — formidability. The word arouses distrust; it recalls the tracking of wild beasts, and the suggestion is hardly acceptable even in reference to criminals. That is why the idea of individualization seems preferable; the criminal is not to be hounded but reformed. Punishment is not to be made the instrument of barbarism but the means of social reinstatement, and for that purpose it must be adapted to the individual. Simple though this be, it would seem to involve a complete transformation of our traditional system; and law is no more hospitable to sudden revolutions than are other disciplines. History, in order to build solidly, endorses only what is slowly evolved; it rejects systems that are forced upon it by authority. Is it then possible to adapt a system of individualization to our traditional legal organization? Is it possible to set forth principles and to supply the general outlines within which may be gradually established the legal evolution that has already begun? Such are the pressing questions. Upon this topic each contributor may express himself, albeit modestly and without pretense, conscious that the final word will not have been spoken. If such contributions are conscientious, scientific in type, and serviceable to society, they will strengthen the cause of criminology.

The problem must be attacked from above. Hitherto a critical review of systems has engaged our attention; we must now attempt a positive construction, not with any immediate finality, for that would be an idle system-making, but in an attempt to weld the several tendencies ready for fusion into an organic whole. Such an organic form determines the life of a doctrine.

Practically we find ourselves in the presence of two opposed tendencies. The one, the neo-classic school, reduces everything to the conception of responsibility; the other, the Italian school, to a determinism. By a strange contrast it appears that what is sound in the one system is its principle, and what is false are the conclusions drawn therefrom; while in the other, it is the conclusions that are inviting and almost convincing but the principle deters. To propose a possible reconciliation between the principles of the one and the conclusions of the other may seem a strange notion; but are not truths in nature and in thought wrought out in terms of antithesis and irreconcilable principles? Therein lies the mystery of things. In every field of reality there appears this mystery of the irreconcilable, reconciled in the actual. Such indeed is the fact of life itself. It is the nature of religion to fuse these persistent antitheses and reconcile eternal contradictions, to make us recognize that an ultimate accounting transcends our intelligence but that the facts remain. All this apparent eclecticism would be such in fact, were it not that it is based upon consistent conceptions and principles and not upon the simple opportunism of conclusions; but for this, one might hesitate to propose so hybrid and so novel a combination.[1]

But upon reflection the contradiction in question is endorsed by two sufficiently authoritative sponsors, — by popular opinion, and thus by history, and secondly, by ecclesiastical law, and thus by moral doctrine in its most explicit religious expression. We need not consider whether the basis of ecclesiastical law represents any objective and generally acceptable reality. We have only to consider it as an historical and social document of intrinsic value; in this respect it commands attention. To disregard it would be unscientific and would run counter to approved methods of sociology.

§ 52. The Popular and Social Bases of Responsibility; Social Solidarity

It is noteworthy that the difficulties of the neo-classic doctrine is not due to the fundamental conception of respon-

[1] It cannot be denied that the recent conceptions of individualization in criminal economics have been regarded, at first sight, as very difficult to reconcile with the traditional conception of responsibility. See, for example, an important article by *P. Cathrein*, S.-J.: "Das Strafrecht der Zukunft," published in *Stimmen aus Maria-Laach* (1896, p. 461, 489).

sibility. This conception of responsibility is generally accepted, although somewhat differently interpreted. The false position lies in reducing responsibility to the concrete evidence of moral freedom in action; and particularly to the degree of freedom thus manifested. This claim is indeed strange and quite untenable, and is in formal contradiction with the philosophical view of freedom. The objection to the Italian position is not its view of the function of social defense and protection. We can hardly decline to regard such protection as the urgent function of penal law and criminal economics, when each year's statistics shows a frightful increase in the prevalence of crime. Moreover this conception appeared among the older criminologists, such as Jousse, Muyart de Vouglans, Rousseau de la Combe. They certainly did not deny the validity of the conception of freedom and responsibility. The classification of criminals and the joint psychological and sociological analysis of crime are wholly commendable. The prevention of crime requires an investigation of its causes. Equally to be approved is the policy of the adjustment of punishment to the degree of the potential criminality and to the temperament of the criminal. If endeavors are to be directed against the inherent criminality, the criminality resident in the man and not merely that which comes to expression in the crime, then punishment must be made an effective instrument of moralization, and not, as at present, a means of corruption. This, indeed, along with the growing demoralization and irreligion, is the most important factor in the increase of criminality. No one to-day doubts that these considerations will become the basis of the penal law of the future. But what appears false and supremely dangerous is that fundamentally the Italian school impugns the only conception that, from the point of view of morality, can preserve the conscience:

the conception of responsibility. It is false to make of punishment something without influence upon the conscience, to make it merely a cruel and terrible weapon in the hands of the State.

A recent and powerful drama presents the analogy of the ties that hold men together in the social community to those existing between the lion and the jackals who follow him in fear and trembling. When the jackals become strong enough, they rebel.[1] If punishment is to be only the lion's paw pouncing upon its prey, if it is to be but the segregation of a human being, like a wild beast placed in a cage, then here likewise the jackals will rebel; and why should they not? The way to assure public safety and social protection is not to overthrow the conception of responsibility, but on the contrary to implant it in the conscience of the masses and to strengthen it by every remaining vestige of belief.

The conception of responsibility is a principle to be preserved at all cost; and social protection is an equally commanding purpose apparently opposed thereto, but whose interests, while including the whole field, in the end are seen to require a large consideration of the criminal nature and but little of the crime.

When we consider the popular conception of responsibility we find therein, as in all conventional notions, many complex factors: in part an unconscious and inherited belief, which is the product of the cumulative social psychology of many ages and must on no account be neglected; and in part a real though somewhat slender and shallow conviction that serves as the needed justification of this antecedent instinct in favor of responsibility. The social and psychological foundation of the conception of responsibility is its true source, which a scientific and observational analysis dis-

[1] *De Curel*, "Le Repas du Lion" (*Revue de Paris*, 1897, p. 548).

covers; but that is precisely what we fail to consider and what the public ignores. On the other hand the formulated reason constitutes the popular conception. It is the abstract and ideal conception with which alone the masses are acquainted. But when we divorce the conception of responsibility from the rational and logical conception which stands in the mind as its support, we subject it to conditions that are opposed to its sociological foundations.

The sociological factor in the conception of responsibility is derived from various sources. In his "Philosophie pénale" M. Tarde has shown the complexity thereof, which, in the last analysis, turns upon the integrity of certain simple and generic feelings. Yet various opinions have been urged in regard to the sociological origin of the conception of responsibility, and doubtless there enters into it, in large measure, certain effects of a social solidarity, or, as M. Tarde puts it, a social affiliation ("similitude"). Such is the feeling of forming part of a common group; the feeling that any one who is capable of responsibility is like ourselves in his psychological endowment and outward circumstances. To combine responsibility and criminality is to begin with social coherence and end with social detachment; it is to imply a feeling of social community and yet admit a disparity. The farther apart men are in race and environment, the less feeling of responsibility they experience toward one another. A man in the presence of a member of a wholly foreign race, — for an extreme example take a savage, — experiences a sense of antagonism, a powerful physical reaction of repugnance. A crime committed under our social conditions by a savage would make the impression of the onslaught of a beast; he would be hounded and assaulted. This would be a popular illustration of the views of the Italian school. All feeling of responsibility would tend to disappear, and, in excuse of its position and attitude, the public would resort to a formula that summarizes its natural and unconscious prejudice: "Such a man is not like the rest of us." However, we comprehend and admit that he would appear to his own kind as responsible, for it is the similarity of individuals that establishes a mutual responsibility.[1] A similar explanation applies to the observed phenomenon that political or religious factions maintain an irreconcilable antagonism to those most closely approaching their own positions, and this side by side with frank sympathy for the supporters of a radically opposed position.[2] The slightest divergence among a very homogeneous group becomes disloyalty, and family relations all too commonly present the same situation.

It is true that in the last analysis this purely sociological factor corresponds to the idea of blame rather than to that of responsibility, inasmuch as the term implies the feeling of a conscious motive power and self-mastery. It is to the latter that the second factor of the personal sense (so well described by M. Tarde) corresponds, which is nothing else than the reflex consciousness of one's personality. This indeed is a decidedly psychological conception, or, if one prefers, one belonging to social psychology. In the relation of responsibility there is a necessary mutual contact. Imagine a man living alone like Robinson on his island. To arouse in him a sense of responsibility would require that he believe in God. He has no responsibility towards himself, unless he sets up by the side of his real self a fictitious self, —

[1] To understand the consistency of this view with the essential foundations of society one should read an interesting comment on the consciousness of similarity as a social bond, in a thesis by *M. Dobresco*, " l'Évolution de l'idée de droit" (Paris, 1898).

[2] On the community of feeling and the psychological similarity of sects see *Sighele*, "Psychologie des sectes," 1898, p. 84.

the ideal self that he ought to be ; and this implies some higher authority towards whom an obligation is felt, such as God or society. Hence responsibility is primarily a social conception; but, this granted, it becomes as well, though only secondarily, a personal conception. It becomes this through its reference to the ego as an independent cause, and to the integrity of our own personality. There is thus involved a relation with others, which is the social aspect ; and a relation with ourselves, which is the individual aspect. This relation of personal origin consists, in essence, in the identity of the self, regarded as it is at the moment, in relation to the true and fundamental personality. Nothing is more characteristic of this relation than the very history of the words, in terms of the metaphors and ideas which they reflect. The insane man is called alienated; that is, he has become another, he has become a stranger to himself and to his fellowmen. Such lapse, which excludes responsibility in the one state for the other, also applies as between the self of yesterday and the self of to-morrow. There is a break in the personality. When a man thus becomes a stranger to his true self as well as to his fellowmen, he is spoken of as he really is, as a being of another nature without psychological contact with his true self; he is no longer responsible.

§ 53. The Subconscious Basis in Feeling and its Logical Justification

This hereditary origin of responsibility suggests further considerations and involves other determining factors.[1] Pos-

[1] As factors to be considered one may take into account the sense of social cohesion, and also the necessity of fictitious abstraction in the field of the contest between the instinct of individual morality and the social needs. See an important chapter in *Giddings*, "Principles of Sociology," Vol. II, chap. ii; and *Gumplowicz*, "Précis de sociologie," Vol. IV, principally chap. v, § 3.

sibly this group of complex instincts may be reduced to a common point of departure in simple and generic feelings, but that is hardly essential to the present interests. Such a conclusion results from a careful and discerning observation of the relations at a given period and the investigation of these same forces at a previous period, and so on, going back as far as possible in history. They are not part of one's own intimate and personal consciousness. They are not the factors which we feel and of which we are conscious. For us all these things take place in what it has been agreed to call the subliminal or subconscious phase of mental experience. In accordance with this historical growth, the sense of responsibility had assumed the nature of an instinct long before a rational conception thereof was framed, and in so far as it is instinctive, its purport and bearing are least perceived ; of that we have slight consciousness. But we require some abstract principle to explain the notion as well as seemingly to engender it ; and thus logic enters and performs its service. We proceed to give the situation a rational appearance, and when we have constructed the argument we congratulate ourselves upon our discovery. We believe that we have created the responsibility ; or rather, inasmuch as the issue is believed to be something real and objective, we conclude that we have discovered it. We take pride in our reasoning that has penetrated to the essence of things and evolved the elements of a living and mysterious reality therein contained. Such is our logical conception of responsibility.

Objectively these historical and social aspects of the conception of responsibility form its sole constituent factors; in them it has its being. But subjectively, and from the point of view of our inner feelings, they do not exist. For our consciousness responsibility is what our reasoning has

§ 54]   DOCTRINE OF RESPONSIBILITY   159

made it. It contains what we have put into it ; and it is as such that it is operative and effective, and becomes a force and a living reality. A reference to history and sociology lays bare the unreality of the abstraction, yet at the same time discloses the skeletal basis of the construction. But to animate it requires something living, the spark of logical reasoning that gives life to every such artificial construction and makes of it a principle, whereby it becomes an effective factor and a motive of action. In other words, it is as a subjective conception that responsibility is efficient and becomes a conscious motive force. It is this subjective reality, this mental image and concept, that the penal point of view must consider. The important point is not to determine its origin in terms of its sociological and psychological causes, but to observe how it presents itself to the mind, how it lives and makes itself felt in consciousness. It is the social conception, and not the sociological analysis of responsibility, that forms the controlling factor of criminal law.

§ 54. Criminality and Motives; Responsibility and the Moral Nature

As a subjective reality the popular mind has but one mode of representing responsibility, and that is under the conception of causality. The popular analysis of this conception finds no other basal warrant for responsibility than freedom. This second stage in the development of responsibility we reached some time ago. There is no doubt that the efforts of certain modern scholars and philosophers to establish a precise analysis of responsibility apart from the conception of freedom have not taken hold of the masses. They accept the finality that in the criminal is presented the proof of his criminality ; the public, to hold the criminal responsible, requires that he be the author of the crime. He is the victim of his criminality but he has not created it. These considerations serve to establish the collective or social indignation against the criminal deed as an index of social injury ; but they do not require the reference thereof to an individual wrong-doer. The criminal appears as the embodiment of criminality ; and it is the criminality that arouses aversion and indignation. Criminality is above all a menace, but it is also a moral deformity, an anomaly, and a social rupture. We suffer by it morally. But has this feeling any other status than that experienced in witnessing a shocking calamity of natural origin, or a tragic death through accident? In witnessing a revolting tragedy there instinctively arises, because of our suffering, an inevitable impulse to investigate the cause, to determine and remove it. When we find this cause in a being like ourselves, we perceive in him the source of present trouble and the menace for the future ; his inherent perversity is his criminality. We have discovered the moral evil, but that is not sufficient. Just as in presence of a material injury we want to get at the cause, so in the presence of moral wrong we want to trace its original source. It is against this source that our indignation should be directed, for the superficial expression thereof is but the mechanical output of an underlying factor which we must reach. In the last analysis the criminal, as man to man, must admit that the initial cause lies in him, that he himself is the cause. Man is the maker of his own criminality. The determinists say that it is part of his personality and that is what makes him responsible for it.[1] But the public adds that he has control of his personality and of his character, and that the latter alone explains and warrants his responsibility. It is a motive within him, a primary factor of his active and living moral-

[1] See *Merkel*, "Lehrbuch des deutschen Strafrechts," § 28.

ity. This idea of a primary cause, which is indispensable to the conception of responsibility, is identified with the conception of freedom. It is part of the logic of the mind and of the inherent justice of things that responsibility is always referred to the series of secondary causes. The public conceives of justice only as that which applies to the primary cause. To hold the agent responsible requires that the series of causes shall stop with him ; otherwise it goes beyond him and the responsibility belongs elsewhere, — to society, to God, if one still believes in God. In that event it is not referred to the man. The public stops with the man, the author of the crime ; and in the logic of its notion of justice it must make him the free cause of his acts. Without freedom there is no responsibility.

This factor in the logical and ideal construction of responsibility is thus the only one to which we must hold so far as penal law is concerned, since in the minds of the masses it is upon this that the whole rests. For the individual, as for the collective consciousness, moral freedom and responsibility are the same. Penal law may in a sense ignore the instinctive elements in the conception of responsibility, it cannot disregard the rational elements. It is through the ideal and fictitious that men are governed and societies regulated ; and whatever may be said or done, government and legislation cannot really run counter to factors and phenomena as they exist, for these form the very structure of society. The relation for society as for individuals is the same as that discussed above, in which the real self, as it is, is set up against the ideal self, as it is conceived to be. In every community there is the real spirit which gives it life, and the ideal spirit which determines the goal of life. The government or legislation that disregards the former will find itself in direct opposition to the laws of society, but if the latter be disregarded the situation will be still more serious. It will bring about not alone conflict and friction within the organism but a radical antagonism. The legal life of society must be in accord with its true social nature. It must also express an adaptation of the ideal personality that directs its impulses and its progress to the demands of the natural laws that control its operations. This should never be forgotten. Nations can at times, and for a short period, exist without bread; they can never exist without justice. Justice is the very essence of the ideal and progressive life of nations even more than of the life of individuals. The composite school of Alimena agrees to hold to these traditional ideas as they are; it accepts the principle that society lives in ideals and through justice. The conception of responsibility is bound up with this resulting conception of justice. There is no fear that it will ever disappear.

But it is important to observe, after having noted the conception which society forms of responsibility, how it practices it and applies it. As an ideal conception we have seen that it rests upon an instinctive belief, the belief in freedom, which is a purely intellectual principle without foundation in experience. How then is this ideal principle brought to a practical actuality?

It is at once apparent that responsibility as accepted in current thought is primarily a condition or possibility. One says of a man, independently of this or that act of his, that he is a responsible being; and this condition of responsibility is not the empirical confirmation of the state of freedom as we observe it, but a claim of a physical or natural order. It means that his condition is regarded as physiologically normal. In the popular view which holds to freedom, the criterion of this condition of responsibility becomes the same as for the determinists, who deny it: it is resolved into the idea of normality. It is true that in the one view normality is but a sign or a symptom, while in the other it is fundamental; and therein lies an important distinction. For the determinists, for whom responsibility is but a conception of a social or psychological origin, the idea of normality, which is its distinctive factor, is at once the sign and the essence thereof. Back of this appearance no other reality is assumed. Responsibility is made one with normality and thereby becomes fundamentally, as well as apparently, a question of moral pathology. One may thus understand the reservations and hesitations that at present prevail. Even from the pathological point of view can there be a clearly traced distinction between the man of sound mind and reason, who permits himself to be overcome by a momentary attack of criminality, and the man who allows such a condition to become chronic, and again, between the latter and a man pathologically abnormal? The distinction between the criminal by nature and the insane is already tending to disappear; and one may anticipate that with the first barrier let down, the second easily follows, for the difference between an acute and a chronic attack lies only in its permanence and intensity and not in the pathological and psychological nature of the criminality which is displayed.

For the public that believes in freedom, normality is the basis of a moral and a legal presumption, the index of a real condition whose probability is assumed. The popular conception refers to the personality all the psychological factors which form its nature. To this personality are referred the impulses and passions, as well as the instincts and feelings, so that all these motives of conduct appear like the strings of a delicately vibrant instrument, of which the personality becomes the controlling regulator and harmonizer. Personality becomes at once the object and the subject of its expression. From this position even the fluctuation of our psychological and moral personality must be ascribed to our nature, considered as active, as itself the subject of its own activity. For the average mind such an hypothesis is necessary to account for the complete loss of the moral nature. This may be recognized and conceded when the fundamental tissues through which the cerebral processes function no longer respond to normal perceptions, and, consequently, to the objective reality of things. Such is the case of a pathological alienation due to a constitutional condition, whether inherited or acquired matters little. It is a pathological lack of conscience. The common conception of normality, interpreted as a symptom, refers only to a physiological normality, any deviation from which must be of a purely pathological character. The man who can think and reason normally remains, according to the popular conception, a presumably free agent. Physiological normality becomes a matter for medical confirmation.[1] The abnormal man, for whom this assumption of responsibility fails, has been removed by pathological defect from the sphere of our psychology; and as thus considered the hardened criminal cannot be regarded as an abnormal and irresponsible being. In his case there is a defect of the moral sense and not of the faculty of free decision; he shows a perversion of morality

[1] I recognize that the limitation of this point of view, in that it regards normality in the sense of penal responsibility, implies that the estimate of individuals shall refer to a common environment and a common sociological group; for, before we can speak of an individual normality within the group, there must be a sociological normality, that may serve as a primary line of division, separating groups, and involving responsibility. But this depends upon an expression of the social consciousness, and furthermore tends gradually to disappear as the sociological idea of the special group extends and becomes more comprehensive. Consult *Gumplowicz*, "Sociologie et Politique" (Paris, 1898), pp. 120-121.

and not of intellectual perception or understanding. He remains responsible, if not absolutely for his actions, then for what he is and for his condition. This responsibility for a passive condition extends indirectly to the actions which emanate therefrom. Such is the popular verdict. The criterion of normality takes on a more fixed and solid foundation than it does in the determinist's position, because the public holds fast to an assumed ideal factor, which is presumed to persist, except when abnormalities of a purely moral nature intervene.[1]

§ 55. General and Specific Freedom of Action

But when once the condition of responsibility is thus established does public opinion demand a further evidence of responsibility in regard to every action as it occurs? Or to

[1] It was believed that a simple and certain criterion had been found in collective intimidation, the "general prevention" of the Germans. It consisted in considering as responsible all those who are amenable to the psychological effects of punishment, for it is well known that the insane are incapable of being affected by punishment. But the practical difficulties were not solved by this step, for the uncertainty was but carried over to the intermediate group of the semi-abnormal; and it was no easier to determine whether they could be affected by punishment than to determine whether they were in a condition of physiological and psychological abnormality. On the other hand, this is a return to a theoretical assimilation of punishment and the disciplinary treatment of the insane, in the sense that these two orders of treatment differ only in their effects, — as Alimena has very clearly shown. But that they are different in effect, and consequently form a different treatment, does not imply that they differ in nature and in status; and when one speaks of responsibility it refers to the justification of punishment. It is reasoning in a circle to pretend that this justification of punishment is present because the effects of punishment make themselves felt, and that the impression may be of a psychological nature. In the two cases the justification of punishment remains the interest of public security without any other distinction. Consult the report of *Löffler* on responsibility: "Der Begriff der Verantwortlichkeit," in the *Bulletin de l'Union internationale de droit pénal*, Vol. VI (1897), p. 388. See also the letter of *Löffler*, published by Liszt in his answer to the stated criticisms against his report of 1896, in Liszt's Review (*Zeit. f. d. Ges. Str. W.*, Vol. XVIII, 1898, p. 242).

put the question more precisely, does freedom, as the basis of responsibility, when once assumed for a man in a normal condition, become the further object of a concrete inquiry for every subsequent act? We reply, decidedly not; and this conclusion, though surprising, is not the less correct. The public consciousness in judging an individual act does not analyze this condition of freedom, which it accepts in principle as the normal condition of every man in possession of his faculties; it does not seek the source or the degree of freedom in the act committed; it accepts the vague notions of freedom and responsibility in their bearing upon the proof of the state of normality; it does not inquire into first principles nor analyze the concrete situation. It is not the degree of freedom which the act implies that determines the degree of popular indignation, but the degree of interest or aversion which the agent inspires. This has long been observed in the verdicts of juries. The jury is confronted by individuals perfectly responsible for the actions committed, but it appears that the defendants have feelings quite like those experienced by the ones who are to be their judges, that indeed they are all of like nature, with similar environment and social affinity. Such considerations unconsciously weigh with the jurors, and they acquit. It is the natural principle of responsibility that unconsciously outweighs the principle which is its assumed justification. The instinctive feeling of responsibility determines the application, while the rational conception thereof follows a logical construction.

In the public mind freedom and responsibility justify the application of penalty. But this popular conception does not serve to determine the degree of punishment. When it comes to determining the penalty, it is the entire man in the totality of his moral nature that must be considered, and not the fragmentary and incidental part of himself that has found expression in the crime committed. It is the entire man, body and soul, that comes under the jurisdiction of the popular conscience; and that is why the verdicts of juries so commonly differ from legal opinion. The law must judge the artificial and fictitious person who is revealed at the moment of the crime, — that is, the man at a single incidental moment of his existence, possibly when he is hardly himself, — instead of judging the real man, who can be correctly appraised only in terms of his entire life and his complete personality.

If then we desire to translate into a legal principle these several factors contributed by popular opinion — factors that thus find their source and support in society — we may say that the conceptions of freedom and responsibility remain the basis of punishment, but that they do not indicate its degree or serve for its individualization. A punishment must punish (that is, it must be an expression through penalty of social disapproval), only when the act is committed in a normal condition, when it is the work of one capable of freedom. But the freedom thus assumed is a fact that escapes demonstration and scientific analysis. For it is primarily an abstract description of a natural phenomenon; it is merely the rational justification of a sociological reality, so to speak. Consequently, to apply and grade punishment does not imply that we seek to discover the degree of freedom, or that we empirically test the abstract principle. What must be considered is the distinctive character of the delinquent, and the social end to which he, as well as every individual member of society, must be adjusted or re-adjusted. The crime is evidence of social abnormality; the task to be undertaken is one of social readjustment. The purpose of punishment is to further the transition from one to the other; and it is thereby that the interference of society is justified. It is towards this service and function that we unconsciously shape the means. We thus reach the principle, which is that of the classic school, that punishment is based upon the conception of freedom and responsibility; but in application we follow the principle of the Italian school by taking special account of the psychological worth of the individual.

If we wish to summarize these sociological conclusions we observe the following stages of transition in passing from the conception of responsibility to its application: first, a positive belief, a profession of faith in the conception of freedom; second, its empirical identification with the condition of normality; and, finally, a concrete application, determined by the potential criminality of the individual, independently of the criminality of the act in itself. Such is the somewhat strange combination and fusion of ideas that we have reached. It proceeds upon the study of the facts, the observation of the social conditions, and the analysis of the popular conscience.

§ 56. Responsibility, Freedom, and the Will

Determinism and freedom are alike indispensable to the social life, and supplement one another. Without the law of causality all would be indefinite; and without the consideration of the circumstances no one would receive a fair trial. But without the conception of freedom there would be neither morality nor justice as popularly understood. For the fate of rationality and progress is bound up with the idea of freedom. Especially when involving personal sacrifice, the popular view can conceive of endeavor only as taking place under the sway of reason and the influence of noble impulses, as an issue of the freedom of effort, exercised under a belief in the value of such striving for the better. To

§ 56] DOCTRINE OF RESPONSIBILITY 169

put forward virtue as a variety of utility would be popularly regarded as a falling off from virtue itself. Freedom and responsibility are words that cannot disappear from common usage without creating an irreparable void in the current stock of ideas.[1] It is not supposed that these terms are popularly used to support practical, logical conclusions. In the popular mind judgments are inspired by a practical determinism that provides the means of anticipating conduct. But it is by laying bare the layers of cumulative ideals that the nature of social realities is exposed. And indeed the rigid conventions that hem us in by reason of the excess of civilization from which we suffer are likely to be more and more closely drawn. It is well not to interfere with the balance of opposing tendencies. Society as realized, in common with other developments, reflects the mystery of forces that offset one another.

We accept freedom as a traditional datum without which every legal construction would be in contradiction with popular sentiment. But must we not go further? For in the end, if we make freedom the foundation of responsibility solely because the masses believe in it, is there not danger of a conflict between our convictions and the legal solutions proposed?[2] Obviously beliefs cannot be imposed, and there will always be those who question the notion of freedom. But that is not the point. The question to be determined is whether, despite the appearance of facts (which it must be conceded are all opposed to the notion of freedom), this conception remains susceptible of a certain rational proof. That

---

[1] The most convinced determinists admit that they cannot eliminate from human language and conceptions the fact that the individual considers himself a personality in the independent sense of the word. See *Félix le Dantec*, "L'individualité et l'erreur individualiste" (Paris, F. Alcan), 1898, pp. 74, 81.

[2] Consult the report of *M. Garraud*, cited above, p. 139, note.

the conception does not come as an axiom is plain, since scientific observation does not come upon freedom as a discovery, which it then verifies. But freedom is not withdrawn from every possibility of proof. Otherwise the principle involved would be but a common fiction, almost an hypocrisy, which the somewhat ruthless reasoning of the popular mind will perhaps throw aside as quickly as it accepted it. Hence it is not sufficient, in order to maintain the conception of freedom and responsibility as the basis of penal law, to declare that it constitutes a traditional postulate, indispensable to the security of social morality; it must be admitted as a conception whose objective reality may be susceptible of at least an approximate proof.

It is difficult to establish such proof as long as freedom is represented as a state of positive action, as a factor that enters to determine the execution of each of our volitions. In this field we perceive only the predominance of feelings or ideas. When we follow an impulse or favor an idea, such impulse or such idea prevails and thus gives the cerebral mechanism its final direction; and this is the very notion of will or of freedom. What is illusory is the exaggeration of the idea of our will when we wish to will; and this idea — which is nothing more than an idea, and often the most tyrannical of ideas, the idea which we form of ourself as a personality — acts as an intellectual obsession upon the mechanism of our volition. In the traditional doctrine the motives or inclinations are the elements of choice at the disposal of the free will. In reality they are the weights that are put on the balance and determine to which side it shall turn. This final impulse and decisive idea is itself derived by way of indirect influences, from the intrinsic nature of our personality and character. It is the totality of our psychic personality, unified and consistent, that determines our actions.

§ 56] DOCTRINE OF RESPONSIBILITY

In reality the radical distinction that is supposed to exist between instinctive and other actions applies only to their reflex action upon consciousness, and not to their mechanism. Every movement has the same point of departure and the same mode of operation. Every idea tends to express itself in action; and it is the idea that imparts the cerebral impulse and, through it, the muscular impulse. In distinguishing between the will and volition the free action must be referred back to the idea. It is the resolution that is free and not the action. But to make sure that the resolution will not change and inevitably give rise to the action, one must suppose a psychological state of obsession persisting in a permanent form. As to the action of the free will upon the resolution, it arises only from the decisive perception that comes to dominate the rest. But in order that this idea, if not of freedom of choice at least of freedom of effort, shall be present, one must suppose in addition that an opposed tendency to the initial impulse has asserted itself, that the idea of a different issue has come to mind; and every idea, as is familiar, tends to express itself in action. Thus it comes to offset the other by the very fact that it exists; however weak it may be, however subordinate the counter-tendency, there exists, through the very fact of there being an opposed idea, a conflict which begins and may grow; for psychologically an idea never exists in a purely passive condition. It is well understood that, if the idea of an opposite action does not present itself at all, — and this is quite too frequent in case of crime committed by an habitual criminal — there can be no question of freedom. If it is present, it is through the growth of the contrary idea that the notion of "not doing" (restraint) may come to be the dominant force in opposition to the notion of "doing." There thus will occur a moment at which one of the two ideas will be expressed in an act of will; then the decision is made. Now there can be no doubt from the psychological point of view that this action of a purely internal character is produced through the same cerebral functioning as is the physical act which becomes the external expression thereof. It becomes an impulse under the sway of an idea that has become dominant and has reached the condition of an acute obsession. Every idea that acts by way of the will expresses itself under the form of a momentary obsession which lasts, it may be, an infinitesimal time, but is of the same nature as an obsession of a chronic order.

In an extreme case it is neither through the volition presiding over the physical act nor through the will translated into an inner resolve, that freedom comes to be realized. It is possibly only through the growth of the idea that the idea of willing is evolved by direct action upon the feeling itself; that is, by the personality acting upon itself, upon its intimate and total character. Freedom, if it exists, extends over several stages; it always goes back to the impulsive feelings, to that which serves as the motive forces within us. It is upon our sentiments, feelings associated with ideas, that the effort operates to oppose or develop them, to further or hinder them. We thus always reach this mysterious point of the psychological nature at which consciousness discovers the unity of the self, individualized and integrated.[1]

§ 57. Freedom and the Principle of Causality

However, here the field of scientific investigation stops;[2] and beyond, the assertion of the law of causality under its

[1] All philosophic and scientific demonstrations bear on this point. The references are endless; it is sufficient, and in the legal field of punishment one can do no better than to refer to *Merkel*, "Lehrbuch des deutschen Strafrechts," §§ 19 and 20.

[2] In the excellent book of *P. Coconnier*, "l'Hypnotisme française," p. 367, *seq.*, will be found a very interesting development of the Thomist doctrines in regard to the functions of the mind and their psychological operation.

§ 57]   DOCTRINE OF RESPONSIBILITY   173

mechanical form is only a metaphysical assumption which has precisely the same value as the postulate of freedom. If one must choose between these two *a priori* data, it is by other than scientific or experimental methods that conviction comes to one. Indeed, when we have reached the very foundation of our personality and of the consistent unity of our nature, we must ask whether this personality constitutes a cause in itself, apart from the physiological mechanism which is its instrument; whether, in consequence, we are by the unity of self a primary cause, of a nature different from that of the skin, nerves, and muscles, that transfer the vital impulse.[1]

We unquestioningly admit the influence upon one another of psychic factors; and we may believe that where the realm of the unconscious begins, the chain of causation continues, and returns upon itself at the point of meeting between the psychic mechanism which closes the process and the physiological organism that begins it. But as we remain within the limits of what is conscious and perceived as an intimate sense-feeling, there is no doubt that along with the influence of a physiological order, which we never escape, there is experienced a background of the basal psychic individuality to which our moral nature is bound. There is likewise no doubt that this psychological individuality is influenced by tendencies by way of the permanent path of actions and reactions. But our consciousness thereof reveals it as at once subject and object, as a primary cause acting upon itself. It thus answers to the action of environment, or in theological phrase belonging to another realm, it answers to a state of grace. The question thus returns to the determination of whether in the last analysis

[1] See the two important chapters of the thesis of *M. Maurice Blondel*, "l'Action," part iii, § 2, chaps. ii and iii (Paris, F. Alcan, 1893).

the psychological personality (outside of the purely instinctive phase of our nature) is the issue of an absolute and complete subjection to the physiological mechanism, — the question assuming that we remain within the field of the conscious and directly perceptible. At this juncture we have passed beyond the field of experience and direct observation. The argument passes to a metaphysical type of explanation and makes the law of mechanical causality, as expressed in unconscious nature, equally the principle of the psychic life in its relation to the organic personality.[1]

This is the type of question which science can answer neither in the affirmative nor in the negative; for it belongs to a realm which science neither commands nor invades. It involves the essential nature of being. Science recognizes only phenomena; it does not consider the essence of things.

However, if this question is answered affirmatively, if this conception of self-sufficient personality is capable of an objective existence, then this personality can exist only in such autonomy, if it exercises a real autonomy over the organism that serves its expression. If a realm other than that of material nature be admitted, it follows that man, as a spiritual being, may be an autonomous force. Bearing upon this position is the able address of M. Sabatier, delivered at Stockholm.[2] While one may not concede all his conclusions, one will readily recognize their high moral and religious import. He sets forth the requisites

[1] On these points see the excellent work of *Stammler*, "Wirthschaft und Recht nach der materialistischen Geschichtsauffassung" (Leipzig, 2d edition, 1906). See also the account given by *Keller* in the *Kritische Vierteljahresschrift für Gesetzgebung und Rechtswissenschaft* (1897, Vol. XXXIX, p. 498, seq.). See also a résumé of Stammler's views in his work on solvency in the German civil code, *Stammler*, "Das Recht der Schuldverhältnisse" (Berlin, 1897), pp. 14–21.

[2] *Sabatier*, "La Religion et la culture moderne" (Paris, 1897).

necessary for the transition from a personal autonomy of thought to a religious autonomy, — an autonomy, by the way, that remains perfectly consistent with a group of universal dogmatic truths, for the reason that it is comprehensible only in terms of the inner life of the soul and not of the objective reality of the facts belonging to a different realm. But clearly such autonomy is meaningless and these conceptions, ably and even scientifically expressed, are but words without other significance than as an abstract construction, unless there correspond thereto an actual natural autonomy without which the rest is but mental illusion and fiction. Such autonomy of the human personality is what the conception of freedom should signify. Freedom is the law of whatever evades the realm of physical nature, as causality is the law of whatever belongs to the world of natural phenomena. Freedom is thus the personality itself, in so far as it is capable of detachment from the organism that serves as its instrument, and thus comes to live its true life and to influence character and all the latent reserve forces that favor virtue and oppose vice.[1]

§ 58. The Human Will as a First Cause

Freedom is not necessarily active. It is a condition; the condition of a man in complete self-mastery, — a condition that accepts and implies an internal determinism, provided that such psychological determinism is eventually connected with a vital cause within the self and part thereof. In the traditional view free will is conceived as a determining influence interposed between the motives and the act itself. Thus the free will operates and becomes the

[1] On the question of freedom and moral responsibility see particularly, apart from the already cited works of *M. Fouillée* and of *M. Fonsegrive*, the suggestive study of *M. Lévy-Bruhl*, "L'Idée de responsabilité" (Paris, 1884).

immediate and efficient cause of the action. In this mode of viewing the matter there is a kind of anthropomorphism derived from the appearance of the action, as though man stepped in to the contest of purely natural causes in order to direct them in defiance thereof ; it is the intervention of human agency. In the psychological conflict there may enter, at the moment of action, an analogous factor, likewise independent of the efficient psychic elements that form the essential human character as opposed to elements of a material order. Would it not be better to say that freedom — assuming its existence as a quality of action — is but the psychological personality acting upon itself and influencing motives and inclinations? Since, however, in this analysis of the psychic personality there still remains a bit of purely artificial abstraction, would it not be still better to speak of it simply as an influence upon character, upon the basis of personality, from which are derived motives, inclinations, and impulses. In this way freedom may be said to act upon the determining factors of the will itself. In the mental experience which constitutes the field of science, there appear only these factors in operation, in a series of actions and reflex reactions up to the final discharge which determines the act. But when it is a matter of going beyond this into the field of causes antecedent to the primary cause, science can reason only in hypotheses, in terms of a fundamental condition of the physiological organism. Offsetting one hypothesis by another, one may assume, along with this unquestioned relation, a factor of a different nature, whose laws escape the record of scientific instruments and whose principle is that of free causality. But precisely because such relation is unquestioned does the condition of freedom, being but a condition, imply variable stages from a complete dependence of the personality upon the conditioning physiological influences up to full self-mastery, by which the personality, conformably to the laws regulating its existence, transcends this organic mechanism, to develop the free conduct of a transfigured and re-established personality. Such transfiguration of the self may be the issue of tedious labor and long effort, by adjustment to a new environment and to new influences. It may also appear as a sudden and profound conversion, which, like an act of will, gives the impression of being free in the traditional sense. Thus is a personal self regenerated and set free.

§ 59. Determinism and the Environment

Obviously freedom does not imply that caprice or break with causality, which the traditional view of free will assumed.[1] It is character developing its normal issues, subject to the continued control of the psychological personality, whereby at any moment it is reinstated as an influence and modifies the direction of its own conditioning factors. So it may truly be said of a man that he always acts according to the law of his character, as one may predict of the poor tree of the Gospel that it will bear only poor fruit. Psychologically determinism bears the same relation to freedom as historically it bears to the will. Whether the will be free or not, it is certain that it introduces an incalculable factor in the sequence of social issues, but this factor is so slight that sociology may disregard it and yet become scientific; moreover, sociology may make allowance for this variable factor by establishing the laws controlling the influences to which human wills are subject, which, in turn, influence the group of automatic personalities of which

[1] On this point see an able chapter in *Prins*, "Criminalité et Répression," chap. ii, § 3.

crowds are composed and by whose actions history is shaped. A similar relation obtains in regard to the psychological determinism of the will with reference to freedom. In predicting how a certain type of person will behave, one may always disregard the intervention of the incalculable. On the other hand one may estimate the influences that are likely to arouse a reaction of the personality and a free adjustment on his part to the influences to which he is exposed; and one may say of this adjustment to the influences of the environment what the theologians say of the responsiveness to grace, that there is neither an absorption of one in the other nor a fusion of the two, but a reciprocal interaction through which the intrinsic freedom and integral nature of the human personality persists.

Freedom, if it exists, is thus merely the power of our ultimate resistance, the fundamental possibility of reaction in opposition to external forces; and this power of resistance, while it may be aroused or excited by something from without, need not necessarily be conditioned and determined, as is the ultimate discharge of the will, by the impulse that comes to prevail. The psychological personality, though in its essence escaping our investigations, may impose its own law of causality. It cannot be denied that all this amounts to a contradiction. But contradiction is the law of all nature, and this break of the law of causality in passing from one field to another is no more mysterious than its universal application; it is like an endless chain returning upon itself, since it ever supposes a primary impulse originating in a free and independent cause, which arouses the next primary cause, and, through it, all the rest.

Freedom thus understood and considered, in relation to each of our particular actions, becomes a potentiality and not a necessary actuality. It is through the influence of character upon our feelings that we are able to direct our actions, and by virtue of this mechanism one may declare that every act is virtually an act of freedom. But to determine to what degree it really is free is a point that will always escape us.[1]

§ 60. Freedom Essential to Punishment

The problem of freedom, like the problem of the soul, of which it is but a special phase, and like the problem of God, is one which cannot be demonstrated by reasoning, nor established by scientific induction, but which demands other modes of proof, which are, however, not essentially different from those that serve to convince us of the objective reality of the external objects perceived by our senses. To believe in the latter requires the same act of faith in regard to the data of our external senses as is the act of faith demanded of our inner senses to believe in those other realities, or, let us say idealities, of which freedom is assuredly a part.[2]

[1] In reality this conception differs more from the traditional one through the psychological mechanism of freedom than through its effect. To consider an extreme case, if one wishes to take account of the purely theological doctrines, and particularly of those of Catholic theologians, concerning this problem of transcendental metaphysics, one may refer to an important thesis of *P. Frins* (S. J.), "De actibus humanis ontologice et psychologice consideratis" (Freiburg-in-Breisgau, 1897), No. 97, and *seq.*, p. 116, *seq.* Within the realm of more modern philosophy, characterized by the most advanced scientific spirit, see the excellent work of *M. Fonsegrive*, "Essai sur le libre arbitre." Consult also *Desdouits*, "La Responsabilité morale," Paris, 1896. But the two authoritative works are those already cited of *M. Fonsegrive*, and the older thesis of *M. Lévy-Bruhl*, "L'Idée de responsabilité."

[2] On these points see the excellent preface of *M. Brunetière*, to the translation of *Mr. Balfour's* "Foundations of Belief"; and the articles of *M. Maurice Blondel*, "Les exigences rationelles de la pensée contemporaine en matière d'apologétique et la méthode de la philosophie dans l'étude du problème religieux," published in the *Annales de Philosophie chrétienne* (January, 1896), Vol. XXXIII, p. 337, *seq.*; and on these articles the study of *P. Laberthonnière*, "Le problème religieux" in the same Review, 1897. See also *M. Payot*, "De la croyance" (Paris, F. Alcan, 1896).

Instinctive convictions that differ from scientific certainty are equally indispensable; they do not command the universal adherence, the objective certitude, if we may so speak, that attaches to the truths of scientific observation. The certitude thus involved is more distinctively subjective and individual.[1] And this is of capital importance for penal law. It is doubtless sufficient, in order to regard freedom as the basis of penal law, that the idea of freedom shall be susceptible of a proof appropriate to our nature; at all events, let us take this for granted. However, such conviction remains a personal issue, even though considered as universally available. For its basis of practical application penal law cannot use a conception that evades scientific investigation and belongs to the realm of faith.

We thus reach, by a different path, the important truths derived from the study of history and popular opinion. We conclude that the conception of freedom determines the character of the punishment; that, without it, punishment can be neither a penalty nor a measure of social disapproval; indeed, that it falls to the level of the brutal measures of protection taken against wild beasts, against the insane, or, in former days of private vengeance, against the conquered and subjugated enemy. It is a return to barbarism. If then this ideal conception is sufficient to preserve the specific character of punishment, one need not go further. The application of punishment thus justified as a punishment, by virtue of the possible condition of freedom to which it refers, does not depend upon the degree of freedom ascertained to be present. The degree of punishment is only nominally and legally connected with the responsibility for the act. It should refer practically and effectively to the potential

[1] See an interesting study by *Erich Adickes*, "Wissen und Glauben," in the *Deutsche Rundschau* (January, 1898), p. 86, *seq.*, and principally p. 93.

criminality of the individual. The conception of punishment implies responsibility. One must believe in responsibility in order that a measure taken against an offender shall be a punishment. But the application of punishment is no longer a matter of responsibility but of individualization. It is the crime that is punished; but it is the consideration of the individual that determines the kind of treatment appropriate to his case. Responsibility as the basis of punishment, and individualization as the criterion of its application: such is the formula of modern penal law. The era of responsibility is completed; that of individualization is beginning. This does not mean the renunciation of the idea of responsibility, but only the renunciation of the dangerous and puerile fiction, whereby positive and practical applications [1] were derived from merely abstract premises.

[1] All this has already been well set forth by *M. Cuche* in an able article published in the *Annales de l'Université de Grenoble*, 1897 — a valuable authority in support of the argument here upheld. *Cuche*, "De la possibilité pour l'école classique d'organiser la répression pénale en dehors du libre arbitre" (Grenoble, 1897). The same ideas have been taken up again by *M. Cuche* in the "Traité de science et de législation pénitentiaires" (Introduction à la science pénitentiaire, chap. 1: les fonctions de la peine, p. 36, *seq.*). See also a report by *M. Cuche* at the International Congress of comparative law held at Paris in 1900 (*Revue pénitentiaire*, 1900, p. 1145, *seq.*). I note also an excellent thesis by *M. G. Mabille*, "De la question de discernement relative aux mineurs de seize ans" (Paris, 1898), in which I find, not without a certain personal satisfaction, the support of these views. They are there presented with remarkable clearness and effect. See particularly p. 62, *seq.*, and the conclusion, p. 155. Consult the able works of *Dr. Grasset*, already cited, p. 98, note.

CHAPTER VII

Responsibility and Individualization

§ 61. Freedom in the Penal Codes.
§ 62. Social and Personal Aspects of Punishment: their Legal Recognition.
§ 63. The Conception of Punishment.
§ 64. Society's Interest in Punishment; Crime and Degradation.
§ 65. The Moral Purpose of Individualized Punishment.
§ 66. Ecclesiastical Law and Individualization.
§ 67. Examples in Penance and Clemency for Special Crimes.
§ 68. Individualization in French Codes: Political Crimes.
§ 69. Individualization in Deportation.
§ 70. Individualization in Short-term and Long-term Sentences.
§ 71. The System of Parole: its Faulty Application.

§ 61. Freedom in the Penal Codes

THESE newer conceptions should bring about a revival of interest in the French penal code of 1810, — not the penal code as distorted by false modern classicists, but that of the original classicists. This remains the model of its kind and requires but little to put it in line with contemporary progress. The possibility of punishment assumes the potential condition of freedom; such is its postulate throughout. But the determination of what is thus assumed, the penal code does not leave to the decision of the judge. It does not even mention the term "freedom;" it remains outside of, and does not invade penal law. It makes freedom exert its influence from above as a comprehensive conception. It does not make freedom a concrete datum to be legally established. This is why the penal code of 1810 — not that of the neoclassic theories, but the penal code in its original and best form — has remained, or has once more become, the most modern of penal legislations. Undoubtedly the penal code of 1810 has serious defects, of which the principal is its assumption of the potential state of freedom in every adult of sound mind, and its further assumption of the identity of freedom and responsibility. The latter it holds by reason of the unity of the will, which it considers as a neutral force entering into each volition; from this it infers that the same crime should carry the same punishment. That is an untenable conception. The assumption of freedom thus conceived stands in the way of the individualization of punishment. There thus arises an incompatibility between responsibility and individualization; and this affected the neoclassic position in its attempt to embody the idea of responsibility in the procedures of individualization. But this fiction became inacceptable, and such a state of things could not continue. A return to the penal code was made necessary, not to set up responsibility against individualization, but to combine the two. The former, as it appeared in the penal code, was in a measure a fundamental and comprehensive conception, determining the character of the exercise of penal justice; the latter was assigned the part of the active and inspiring motive of the practical organization of punishment and of its application.

If freedom is thus a condition of the personality rather than an act of will, it is this condition that punishment should accept as a basis and a standard; and the conception of freedom, far from being set up against an individualization based upon the existence of criminal condition, argues in favor of such process of individualization in its most subjective form. It favors it by its opposition to the view of the older system, in which the responsibility of the individual was made dependent upon an abstract will exercised in the crime, a fictitious personality considered at a single moment of existence. It sets in its place the entire personality in its unity and integrity, viewed as the active force of the moral nature, considered as capable of moral conduct. The distinction is fundamental. In the newer view the personality qualifies for moral action, and becomes amenable to a precise psychological analysis.

§ 62. Social and Personal Aspects of Punishment: their Legal Recognition

In this view punishment retains its specific character and thus remains a punishment in the traditional sense of the word, but at the same time it becomes a measure of social protection; and in addition, the penal law retains in part its objective aspect. The purpose is not to substitute a purely subjective examination for the classic system of offenses and legal punishments but to combine the two. It may further be noted that the attitude toward the objective side of punishment is not quite that represented by Liszt's theory; for he considers it as a practical concession to guarantee personal freedom. So long as one holds to the principle of moral freedom the conception of penalty must be retained; and the objective point of view follows directly from the notion of penalty. Under the conception of freedom one is doubtless responsible morally and religiously for what one is, but socially one is responsible only for what one does. Freedom, considered as a personal capacity, is correlated with the responsibility for the actions committed, since they are the issue of such moral and mental personality. But socially, it is through his actions that the individual injures society. Society does not control what he is, for it must respect his freedom; it acquires authority over him only through what he does; it has authority only over his actions. Indeed, individual responsibility, which is purely moral or religious, must not be confused with social responsibility, which is involved only to the extent to which society controls individual liberty; and such authority is legitimately applied only through the consequence of an action harmful to society. But at the same time that an act has been committed which confers upon society the right of intervention, evidence has been given of the danger to which one of its members may expose it; and the penalty, which it is the duty of society to exact for the act done, must be so disposed as to make it a safeguard against future exposure.

The idea of penalty implies that punishment is the expression of social disapproval, the expression of public condemnation based upon the disturbance and excitement brought about by the crime. This implies that there is crime and also that the social, and therefore the formal, aspect of the crime must be taken into consideration. Socially the crime is of account only through its consequences, and not through its antecedents or causes. A murder, whatever may be its cause or whatever the motive that accounts for it, remains a murder so far as concerns the social community in which it has occurred; that is, it remains the supreme violation of personal right. If it is judged in terms of the injury effected, the consideration of purpose and motives disappears altogether. In so far as it may become the center of a series of waves of suggestion, to use the apt expression of M. Tarde, it is significant only through its results and its formal status. By virtue of its legal definition it acquires a real status in the law. The law can prescribe and define offenses only in formal terms and must disregard their concrete setting and their detailed circumstances. But the application of punishment requires the consideration not of the abstract crime and its legal status, but of the concrete crime with all its complex psychological factors, which in turn must be ascertained, judged, and punished. At present we are treating of responsibility only from the social point of view, and of the penalty in terms of the social injury. This implies that crime should be defined by its formal status and taxed according to its social value; that is, according to its objective gravity for society. The meaning of this is definite: for an action to be punishable and justify prosecution its formal features must correspond to one of the legal prescriptions. It is the crime as defined that alone permits prosecution, but it is the criminal act, or rather the agent, the author of the crime, that should be the object of punishment. The objective aspect of crime determines the prosecution, and the subjective aspect determines the punishment. Such is the division to be made between the two considerations. A place remains and should always remain for the objective side of crime and punishment.

This is essential not alone for the determination and warrant of the prosecution but equally for setting what is called the legal punishment. The legal punishment is at first a maximum. It is the limit set to the discretion of the judge. The abolition of such upper limit will never be permitted, but we are quite willing, as has been done in the Dutch penal code, to abolish the minimum. The system of ancient law that permitted the judge to go beyond the maximum legal punishment, or rather, to choose among the legal punishments by taking the most severe, even though it may not have been a punishment prescribed for the particular crime, would be in total contradiction with the principles of our public law. Thus legal punishment is primarily an upper limit, but it is otherwise significant; it is a social appraisal of the deed considered as a crime; it is a tax. If the penalty aspect persists, the penalty should be proportional to the objective gravity of the deed. It must then have a legal tax serving as a scale to measure society's interest in the prevention of that crime. Thus there must be a proportionate social indemnity, precisely as a personal indemnity is appraised according to the injury done.

For this reason, apart from the demands of public law, there must continue to be a scale of offenses with a legal maximum of punishment. But this scale is only a relative one, indicating the maximum for each crime; and the judicial sentence for each particular crime follows a similar relative scale in terms of the punishments. It is not an exact dose that can be applied to the letter; it is a relative and general prescription. It but indicates to the judge in what degree and in what proportion, in each particular case, he should consider the social gravity of the crime. Yet the gravity of the crime is to be considered only secondarily, after the fundamental consideration which remains dominant in the application of punishment; namely, that of the individual concerned and the degree of morality which he retains. As will appear later, the subjective consideration of the individual determines the nature of the punishment; and the objective gravity of the crime is also to be taken into consideration as one but not the only factor entering to determine the term of punishment.

§ 63. The Conception of Punishment

The system of individual adjustment requires that the nature of the punishment should be determined by the nature of the individual. This is the very definition of individualization. Punishments should be differentiated with reference to the classification of criminals, and not to the categories of crime. But the term of punishment will depend also, in greater or lesser measure, and in accord with the relative scale provided by the penal law, upon the objective gravity of the crime. Such is the accepted compromise between individualization as the criterion for the application of punishment, and its relative objective status, which is likewise to be retained.

It is well worth while to note that this combination stands in complete harmony with a legitimate attitude towards the problem of freedom itself. Freedom is not a necessary datum indispensable to the practical construction of penal law; it is a moral conception based upon an individual belief, a datum of the personal consciousness. Thus it bears only upon the conception of punishment and the notion thereof to be entertained. It does not bear upon 'ts administration. The administration of punishment considers actual social needs with little concern for our theoretical beliefs. It grows out of criminal sociology. But while criminal sociology operates subconsciously those who apply its laws are influenced by moral conceptions, and it is to such conceptions that punishment must be adjusted. To keep in touch with current beliefs punishment must be given a rational setting. The conception of freedom and responsibility must be retained in the administration of punishment only as a conception, and it must not interfere with the requirements of social protection. There should be organized a protective penalty for society against responsible evil-doers, and a penalty so far as there is responsibility.

But a further important point remains. The value to be ascribed to the psychological aspect of punishment has been considered; accordingly, in a way, the conception of punishment may be exclusively reserved for such measures as have an influence upon the psychic personality. Punishment does not become equivalent to any and every punitive measure based upon responsibility. It comprises only such measures as in their application to responsible agents may be directed to those susceptible to psychological appeal; and this may be properly interpreted to include *all* the results that may be expected to come from punishment. Such was the view of ecclesiastical law, as well as of other systems, in regard to the function of correction and reform. It was also the position of Feuerbach based upon the curious notion of a psychological balance of forces: as punishment was the threat of a given degree of suffering, it should stand in the mind of a man contemplating a crime as the exact balance of the profit which he expects of its accomplishment. But there is yet another aspect of the problem, too commonly overlooked. Before knowing how the execution of the punishment will affect the individual concerned, one must know (for the one depends upon the other), how he will be affected by the very idea of being condemned to punishment; and this question involves yet another, which is but the public phase of the same, namely, what impression is the condemnation going to produce upon others?

§ 64. Society's Interest in Punishment; Crime and Degradation

The future of penal reform centers about this question, for sociology has definitely established the influence of social community upon social adjustment. Adjustment to a socially organized group occurs only when there is a feeling of a certain similarity of character; a similarity that is interpreted legally as the conception of equality with the rest of the community. Any deviation from this standard implies the existence of a difference, a more or less radical withdrawal, an exclusion; hence a social mal-adjustment. The psychological effect of a lapse from social standards upon a member of a social group is the loss of the feeling of self-esteem, and frequently what is called shame — and shame should not be confused with remorse — is but the first realization of such personal lapse and the effect thereof. No character can resist it. Society may pertinently say: Whoever is not with me is against me. There are ever two groups: the pros and the cons, those on the one side and those on the other, organisms of a different structure but a like power. One may belong to the party of the opposition by natural tendency, or, possibly, by the emotional effect of the first offense. But if it happens that neither one's natural attitude towards crime nor the reaction subsequent to the actual commission of a crime is a sufficient protection against crime, there remains yet another alternative, a last chance of losing or of saving one's soul, the choice of remaining a useful member of society or of passing over to the enemy's camp. This choice depends upon the psychological effect of punishment ; to which camp will punishment send one?

Now in this connection one may indicate three or four tendencies corresponding to various historical aspects of punishment. The first belongs to the primitive theory of criminal risk. What we look upon as crime appeared in primitive conditions as a normal condition of life in which one simply took his chances. There was no degradation in crime. A cyclist who runs into and injures a pedestrian pays the damages, and is not considered disgraced. No one would think of him as wicked. The same is true of the soldier of the period of private wars. He agreed to a settlement and paid the Wergild; and clearly the payment of the Wergild did not disgrace. Ecclesiastical law, at the very time when the conception of sin and responsibility was spreading, presents a conception, which, along with considerable differences, has points of resemblance with the former view. Crime constitutes a fall, but a fall that does not degrade. Christianity has impressed upon the world the notion of sin, which it has made the normal condition of humanity. We all are more or less sinners, and among those fundamentally much in the same condition, sin can arouse only commiseration and pity; it does not arouse aversion. The sinner is a brother to be helped; he is not an outcast from the community. Heresy alone can break the common tie. As between those united in a common faith, a lapse, even a crime, does not degrade. One should chastise, and chastise ruthlessly; but punishment implies the certainty of reinstatement and not an ultimate ruin. And in communities that have retained something of this monastic spirit, it is indeed strange to observe the feeling of tolerance for wrong-doing so long as faith is professed. Many instances of tolerated fraud thus find explanation, but this circumstance proves as well the persistence of the curious social fact that crime in itself does not degrade.

The association of degradation with punishment appears in the rationalist theory of responsibility. If every offense is the result of a free but perverted choice, punishment becomes the chief clue to the sinners of this world. It serves to mark the division between those of evil intent and those regarded as righteous. For the former, penalty becomes a burden of shame and disgrace, which should be apportioned to the criminal intent; and the intent may be regarded as the free expression of evil, since it is the issue of a choice made in full and absolute freedom. And since wrong-doing is represented as a social offense and not as a personal sin, the conception of fraternity and community in sin disappears and gives place, somewhat as depicted by primitive painters, to the idea of a separation between the righteous and the vicious, between those accepted by society and those rejected. Such is the army of the wicked that likewise forms an organized portion of society, scattered, it is true, but for this reason more elusive and more dangerous.

The new theory of *témibilité* (formidability) is hardly more respectful of the self-esteem of the fallen man. Its classifications may indeed recognize the possibility of a criminal being an honest man who is the author of a material crime without being the embodiment of criminality. In his case punishment becomes, as in the Salic law, the payment of a risk incurred. In a theory that does not believe in freedom in any form there is no place left for self-esteem. To retain the feeling of self-esteem there must be self-control and a consciousness of will and freedom. On the other hand, without freedom there is no hope of a return to virtue; and thus arises the tendency to recognize only criminals by nature, to regard them all as beset with an incurable criminality, as belonging to the lost. They form a part of the increasing army of the wicked, yet further increased by the moral effect of the hopelessness here attaching to criminality. It becomes an indelible taint. The criminal is of another race; he is the savage come to life again, and is to be hounded without mercy; he is the extreme anti-social being, wholly refractory to the requirements of social life.

§ 65. The Moral Purpose of Individualized Punishment

In a view that combines responsibility and individualization these trends of opinion are likely to be modified in deference to traditional institutions. Thus a conditional sentence like parole carries with it the benefit of the tolerance attaching to the "penal risk" view of crime. Parole is just such a punishment that does not degrade, for it was devised for that purpose. The same applies even more strongly to deterrent punishments and merely technical penalties, which are imposed upon offenders with no criminal tendency. At the other extreme there is the army of hopeless outcasts, unfortunately but undeniably on the increase. But it is likewise true that so long as we believe in freedom and in the value of a personal effort, we shall hold to the hope of a possible regeneration. We do not close the door upon any one for whom a return to the conditions of social life is possible. And this possibility, in the absence of a proof to the contrary, we may accept as a definite principle—analogous to certain presumptions of civil law. Lastly, there is the rank and file of the army, the battalions of true delinquents, susceptible to remedial punishments. They are not to be discouraged nor degraded; their sense of personality and self-esteem is to be restored and not destroyed, for self-distrust leads to vice. It should be recognized that the critical point lies in the type of individualization. A severe punishment imposed without probing the offender's conscience may in some respects be considerate of the personality, but at the same time it is also considerate of vice and criminality. It is as though society, indifferent to the past immorality and wickedness of its enemies and exploiters, should say: "Let them pay and return to their careers." Such a system encourages crime; it is made for those who scoff at virtue and boast of vice. Such self-esteem it is not important to preserve. On the contrary punishment must carry with it something deterrent, by virtue of that social force that differentiates individuals by their character, and self-esteem of the type expressed by the vanity of vice will in that event find itself decidedly at a discount. As, ordinarily, criminals of this type, even when susceptible to reform, have hardly any other form of self-esteem, the loss thereof is not to be regretted. But to build up the other and true self-esteem that consists in believing oneself fundamentally and conscientiously the equal of honest persons, requires the revival of the feeling of virtue; and such these criminals no longer possess. It is not the brand which they bear that affects their moral character, but the discipline to which they are subjected that alone can restore a sense of virtue and of self-confidence.

A reformatory punishment imposed upon the weak and the victims of our extreme civilization can hardly be effective except through the feelings of deep compassion that were appealed to by the ecclesiastical law. A man who could be saved was not treated as an outcast. His regeneration was to be sought; he was not to be abandoned to the army of the wicked, but was to be reinstated among the honest. Society was not to brand him with an indelible stigma. Upon such basis rested the fellow-sympathy that avoided degradation and a definite social exclusion. In a system based upon free will, that regards every crime as a freely made compact with evil as formerly it was made with the devil, every crime becomes a permanent mark of disgrace; but a system admitting a more general freedom, without assuming the concrete freedom of any given act, approaches this religious fellowship, that believed in a like temptation for all and assumed for all a like capacity to be free. The sense of social estrangement is less marked. There remains a bond of attachment to the social organism in the feeling that all of us may qualify for a life of freedom, and no one need necessarily remain in a career of crime and in the conditions that lead to it. The restoration to freedom requires an appeal to the inmost nature and its liberation through punishment. Crime seems thus conditioned by the determinism of human fate while yet it begins with freedom of action. It is due to this determinism that there arises a fellowship in moral unworthiness that may develop to a fellowship of pity. Yet the fundamental freedom of action and character inspires the hope of an ultimate regeneration. This very hope forms a bond of attachment to society, which punishes but does not exclude. Thereby it makes possible the restoration of self-esteem, for the punishment that is to restore must not debase. Punishment should make a man feel his moral but not his social fall, and the society that inflicts it should express a moral condemnation that does not definitely degrade or cut off. The psychological effect of punishment should be directed to the future and not be obsessed by the past. The constant thought of remorse and, still more, of shame, becomes the greatest hindrance to individual regeneration. Faith in the future remains the sole source of initiative and moral progress, even for the fallen, indeed, especially for them.[1] Such faith leads to a more comprehensive view of freedom. The concrete loss of freedom in a given crime should not involve a persistent and oppressive retrospect; the surviving fount of freedom of every spiritual nature should direct endeavor to the future. Such is and must be the place of the psychological effect of punishment in a reformed penal law. Such reform involves a re-education of public opinion, and to this end the practical application of punishments based upon a strictly psychological classification will contribute effectively. For such application the Bérenger law may successfully serve as an introduction.

[1] It is pertinent to apply the fine words of St. Paul: "But one thing I *do*, forgetting the things which are behind, and stretching forward to the things which are before, I press on toward the goal unto the prize of the high calling." *The Epistle of Paul the Apostle to the Philippians*, iii, 13–14. One cannot better emphasize the duty to forget the past and to consider only the future.

§ 66. Ecclesiastical Law and Individualization

We have still to review the position of ecclesiastical law upon these issues, considered in its historical rôle. The association of the idea of penalty with that of social purpose may be reached through a sociological analysis of popular conceptions. May it not have like relation, despite the radical difference of approach, to ecclesiastical law? To find that such is the case would be of importance, and not merely in the interests of historical truth. It would appear that ecclesiastical law has everything to gain by detaching its origins from a certain spiritualistic philosophy with which it is affiliated, yet which is fundamentally an aspect of rationalism.[1] However, the guardianship of the good name of the ecclesiastical law belongs to those officially qualified to express an opinion. We are concerned only with historical evidence.

And first of all, may we not recall, in connection with the popular as well as the traditional conception of freedom, the very perplexing parable of the Gospel? I refer to that of the seed cast upon good soil, that increases of itself by virtue of the soil that has received it, without personal effort and, as it were, in complete unconsciousness. There comes a time when the plant has grown and become a tree with spreading branches wherein rest the birds of the air.[2] Where then does individual effort enter? Where does freedom, as a positive act, come into play? Where shall we observe the appearance of responsibility for the good issue that results? The original personality is the sole explanation; it alone creates, by a force inherent in its nature that suffers

[1] In regard hereto, and under a title that explains itself, see a curious article of *M. l'Abbé L. Picard* (of the diocese of Lyon), "De l'insuffisance du spiritualisme," published in the *Revue du Clergé français*, 1897, p. 481, *seq.*
[2] *St. Mark*, iv, 8, 26-28, 31-32.

no interference of an alleged free will. The soil is well prepared; nothing remains but to deposit therein the seed that is to thrive. The sower has done his work, the germ develops by virtue of its inherent fertility. It is a purely organic process. Freedom and responsibility, if they have any part in the personality, are a part of the whole in its unity, and, let it be added, in its variations and successive transformations. But we do not observe them in each particular action. The actions taken individually are the fruits of the tree, — good if the tree is good, bad if it is bad.

In a doctrine of this kind man does not necessarily appear as free in his actions but as free in the development of his moral personality. We do not know whether freedom is the power to act independently of every antecedent condition, but for man it is the power to act on the basis of his moral nature, and to be constantly active in transforming and improving his personality, and thus in determining, through this sequence of causes, the resulting actions. Freedom may be the power to prepare the soil, to make it good or bad and to conserve it as the depository of the good, which according to the Gospels is made a part of one's ancestral or rather divine inheritance.[1] But the soil once prepared, nature asserts its rights and the fundamental law of physical causality prevails. Freedom prepares the soil, determinism receives the seed and makes it fruitful. This is our first consideration.

So far as responsibility appears in the Gospels it is never attached to an act considered in itself as the product of the freedom of choice, but as an expression, a condition, what we now call a state of mind. The expression appears in St. Bernard: "Et enim libertas habitus animi liber sui."[2] From this results the triumph of a state of faith. The predestina-

[1] *St. John*, i, 4, 9. [2] See above, p. 40, note 2.

tion of the apostolic calling has no other foundation. It is the reward of an inner latent faith.[1] The same holds of the miracles of the Gospels. They are the reward of a positive and efficient faith,[2] and to this state of faith, as revealed in the Gospels, there corresponds a state of grace with the dogmatic interpretation ascribed to it by St. Paul.[3] Personalities, not actions, are to be rewarded or punished; and if at times the act appears as the object of penalty — the sin committed rather than the state of sinning — this must be looked upon as the expression and issue of a corrupt personality in revolt against the spirit immanent therein. Is not theological teaching merely the development of these views? A state of grace or a state of sin makes the distinction between the righteous and the wicked, and good or bad deeds are significant only as the consistent expression of our inner nature. The theologians tell us that sin, as such, withdraws from God; it leads to death. This is doubtless true; but even within the theological position there has not been sufficiently considered the subjective factor necessary to bring about such withdrawal. This factor consists far less in the free yielding to the circumstances of the action than in an open and conscious revolt against a part of the divine inheritance. It is of this human element of regeneration that St. Paul speaks as living and moving within us, from which the soul withdraws when, by a critical act, it rests in the common human element of sin.[4] Is not this the true basis of the theological view?

Such is the general impression of the situation, doubtless

[1] *St. John*, i, 35-49; iii, 19-21; v, 38-44; compare with viii, 34; *St. Mark*, ii, 5; v, 34; vii, 29; x, 52; *St. Matthew*, viii, 10-11; ix, 2, 29.

[2] *St. Luke*, v, 5, 12-13; *St. John*, iv, 50; *St. Matthew*, ix, 22, etc. See preceding note.

[3] See the *Epistle to the Romans*, especially chapter vi.

[4] *St. Paul:* Epistle to the Romans, vii, 18-24.

not to the professional theologian with his acceptance of the objective reality of theological truths,[1] but as it appears to one who looks upon theology from the historical side, in its relation to intellectual movements and to the influence which it has exercised upon the growth of popular opinion. No one with a sociological interest has the right to neglect this historical aspect.

§ 67. Examples in Penance and Clemency for Special Crimes

If we set aside theology, which in this respect forms a sort of spiritual psychology, and take up the practical organization of society, we shall see that ecclesiastical law is but the development of these several conceptions. The primitive law of the church is comprised in the penitential reports;[1] and these distinctly approach the position of the Salic law, yet with this difference, that in place of the Wergild there are years of penance, corresponding to each of the deeds concerned, — so many years of penance, as it were, instead of the pieces of gold exacted by the Germanic laws. The one replaces the other. It is familiar that later, with the practice of indulgences, the pieces of gold again replaced the years of penance. From the rationalistic position of the freedom of the will it is natural enough that this should seem scandalous. But does not this throw light upon the purely superficial character of these penances? The fine thus imposed

---

[1] As an example of the intrinsically theological position expressed dogmatically, see the thesis cited above by *P. Prins*, "De actibus humanis," p. 116, *seq.*

[2] On the Penitential Books, see *Viollet*, "Histoire du droit civil français," last edition; *Schmitz*, "Die Bussbücher und die Bussdisciplin der Kirche"; *Henry C. Lea*, "History of Auricular Confession and Indulgences in the Latin Church," Philadelphia, 1896; and a remarkable study by *M. A. Boudinhon*, on the subject of the preceding work, in the "Histoire de la Pénitence à propos d'un ouvrage récent," which appeared in the *Revue d'histoire et de littérature religieuses*, Vol. II, 1897, p. 306 and p. 496.

is wholly objective and relative, and consequently nominal; it corresponds, in a somewhat symbolical way, to the objective gravity of the offense and to the reprobation it is likely to arouse. The penance has the simple purpose of exacting payment to make good the offense and to require its confession by the offender. The question of the conscience and that of the moral status of the action is a very different one. In this respect the action is but secondary; the paramount consideration is the return to a moral state, the substitution of a state of grace for one of sin. To that end it is necessary that punishment heals, as the ecclesiastical expression puts it, or as we now say, reforms. The end to be attained is the moral reform of the sinner, and in the primitive church the psychological effect of penitence was relied upon to effect this. At a later day, in consequence of moral laxity, alternates and substitutes were found of a more tangible kind, and the almost nominal fine was retained only to mark the relative gravity of the action. It was replaced by prayers, pilgrimages to the Holy Land, and almsgiving. Still later, indulgences were introduced in the form of symbolic recognition of what was originally an objective penalty.

Let us take an example, that of infanticide, that will well illustrate the subsidiary status of the objective aspect, and the dominant influences of personal subjective considerations. It is generally acknowledged that it was an advance in the philosophy of the eighteenth century to admit strongly extenuating circumstances for this crime when the case was that of a mother driven to the crime to conceal her sin. Such a view seems decidedly modern; and, indeed, the ancient law under Christian inspiration regarded only the protection of the child. For this it was necessary to defend its weakness, as every human being had to be defended, because in the eyes of God the child was a soul with a destiny on earth; and thus the conception of murder as imperilling a soul's salvation was introduced. This likewise impresses us as a modern tendency. However we find a similar provision in the fourth century in the Council of Ancyrus (314), from which arose the penitentials as they survive.[1] Doubtless at the beginning great severity of punishment prevailed. Infanticide was looked upon as homicide by reason of a reaction against the established pagan custom.[2] But at the Council of Ancyrus the question of the desire of the mother of an illegitimate child to conceal her sin was considered, and in regard to her alone (and here is the modern point of view), instead of a life-long penance, as would be imposed for homicide, the punishment was reduced to a period of ten years, — owing to humane considerations, as the texts put it. From then on all the penitentials reassert this provision. They even disclose a deeper and more humane insight; they speak of mothers who allowed themselves to be led into the sin of the flesh, as it was called, and disposed of the child. Such murder is considered only as the consequence of the first sin and becomes one with it. It entails no special and distinctive penance. The case is judged as a whole, as the case of an erring woman in permitting herself to be seduced. The rest is looked upon as the inevitable consequence of the seduction. The punishment is mitigated by considerations of humanity, say the texts;[3] and no more humane, more individual, or more subjective point of view could be conceived. It is not the crime but the criminal alone that is to be regarded. It becomes a subjective individualization under cover of a

[1] See *Schmitz*, cited above, pp. 259, 356, 412, etc., and *Hefele*, "Concilien-Geschichte," I, chap. i, 240.

[2] On this point see a good thesis by *M. R. Bouton*, "l'Infanticide," Paris, 1897, p. 33, *seq.*

[3] See *Schmitz*, cited above, pp. 624, 629.

wholly objective legal sentence; and this is what we now demand. This subjective individualization derived from this very conception of responsibility and freedom is the same formula which we of to-day have reached.

This formula applies to that condition of virtual and general freedom that inspires, though it does not create, each particular action. When only the freedom of the action was considered, it followed that the penalty was attached to that very act. The punishment was determined by the exclusive regard of the act committed and was directed to the past. But when one no longer considered the act committed and realized that freedom goes back to the deeper strata of the psychic personality, while yet unable to demonstrate its definite intervention for each act in particular, the moral and personal status of the act was decidedly lessened, and consideration was turned to the restoration and reinstatement of morality. Freedom was looked upon with reference not to the past but to the future. One could not prove what it was that directly inspired the crime; but one knew what alone could arouse a struggle against the criminality resident in the soul. Since punishment is again directed towards the restoration of freedom, it is this very freedom, the seed of the moral future of the condemned, that should be considered, far more than the freedom of action which had turned the wrongdoer towards evil ways. There is something definite in the former which can be reckoned upon as the lever for his regeneration; in the latter there is nothing tangible. It is a matter of belief which cannot be defined. In a theory of this kind, punishment considers only the condition of responsibility which alone the Gospels recognize, and not the state of responsibility which is a construction of abstract reason and does not reflect the facts as they are. If punishment is directed to the production of a condition of responsibility it will individualize according thereto; and it is in this manner that the conception of responsibility in the Gospels, far from being opposed to the conception of individualization, prescribes the practice and discipline thereof as the necessary adjustments to practical conditions. These form the foundation of its position, quite apart from all purely rational and dogmatic abstraction. The practice of penitence and punishment in the Church never looked to any other purpose. The conception of "castigatio" was allied to that of "disciplina" and "remedium." [1] It may be said in all sincerity, and with reference to the spirit of the ecclesiastical law, if not to the practice,[2] that, from the penitentials to the foundation of St. Michael at Rome by Pope Clement XI, "Parum est coercere improbos pœna, nisi probos efficias disciplina." [3]

§ 68. Individualization in French Codes; Political Crimes

If this combination of terms seems strange, and if dogmatic minds, following a purely deductive reasoning, still refuse to reconcile these two conceptions of responsibility

[1] On the "Pænæ medicinales" of the ecclesiastical law see *Vargha*, "Abschaffung der Strafknechtschaft" (Graz, 1897), II, p. 151 and pp. 217, 218.

[2] It is indeed necessary to make this reservation as between practice and theory, and not to confuse the principle by which the system was inspired and the compromises determined by circumstance, by reason of the social requirements that in the end ever determine measures. This is observable from the beginning of ecclesiastical law, which indeed found its positive inspiration in Roman law, in a legislation strictly shaped by the prevalent social conditions. These distinctions will aid the understanding of the ideas which at first seem somewhat paradoxical, and by which *Hinschius* in his "Kirchenrecht," Vol. V, § 265, p. 123, *seq.*, attempts to challenge the traditional conception held in regard to the penitential discipline of the ecclesiastical law. On this point see *Günther*, "Geschichte des Strafrechts" in *Liszt's* Review, *Zeit. f. d. g. Str. W.*, Vol. XV, 1895, p. 166. His presentation is the result of a too one-sided and inaccurate consideration that does not take sufficient account of all phases of the problem.

[3] Motu proprio of Pope Clement XI of November 14, 1703.

and individualization, it will not be profitless to show that this paradox characterizes the present French school. Is it proper to speak of the French as the classical school, or shall it be called the corrective (*pénitentiaire*) or by yet another name? This is not easy to determine. It is clear, however, that it is a school that accepts truth wherever it finds it, without too close allegiance to systems, — a school of practical methods and happy solutions, one of good sense and fine Gallic insight. It has given rise to the three following measures: to the provision of special punishments for political crimes; to conditional sentences as embodied in the law of parole; and to the banishment (*relegation*) of habitual offenders, as prescribed by the law of 1885. A school that may be credited with these three results stands for distinctively subjective individualization.

Let us examine first the current distinction in the scale of criminal punishments, between political punishments and those of common law. It appears at first view to be a reversal of all traditional principles. For general welfare, political crime (formerly a crime against the state or *lèse-majesté*) was the most serious of all, as it affected the safety of the State, which under every system was one with the government. Such crime was pitilessly and severely punished without regard for the individual. The objective aspect of the crime was commanding and dominant. Indeed it may be urged that the more engaging, genial, and respectable the individual, the more dangerous he was as a political criminal, — the more his influence was to be feared, the more the example set by his rebellion was of grave import, the more dangerous became his crime in its outer aspect; consequently the more severely was he to be punished. In classic antiquity, as in ancient law, from early mediæval times up to the darkest years of the French Revolution, political crimes were invariably accorded the most severe punishments, and they were the more ruthlessly executed when the victims commanded interest and sympathy.

But a new conception emerged from the carnage of our civil wars. It was born of the horror of bloodshed and welcomed as a breath of peace, that might make one forget its origin. While under this view a political crime, on its objective side, remains the most serious of all offenses, subjectively it bears no relation to common-law offenses. The political offender is not a common criminal; he is not necessarily an evil-minded man, not an enemy of society, or one who cannot be assimilated as a social unit. He may be a political opponent, but he is not antagonistic to the social idea. The anarchist is anti-social; but the anarchist is not a political criminal. There must be protection against the danger which the political criminal offers to the State, and it is the State's duty to protect itself against him. But there is no occasion to reform him by punishment nor to influence him by the social disapproval of which punishment is the expression; and still less to attempt an educational punishment. He is not a pervert. Punishment will have no hold upon him. It may arouse hesitation and fear by the threat of the deprivation of his liberty; but to attempt a reform of his conscience and opinions would be an absurd pretense. What he needs is a political, and not a moral conversion; and prison discipline will hardly change the politics of any but those whose convictions are readily shifted. The influence of fear does not effect a moral reform. Hence political punishments should not be in the same class with those of common law.

As soon as this idea was accepted it brought about a revolution in our laws. The subjective view and the conception of individualization were substituted for the objective view of the material gravity of the crime. The modern view that punishments should be differently organized for different classes of criminals prevailed; and in the sequel will appear the further consistent results of this double scale of criminal punishments. At all events the conception that directly resulted therefrom was that, side by side with the punishments that apply to the evil-doer and make him the mark of public disapproval, there must be punishments for honest men, who, by the manner of their behavior have become a public menace. Such punishments should not be degrading or educational or corrective. They should be purely and simply deterrent, or punishments in behalf of public safety without other pretense.

§ 69. Individualization in Deportation

That this was the precise position of the French penal code is evidenced by the fact that at the extremities of the scale we find two punishments of the same character, involving imprisonment, that do not entail hard labor — which is regarded as the sign of penal servitude — and which are free from "legal" infamy. The one is detention, the most serious political punishment, since it may last in theory from five to ten years; and at the other extreme, city-jail imprisonment for infraction of an ordinance, a punishment that carries with it no infamy and has no other status than a penalty legally provided. It is simply a means of forcing citizens to respect the law, and is a very light punishment, with a maximum of five days' imprisonment. Viewed formally as provisions of the same system, these punishments are of the same nature and are purely technical penalties, not measures of social disapproval. They involve the payment of one's obligations in taking one's chances. As a punishment they have no other bearing.

This group of punishments is withdrawn from the field of common-law punishments. It is not until the year 1885 that we find a special punishment that likewise is withdrawn from the list of ordinary punishments. I refer to the deportation of incorrigibles, which measure is a direct result of the Italian school. Among the prized ideas of this school is that of the existence among criminals (and including the majority thereof) of a class not amenable to punishment. They form the class that cannot be assimilated: whether criminals by birth or by later development matters little. Crime is their profession. There is no purpose in punishing them, for punishment has no effect upon them. They must be segregated, and society must be relieved of their presence; especially must the great cities be cleansed of this social refuse. To receive these social outcasts, let there be set apart a colony to which they be sent. Despite all they may develop into good colonists; and that would result to the benefit of society. The source of danger would thereby be removed, and a possibility exists that in the end they would confer a benefit upon the tropical colonies to which they are sent. Such punishment constitutes a measure of criminal economics in the true sense of the word, but obviously not a measure of penal law, merely a measure of social economy.

It is true that the authors of the law of 1885 were restrained by certain scruples which made them commit some serious errors. They started from the idea that deportation was not a punishment, that it was liberty outside of France, which made of it merely a supervised and regulated exile. Since the law had been broken, it followed that a punishment should be imposed and the debt absolved. Thus the man liable to deportation had to pay his penalty in France before being eligible to deportation to the colonies. This was a two-fold mistake. Deportation is doubtless not a punishment in the classic sense of the word. It is, however, still a deterrent measure that should be administered in progressive stages. It is a punishment for incorrigibility, or, if it be preferred, of a series of infractions that prove incorrigibility. The view does not tally with a notion of a series of debts to be paid, for when an account is once settled, it wipes out the whole. On the other hand, it falls in well with the idea of a criminality to be overcome and minimized. It is clearly and primarily a preventive measure. But this preventive measure remains the penalty for a series of criminal actions that furnish the proof, in those thus guilty, of a condition of chronic insubordination. It is this condition of insubordination that likewise demands its special penalty. Why should the deported, inasmuch as they undergo an actual punitive treatment, be subjected in France to a preliminary punishment? Why particularly a punishment of the older type, a punishment of an educational kind, when they are assumed to be refractory to all punishment? They should be put to work in the colonies as quickly as possible, instead of still further having their powers drained by the routine of the prison and solitary confinement.[1] This involves a two-fold mistake and a

[1] See the excellent study by *M. Leveillé* in "Les institutions pénitentiaires de la France in 1895" (Paris, at the meeting of the Société générale des Prisons, 1895), p. 284, *seq.* There are many defects involved in this law of 1885 of which this is not the place to speak. It is sufficient to indicate the most serious, the idea of a purely legal criterion of incorrigibility, depending in an arbitrary fashion upon the number and kind of offenses without regard to the opinion of the judge. The discussions at the Congress of St. Petersburg show how difficult is this criterion of incorrigibility. The French system constantly tends to leave everything to the law and nothing to the judges. This is a spirit of unfortunate distrust. On the other hand the law of conditional discharge makes it possible to apply it to punishments imposed upon those eligible to deportation, in so far as that, if one thus discharged conducts himself well for ten years, he is not liable to deportation. But as it

double misfortune. It arises from the belief that deportation could be made a sort of exile with theoretical freedom, while in reality it is a punishment, though of a different kind and imposed as a measure of social security rather than of personal reform. But it is a punishment by virtue of its legal basis (which goes back to the conception of responsibility) as well as by the treatment that it entails. The position maintains that the incorrigible man, in so far as he is legally responsible for his incorrigibility, shall submit to the punishment which his condition demands.

The penal code instituted deterrent punishments for offenders who were not criminals by nature. The law of 1885 in turn established a penalty of elimination for incorrigibles. There is thus clearly indicated in French legislation a three-fold classification of criminals with corresponding punishments: delinquents, without criminal perversion; incorrigibles; and, between the two, the large group of offenders exhibiting a perversion of greater or less degree, but presumably susceptible to reform. This is the three-fold classification in French law at present.

§ 70. Individualization in Short-term and Long-term Sentences

But the French school has gone beyond this. Within this intermediate group with which common law deals — that of offenders who psychologically are criminals but are supposed to be susceptible to reform and punishment — there are distinctions to be made. There are the first offenders and the rest; next, within both groups, and par-

is the administration, and not the judge, that takes the initiative in conditional discharge, it results that in fact the determination and sentence are put in the hands of the administration, and not of the judiciary control. (Law of April 14, 1885, art. 12.) Moreover this is quite a fortunate solution, since it is by the testing of his freedom under surveillance of the administration, that the evidence of incorrigibility of the criminal may be afforded.

ticularly within the former, there are the chance victims of a vicious, passionate, or dishonest impulse; and again those by nature vicious, who though already given over to the habit of delinquency, are not hopelessly lost but have still a chance of regeneration. But the indifference of the law draws no distinction between them.

However, before reaching the law of 1891, prescribing conditional sentences, we come upon reforms due mainly to the administration, and in the direction of individualization. It is well to recall that many of these reforms following upon the legal provisions, had as their direct cause the requirements of the budget. Their effect has been not the less beneficial. So, accordingly, the penal code admitted punishments of different nature, corresponding to the several types of violation committed. This was peculiarly reasonable with reference to detention in general of which there were four varieties. In particular, imprisonment was to involve a different discipline according to the crimes or offenses concerned. Those sentenced for true crimes and those sentenced for merely legal infractions were to be placed in different institutions. The severity of the treatment was to be proportioned according to the severity of the offense. The resources of the budget did not permit the enforcement of such distinctions and the provision of separate institutions. The differentiation was then made upon another basis; it was no longer in terms of the nature of the imprisonment but of its duration, resulting in short-term and long-term sentences. The former were served in jails and the latter in penitentiaries, without considering whether hard labor or corrective discipline was involved. This was in direct violation of the law, but it produced excellent results, for the short-term sentences were almost always applied to first offenders. It would be rare for an habitual offender to be sentenced to a few months in jail. The incidental offenders were kept apart, and the professional criminals were sent to the penitentiaries. This amounted to dealing with those guilty of repeated misdemeanors in much the same way as with first offenders in crime; and this is quite right. Those committed for a second or third theft, although keeping to petty larceny, are differently tainted, in most cases, from those engaged in their first crime. It is not the gravity of the offense by which the criminality of the individual should be judged; far from being directly related, the two are most commonly in inverse ratio.

This distinction was in the end legally recognized in the law of 1875 on solitary confinement, applicable only to short-term sentences. Moreover, it was recognized, quite apart from the question of subjective criminality, that the treatment for short-term sentences, for the very reason that their duration did not permit of the supervision and the stages of progressive education of the long-term sentences, should be assigned to a distinct administration; and this, not only with reference to labor, but also where solitary confinement is not in use. It was owing to these considerations that the important decree of November 11, 1885, was issued, concerning the organization of short-term imprisonment where promiscuity was in vogue. As a consequence, since 1875, all those sentenced to less than a year of imprisonment must serve their sentences in solitary confinement, and since, in view of this material provision, the jails had to be rebuilt and refurnished, they were subjected to a more or less communal routine, very different from that of the penitentiaries. On the other hand, all those sentenced for long terms, that is for more than a year, whether they had committed a crime or a statutory offense, whether involving hard labor or corrective discipline, were sent to the penitentiaries. Since the law of 1875 the like status of corrective discipline for long-term sentences and hard labor has become a legal fact, sanctioned by law.

The arrangement meets with approval. It is better than that of the penal code founded upon the distinction between crimes and statutory offenses. It has as its basis a principle of individualization, the distinction between the incidental offender and the offender by nature and psychological condition. Yet all this was not adequate; and the next advance was towards the law of 1891, the credit of which belongs to M. Bérenger. It is but fair that it should be known by his name and that posterity should thus render a permanent tribute to this great philanthropist, who, despite prejudice and bias, ever courageously directed his efforts to the improvement of moral and penitentiary conditions. The law of parole should mark a turning-point in the trend of penal law. It is the definite abandonment of the conceptions of absolute justice in favor of that of a criminal economics in the best sense of the word. The best justice is that which saves its victims; and that is the very purpose of conditional sentences. Here we approach the last stage of individualization; one can hardly go further. All we ask, indeed, is that punishment should be differentiated according to the nature of the individual; we do not ask the suppression of punishment. Punishment is indeed suppressed in its outward appearance. However, from the point of view of justice, an infraction has been committed and a punishment must be forthcoming. The penalty must be enforced. Society thus proceeds like a creditor who concedes to the debtor a discount of his debt. Society does this by reason of the interest which the individual presents. Moreover this favor should be granted only to first offenders, and here the distinction between first offenders and others becomes legally sanctioned. The purpose is to prevent confirmed criminality. The Bérenger law is such a preventive measure.

The preparatory steps to this issue were taken long in advance. In 1875 the short-term sentences were separately considered, the idea being thus to make the treatment of short-term offenders as morally effective as possible. It was thought, as every criminologist of to-day believes, that the short-term punishments form the critical point of the penitentiary régime. The many objections made by criminologists (Mittelstädt, Vargha, etc.) [1] against punishments that deprive one of freedom apply particularly to imprisonment as a punishment for first (or early) offenses, broken up into fragments of quite insignificant length. Punishments of this type do not last long enough to reform, but they last long enough to contaminate. Imprisonment, even when served in solitary confinement and free from all promiscuous association, is, in its first impression, of itself corrupting because it destroys the sentiment of self-esteem.[2] Thus since 1875 it has been recognized that there was more to be done in this field. In 1885 a further step was taken by the general introduction of conditional discharge. This was

[1] *Mittelstädt*, "Gegen die Freiheitsstrafen" (second edition, Leipzig, 1879); and *Vargha*, "Die Abschaffung der Strafknechtschaft" (2 vols., Graz, 1896 and 1897).

[2] All this is well known and, sadly enough, too well established to need further corroboration. It is interesting, however, to note the testimony of one who is not a criminologist or an expert but is indeed a psychologist with large heart and clear insight, the late Dostoiewsky. His adverse opinion of the treatment in convict prisons and, as well, of solitary confinement, is familiar. See *Dostoiewsky*, "Souvenirs de la Maison des Morts," pp. 17 and 18. Likewise consult *Paul Hymans*, "La Lutte contre le crime" (Brussels, 1892), especially p. 53, *seq.* Moreover consult *M. Montgomery*, an old prisoner, and his opinion in regard to long terms in the article cited above, p. 135, note 1.

no longer limited to minors sent to prison colonies, irrespective of the nature of their previous sentence. The conditional discharge was not an act of administrative clemency but a recognized mode of serving a sentence at large under a kind of patronage or moral surveillance. Why then may not this method of serving a sentence in liberty begin with the very beginning of punishment? In the progressive system, conditional discharge is but the reward of good conduct; it assumes that part of the debt is paid and part of the sentence served. But for those who are in need of oversight and not of prison discipline, why should not this form of discharge under surveillance and moral protection begin at the outset?[1] Vargha proposes such measures as a general substitute for all punishments by imprisonment and penal servitude. In that form the proposal is quite Utopian.[2] But as a limited provision for certain special offenders, whom it is desired not to withdraw from their work or their vocation, this serving of a sentence while at large would be an excellent provision. It is probable that in the future this will be the great substitute for prison discipline; and especially so in view of the fact that such conditional sentence proves to be more effective. It admits of full and entire liberty, omitting all guardianship and oversight, and yet does not assume that the punishment has been satisfied. The punishment is withheld or suspended, conditionally suppressed. At all events the example of conditional discharges has served as a transition and approach to the conception of a purely conditional sentence.

[1] See *Aschrott*, "Strafensystem und Gefängniswesen in England," p. 98, seq.; and as precedents for conditional condemnation, see *Mumm*, "Die Gefängnisstrafe und die bedingte Verurtheilung," p. 25, seq.

[2] See the account given by *Oppenheim*, in *Kritische Vierteljahresschrift*, Vol. XXXIX, 1897, p. 571.

§ 71. The System of Parole: its Faulty Application

Moreover, when the law of 1891 was voted upon, there was very little discussion of principles; but, what was more to the point, the facts were emphasized. Statistics proved that short-term punishments, and even the simple contact with prison-life, whether of solitary confinement or not, was enough to make a confirmed criminal of any one exposed to its influences. Of what benefit is it for society to incarcerate a first offender when there is reason to believe that he is simply a misguided person, not likely to repeat his offense? His only means of salvation may be that of escaping punishment; and salvation is everything. Moreover, wherever disciplinary authority exists, whether in the family in favor of the father, or in government in favor of superior officials, the first law of good discipline — if that indeed is the object — is almost always, except in absolutely serious cases, to pardon the first offense. Shall society alone refuse to exercise pardon?[1] It is only in deference to an outgrown abstract system of absolute equality that the law is law, and that to suspend its application requires the authority of those who make the laws. Those who have the power to make laws have only to delegate to others the power to suspend or to regulate their application. That is what was done in 1891, to the advantage of the judiciary authority. The judges were given the means of saving those who appeared before them for the first time. They of necessity had to probe the motives and sentiments of the defendants; it was for them to appraise and judge, and the law prescribed

---

[1] On this point see the precedents dating from mediæval times and the ancient law reported by *Chiaroni*, "La condanna condizionale" (Treviso, 1897, p. 21). See what I have said elsewhere in regard to the law of pardon, in the volume of *M. Octave Aubry*, "L'indulgence et la loi," Paris, 1908, p. 190, *seq.*, particularly pp. 196–197.

no further or partial instruction. The law of 1891 did not even make a distinction in terms of the gravity of the offense. It considered all cases of corrective imprisonment irrespective of duration, even cases involving the maximum legal period of five years, and cases assigned a corrective punishment by reason of provocation or of mitigating circumstances in the charge.

The possibility of granting parole, even for those sentenced to an imprisonment of five years, seemed objectionable; and it still appears so, possibly more than ever. In the proposed revision of the French penal code it was thought desirable to accede to these protests; and the field of application of the Bérenger law was decidedly reduced.[1] This involves a misunderstanding of the Bérenger law. It makes the parole a kind of grace or favor depending upon the gravity of the offense, and requires a consideration of the deed committed. This totally changes the spirit of the law. It was the law's intention that the judge should take into consideration not the objective gravity of the deed but the chances of reform of the individual; and upon that the crime has no bearing. Take the case of a young thief who has the temperament of a true malefactor. He commits his first theft, or rather, it is the first time that he is caught in the act. The offense itself carries not more than three months' imprisonment. According to the proposed amendment it would come under the conditions of the Bérenger law. Take the case of an honest cashier, faithful and steady, who is drawn into an irregular life. He gets into debt, takes money from the cashbox, sincerely believing that in a few days he will be able to replace it. He is discovered before he can do so. It is a seri-

[1] See the just criticism on this subject in the essay by *M. Le Poittevin*, "Le projet de réforme du Code pénal" (*Revue pénitentiaire*, 1893, pp. 174–175).

ous offense. To make this offense punishable by nothing less than imprisonment makes it impossible to grant the parole, which, however, is granted to the petty thief who has no need of it. To give the latter his freedom is to restore him to his environment and to the temptations that it entails. What he needs is a corrective and educational discipline that may lift his life out of vagrancy and induce different habits. On the other hand, because the cashier's sentence exceeds three months in jail, he is refused the parole, although he but yielded to the temptation of a moment. Intrinsically he has not thereby become a dishonest man; he is repentant, has given up his evil ways, and gives assurance that he will not return to them. His condemnation is demanded; he must undergo his punishment. It is easy to anticipate what the result will be and what will become of him on leaving the jail. His position and his future gone, his career forever spoilt, reinstatement hardly possible, he has to face poverty and shame. Almost inevitably he drifts to dubious callings and a career of fraud. He does not join a band of thieves, for such is not his temperament, but he can find occupation only in such suspicious callings, followed by shady characters, as are open to persons who have lost honor and self-esteem. The chances are nine in ten that he will become one of their number. Parole permits the one man to return quite too readily to habits of idleness and vice, and the deprivation of parole makes the other more or less a knave for life. Can it be said that a provision able to bring about such results is a fortunate change?

A proper estimate of the Bérenger law requires that it be considered in the spirit in which the eminent man to whose fine initiative it was due intended and framed it, as it was enacted in 1891, and not in the form given it by those who were imbued solely with the predominant and almost exclusive consideration of the objective gravity of the crime. Of all forms of individualization this is, if possibly not the most thorough, at least the most adaptable and elastic; and that for two reasons: the first, because no prescription is imposed upon the judge and he need be guided solely by his personal impression; and the second, because under the pretext of individualization there is involved, not a change of punishment but an actual suspension of the punishment itself.[1] Without going to the extent of pardoning altogether, one can go no further.

In the end what is needed is a legislation such as ours, which, disregarding the outer form of the offense, admits the legal distinction between short-term and long-term sentences, between political and common-law punishments; which accepts elimination — or deportation — for those presumably incorrigible, and on the other hand a purely conditional sentence for first offenders whose reform seems certain, and who, despite this first offense, may still be classed among honest folk. A legislation of this type is legislation upon a purely subjective basis, favoring the individualization of punishment, applying it, and practicing it. Such progress must be a matter of gradual advance and involves reforms to be added from time to time to the body of our old penal code. The present problem is to bring together these several innovations and to develop their logical consequences. The reforms of 1875, of 1885, and of 1891 must be taken as the basis of this new construction. Instead of

[1] It is as a measure of individualization of punishment that conditional sentences should be regarded; and as such it is different from all other regulations with which it may be compared. See for the movement thus brought about in Germany, and the criticisms that have been advanced on this point, the two pamphlets of *Bachem*, "Die bedingte Verurtheilung" (second edition, 1895), and "Bedingte Verurtheilung oder bedingte Begnädigung?" 1896. See also *Liszt* and the works to which he refers (edition 1895, § 15, text and note 3, p. 76).

advancing the cause the proposed amendment retards it; it is a step backward. It is at best a sort of revival of the old penal code of 1810. The latter is indeed better in its somewhat severe rigidity than when arrayed in the legal details which its remodeled form is made to wear. What is wanted is a new construction built up on the sound premises of the penal code of 1810 and taking as a guide the laws of 1875, 1885, and 1891. These have only to be developed in regard to certain simple issues in order to bring about an excellent legislation which shall apply individualization upon the basis of responsibility.

To trace the larger outlines of such an attempt is our present task. It does not involve the consideration of further details. The principles are at hand; there must be supplied an outlook that will show the special measures by which the newer conceptions may and should find their application.[1]

[1] Since the law of March 26, 1891, the institution of parole has been adopted in the Canton of Geneva (law of October 29, 1892), in Portugal (law of July 6, 1893), in the Grand Duchy of Luxemburg (law of May 10, 1892), in Italy (the Ronchetti law of June 26, 1904). In Germany, as already noted, a movement in favor of the parole has been on foot for several years. If it has not, as yet, been admitted for *all* first offenders, there has been, on the other hand, an advance beyond parole in that a system of pardon, with a verbal reprimand, has replaced the sentence of first offenders under eighteen years of age; this was done by authority of the law of July 2, 1900. On this law see *Liszt*, id., 1905, § 15, note 4, p. 75. In Russia conditional sentences have been made the subject of a recently proposed law. (See the report of *C. Sacharoff*, of Moscow, on the reform of justice in Russia: *Bulletin de l'Union intern. de droit pénal*, 1907, pp. 275, 297, and 371).

There should be mentioned the proposed law of *M. Emile Morlot*, for France, having as its object the introduction in our legislation of the system of pardon, pure and simple, without reprimand. (See the text of the proposed law, with the report that preceded it, in the *Journal officiel*, attached to the protocol of the session of December 19, 1907.)

CHAPTER VIII

Legal Individualization

§ 72. Legal Individualization necessarily General.
§ 73. Examples of False Individualization.
§ 74. Approach to Judicial Individualization and the Cases concerned.
§ 75. The Proper Education of Magistrates.
§ 76. The Place of the Jury in Individualization.

§ 72. Legal Individualization necessarily General

In a general survey of the subject three distinct types of individualization appear: the first, or legal individualization, is determined by the law in advance as a penalty; the second, or judicial individualization, which is the best, is determined by the judge; and the third, or administrative individualization, is determined in the course of punishment.

In reality there is no individualization by law. The law can distinguish classes of cases; it cannot recognize individuals. All that individualization by law can consider are the reasons for the extenuation or aggravation of punishment, based upon the relative gravity of the crime, and, in so far, upon the degree of responsibility. Such individualization is based upon responsibility and returns to the position of the neo-classic school. It is a false individualization. It is easy to understand that the law should admit reasons for the extenuation of punishment when the offense in its outer aspect is not serious. This amounts only to a reduction of the penalty and is fair enough. In many instances it may properly apply; for example, in the well-known form of what is sometimes still called contingent liability wherein the nature of

§ 72] LEGAL INDIVIDUALIZATION 221

the offense is altered undesignedly.[1] Let us suppose an assault with the intent to incapacitate. It may be urged that the possibility of a serious consequence of the assault may have been foreseen. Let us assume that such occurs and results in a murder. Inasmuch as the affair was in fact premeditated, one may regard it as an intentional murder. However, the crime committed is not the crime that was originally planned. There thus results a change of the objective status of the crime; and this is recognized in the legal mitigation of the punishment. The same is true of an act of negligence in which there was a similar possible anticipation of a criminal issue. Such is the case of a hunter who, in firing upon something passing within range of his gun, may reflect that he is taking the chances of killing some one. The quarry moves, the hunter fires. He runs the risk of a murder, and a murder ensues. The act may be regarded not as an accidental homicide but as an intentional murder; it should however become a murder with extenuating circumstances. The same applies to an accomplice who performs his part in a venture, knowing full well to what kind of a crime he is lending his aid. Such is the case of a druggist knowingly selling a poison, or of a locksmith consenting to make fase keys.[2] Even in the classic conception of complicity it may and has been regarded that there is not an identity of crime for principal and accomplice.[3] The latter's crime may well be regarded as the same as that of the prin-

---

[1] On contingent liability see a very suggestive report of *Liszt* to the 24th Congress of German jurists (Verhandlungen des XXIVten deutschen Juristentages, 1897, I, p. 107, *seq.*). Also the thesis of *M. Raoul Duval* (Paris, 1900).

[2] See the notable thesis of *M. Thibierge*, "La notion de la complicité" (Étude critique), Paris, 1898, passim, and principally pp. 45–46, 53, 65, and 73, *seq.*

[3] See the subtle and engaging theory of *M. Garraud*, "Traité théorique et pratique du droit pénal français (edition 1888), Vol. II, p. 390, *seq.*

cipal, but accompanied by extenuating circumstances. The assumption of a necessary mitigation of punishment in all cases of complicity would be indefensible, in that it would imply a lesser degree of criminality on the part of the accomplice. The contrary is often the case. The best system is that incorporated in the Swiss draft, which permits the judge to reduce the punishment when there is a difference of culpability.[1] The above are instances of wholly justifiable mitigation. They involve only extenuation with reference to responsibility; and this does not consider the individualization of punishment in its true sense.

One may however conceive a legal provision so framed as to provide a true individualization of punishment. This implies a legal classification which shall indicate by what criterion each of the classes considered shall be recognized; following upon such a scheme, a systematic punishment adapted to each class must be prescribed. Such provisions fall within the province of the law; and it is along this line that the penal legislation of the future should be directed. But there remains a possible distinction. The law clearly provides only the general basis and the very variable factors entering into a sentence, leaving to the judge the duty of making a strictly individual classification after a special study of each individual; it thereby becomes a most desirable legal form of a judicial individualization. But the least desirable system is that by which the law assumes to supply the necessary criterion of the classification, as does our law of 1885 on the deportation of incorrigibles. It rests upon an assumption that is always uncertain and often mistaken; for the only indication of the nature of the criminal which it considers is that supplied by the character of the offense; and that is wholly inadequate. Thus it is often

[1] Preliminary draft of the Swiss penal code (wording of 1903, art. 22).

said that infanticide implies a perversion of the maternal sentiment, and that only a degraded woman would be guilty thereof. Ecclesiastical law, however, considers that infanticide may often be the act of desperate or unfortunate women, and that it would involve most questionable assumptions to judge these persons by the odium of the crime which they have committed.

§ 73. Examples of False Individualization

To make an individual classification through an automatic application of the law would be a true form of legal individualization; and the law of May 27, 1885, furnishes a very sad example thereof. It is an individualization made at random with the hope that in the long run justice will be done; and this may be true of this law, for the sentence of deportation is imposed according as the individual comes under one or another of the categories of the law. There is thus a considerable chance that the legal charge will indicate the defendant's incorrigibility. But why should not the decision be left to the judge? He alone should have the last word in such cases. He deals with real cases, while the law deals only with abstract considerations. Hence the law can but supply the judge with the basis of individualization. It should not itself assume to make the individualization.

A similar consideration may be advanced in regard to the effect of the motive upon the severity of the sentence.[1] It has frequently been proposed to introduce into the law a classification of the various motives concerned in crime,

[1] See particularly the excellent work of *Holtzendorff*, "Das Verbrechen des Mordes und die Todesstrafe: die Psychologie des Mordes." Also the account, by *Garçon*, of *Alimena's* "Le Premeditazione," in the *Nouvelle revue historique du droit français et étranger*, 1889, p. 792, seq. Also the thesis cited of *M. Legrand*, on "Préméditation" (Paris, 1898), and that of *M. Rigaud*, "De l'influence du motif en matière criminelle" (Paris, Rousseau, 1898).

with the purpose of enabling the law to judge the nature of the criminal according to the motive, and to adjust the punishment accordingly. Thus a murder may have been inspired by very base and perverse motives, — for purposes of robbery, or possibly by mere wanton violence. But it may have been inspired by motives shared in common with upright men, such as indignation or an outburst of justifiable anger. It was proposed to have the law consider these several motives, classify them carefully, and according to their nature and character reduce or increase the punishment. Such provisions were made by Stooss in the first Swiss draft. There would thus be a form of legal individualization based upon an assumption derived from the motive. But the question at issue is precisely whether the motive should serve as the proper basis for individualization of punishment, or whether it should preferably be regarded as the true criterion by which to gauge responsibility. This issue should likewise be committed to the authority of the judge; for it is the judge's place to gauge the punishment. Such questions properly belong to judicial individualization. We thus return to the principle, above set forth, that all individualization by law is false, in that it is based upon the question of responsibility and in that it ignores the true nature of the criminal.

Let us consider some examples taken from the Italian penal code. The punishment is lessened in cases of abortive attempt, in cases of complicity, in cases of crimes committed in foreign lands.[1] It is self-evident that these several causes of extenuation refer to a modification in the objective character of the crime and not to the relative psychological criminality of the individual. Thus the extenuation in cases of attempt arises from the fact that the agent was

[1] The Italian Penal Code, arts. 61–62, arts. 63–66, arts. 3–6.

stopped at a time when, through no merit of his own, he had not yet achieved his purpose. This is a matter of chance. In what respect does this lessen his culpability? It is true that the injury has not been effected; but the punishment is not intended as the expiation of a material injury, otherwise it should be completely cancelled in case of a wholly unsuccessful attempt. It is the guilt that is to be punished, and the guilt is the same. So far as concerns the sinfulness of the individual and the punishment that he deserves, it cannot be urged that the fact of having been stopped in the course of the execution has any bearing upon the question. Extenuation in cases of complicity arises from the fact that the accomplice is only the accessory and is subject to a leader whom he follows. But it is a common practice for criminal gangs to assign the several parts; some attack and strike the blow, others keep guard, or perform some minor part. With due consideration of these circumstances how can one be sure that some are less culpable than others? Perhaps those least incriminated are the very ones who devised the crime. The man who struck the blow may have been forced to act, possibly drugged to give him courage; the others took it upon themselves to safeguard the execution of the crime. Viewed from without, their part may appear quite accessory, but they should be judged and punished according to their inner moral participation. In lessening their punishment the Italian code decides in advance that their criminality is of a minor degree. This assumption is quite gratuitous. A like consideration applies to crimes committed in foreign lands. The ground of extenuation is that the act has caused no injury or excitement in the land in which it occurs. But the very presence of the criminal may of itself be a considerable disturbance. Next is urged that the danger or injury caused by the crime does not affect the fellow-citizens of the country to which the criminal belongs. But the danger lies not in the crime and not in the past; it is in the future, and in the person of the criminal. A released criminal becomes a common danger. What matters the place in which the crime has been committed? The criminal must be treated according to what he is, with a view of lessening the danger that he himself carries. Even if he be considered only in terms of responsibility, how does his removal from the boundaries of his country diminish his culpability?

As a last example, take cases of alleged diminished responsibility, such as applies to persons of neuropathic disposition. They are the more dangerous in that their tendency to crime is purely pathological. They are not entirely irresponsible; hence they should be subjected to punishment. But it is urged that as their responsibility is less, so their punishment should be very brief, that they should be restored as quickly as possible to freedom, — a procedure that is the more dangerous in that such offenders are apt to act on a sudden impulse. Seemingly their greater menace results in the prompter restoration of their freedom. The true question is to determine whether in place of punishment it would not be better to provide special treatment in an asylum. That a minimum of detention should be fixed in accord with the degree of responsibility is right enough, but it is yet more important that the judge should be permitted to prolong the detention if public safety demands it and if the person concerned is approaching the stage of dementia.

It is thus seen that all the alleged cases of legal individualization are but cases of false individualization. Let us accordingly leave the field of the law and reach that of judicial individualization.

§ 74. Approach to Judicial Individualization and the Cases concerned

That the judge alone is capable of knowing the offender and of taking account of what he is may be conceded without further argument, but this arbitrary power of the judge (for so it must be called, even though the term be used without prejudice) nevertheless raises serious difficulties.[1] There is a special difficulty in countries where the jury system obtains and where a division of function exists between the professional and these temporary judges. To which of the two shall matters pertaining to the individualization of punishment be entrusted?

Account must first be taken of the kind of decisions that the judge was formerly called upon to render. If individualization is mainly designed to place at the disposal of the judge punishments of different nature according to the character of the criminals, the judge will have two types of problems to solve, the one, and the more serious, relating to the choice of punishment, the other, to its duration. The latter will hardly differ from that which is now exercised in the French law, particularly under the system that recognizes extenuating circumstances. Our magistrates already exercise considerable authority in this respect. Yet such authority could be made yet more extensive, as is provided by the penal code of Holland.[2] However commendable such provisions, the existing provisions involve delicate questions of degrees of penalty, and the difficulty would not be increased if the judge were given further authority

[1] *M. E. Carnevale* in a series of notable articles "L'arbitrio del Giudice nell' applicazione della pena" in the *Rivista penale*, 1897, p. 109, *seq.*; p. 333, *seq.*, has touched upon one of the most difficult points. See also an article by *M. C. de Vence*, in the *Revue pénitentiaire*, 1898, p. 507.

[2] Penal Code of Holland, art. 10 and *seq.*

to reduce the punishments; indeed, the reverse might be the case. It is not the recognition of the extreme cases — the least degree of criminality, and again the most pronounced — that is troublesome, but the disposal of the doubtful and intermediate cases. It is easy for the judge to reach an opinion in regard to an individual who might be given the benefit of what our legal provisions call extenuating circumstances; what is peculiarly difficult for the intermediate cases is to find the exact degree of clemency that the case warrants and that also satisfies the demands of a sound justice. What we already have is an arbitrary judicial power; though by this we understand not an unequal and partial justice but a justice unhampered by a legal criterion. No objections are made to the present system; and we may admit that our magistrates, with the aid of the jury, have proved its worth. They may be said to have made the best of the situation; and yet further progress is possible. No one proposes a return to the hampered and legally restricted procedures of older regulations: such barriers serve only as technical protections for the worst and most objectionable forms of justice. The desideratum is a better preparation and education of future magistrates.[1] At present only their legal education is considered. If this comprises merely an ordinary knowledge of the statutes and their more or less intricate interpretation, it may well be of secondary importance for the criminal judge. A knowledge of men is of prime importance. In place of an off-hand impressionism such as at present characterizes the decisions, there should be substituted, as M. Carnevale demands, a true scientific procedure. Their present technical preparation is presumably adequate to enable them to judge the

[1] See the cautious but well put comments in *M. Cruppi's* "La Cour d'assises," p. 123, *seq.*

degree of punishment as conditioned by its duration, for this, as before, is still to depend upon the crime and its subjective gravity. In this respect any one with a little judiciary experience would be competent.

But the further and serious question relates to the choice of punishment in accordance with the psychological classification of the criminal. In this respect an organized system of individualization will likewise not make the function of the judge any more difficult than it is now under the application of the Bérenger law, or as it would be in dealing with the incorrigible classes, if the criterion of incorrigibility were left to the verdict of the judge, as the Swiss draft provides. This does not imply that at present the procedure is perfect in those exceptional cases — such as that of parole — in which the magistrates undertake penal individualization. Their education inclines them to pay special attention to the crime; and it is with reference to the crime that they are tempted to grant or refuse parole. This tendency does not appear in the statistics of court decisions, for these do not disclose the motives that have guided the bench in the application of the law of 1891. But this tendency may be inferred from certain criticisms made by the magistrates against the extension of the Bérenger law to certain serious offenses;[1] and likewise from the confusion that tends to prevail between the admission of extenuating circumstances and the granting of parole, the one being considered as a first step of clemency necessary to pass on to the other. This involves a confusion of principles and points of view. It might well be the case that the offender is worthy of parole, when the crime in itself would not warrant the admission of extenuating circumstances. Different points of view are involved, and a further training in such distinctions

[1] *Revue pénitentiaire*, 1897, p. 491.

is needed. That the distinctions seem to be somewhat delicate and their introduction difficult is no reason for abandoning a worthy procedure or for returning to unwise measures that have proved inadequate. The adaptability of the Gallic mind should readily acquire the needed technical attainments. Although in fifteen years we have not been able to develop a truly scientific regulation of pardons, it does not prove that our magistrates are incapable of worthily applying individualization. It proves only that ways and means must be established, and that this cannot be done in a day. Our magistrates, impartial, unquestionably honest, and thoroughly trained professionally, are most capable to outline a desirable policy, but a period of tentative experience is inevitable.

The special difficulty in the application of a system of parole — which obtains equally in dealing with extenuating circumstances — is the lack of scientific principles of a directive conception and point of departure; and this should be decidedly reduced under a system of well-regulated individualization. The present form of individualization is sporadic because it is not organized. An organic and scientific individualization must be developed; only when this shall have been done, will our magistrates understand what is expected of them, and meet the expectation. If, for example, they are authorized to determine punishments for incorrigibles, they will know very well that they must consider not alone the last crime committed but the entire life of the individual and everything that may shed light upon his character and temperament. Likewise, if they have at their disposal purely deterrent punishments that make no pretense to a reformatory discipline, they will know that they have to ask only one question: Does the individual stand in need of a reformatory education or not? To face a problem clearly put is a step in advance; indeed, it is the decisive step.

§ 75. The Proper Education of Magistrates

The question how the magistrates shall become capable of solving the problem remains. Perhaps a psychological, as well as a legal education is necessary. Could it be otherwise in an issue that is a matter not of handling arguments, but of dealing with the realities of life in a field involving the management of men and the regulation of careers? Are not magistrates, through their profession, engaged daily in psychological problems? Whether they desire it or not, they must consider things psychologically, at first feeling their way by intuition, and later by professional acumen. But judgment of this type they must make and cannot avoid. The mistake consists in not insisting openly and professionally that such is their chief function. We ask that they be thus instructed, and that they thus qualify for the rendering of decisions.[1] When so qualified their judgments will be sound because based upon sure foundations. Their formal education which now teaches them to look upon the facts uninfluenced by the consideration of the individual, will no longer be at odds with their loyalty to a humane justice, which equally serves the interests of society and leads them to judge the man rather than the deed. At present they practice a compromise, a thinly disguised combination of the two tendencies, and reach results that are satisfactory to no one. To enable them to act for the welfare of human and social justice, a clear and frank allowance must be made for both interests and tendencies. Let

[1] See my letter to M. Paul Desjardins on the teaching of law, in Correspondance mensuelle de l'Union pour la vérité (cahier annexe formant postscriptum a la troisième serie des "Libres entretiens": Sur la réforme des institutions judiciaires, 1908).

them argue in terms of the law in so far as concerns the status of the deed and its objective appraisal; let them increasingly consider the subjective element in the appraisal of the subjective gravity of the offense in its bearing upon the severity of punishment, thus at once considering the motive as well as the objective gravity of the crime. Here lies the practical field for concessions such as now obtain between the spirit of legal abstraction and that of psychological observation. Finally in a third respect, that of the choice of punishment, let them consider only the individual and his character. When they come to realize that all this is their function and when the law tells them this in the very manner by which it organizes punishments, they will be in full exercise of their prerogative. The question will be clearly put. We may have full confidence that they will know how to meet it. For the present, it is enough to state the problem.

§ 76. The Place of the Jury in Individualization

The problem presents other difficulties in determining the proper division of function between the court and the jury; and it must be recognized that almost all writers and projects that mention individualization or attempt a preliminary legal formulation thereof have neglected to consider the jury. They have argued as though juries did not and should not exist. The impression obtains that the jury system does not readily lend itself to individualization. In the first place it seems impracticable to commit questions involving psychological analysis to so emotional and impulsive an expression of justice. Yet on the other hand, if the power of determining the sentence is withdrawn from the jury (as occurred in 1824 with reference to extenuating circumstances) juries will acquit in a spirit of defiance.

§ 76] LEGAL INDIVIDUALIZATION 233

There will be the latent conflict between the two judicial factors in the court of review. Possibly the most favorable solution will be to associate with the magistrates (somewhat as in the German municipal courts) a second jury of experts appointed to determine the punishment. Such would be composed chiefly of physicians, directors of reformatory institutions, professional educators, and others qualified by their calling to judge and deal with men. It would be not an ordinary but a technical jury, the members of which would be obtained by an eliminative process of successive selections. The ordinary jury, drawn by lot, as at present, would remain the judge of the facts; it would report upon the material circumstances and upon the question of intent and mental condition, but it would render this opinion without any technical fitness. Next a technical jury would determine the punishment and become a jury of individualization. Lastly, the court, as at present, would set the term of sentence.[1]

Such a plan involves the admission that the ordinary jury acting without assistance, is not and cannot be the judge of questions of individualization. The point needs no detailed proof. The purpose of the jury system is to furnish an approximate safeguard of personal freedom and reputation. It has also a second purpose. No mundane social system can hope to attain absolute justice, for all social justice is but a procedure of the social order. Such procedure cannot approach an ideal justice that scrutinizes the individual conscience and ascertains the measure of freedom exercised. When once this is recognized we shall admit that any such pretense will but lead to unfortunate results; we shall recognize that human justice cannot replace divine justice; and that the greatest and fairest satisfaction will

[1] See note, p. 293, at the end of the chapter.

be given by following the popular conception of justice and the highest approved standards. Society must ever confirm and endorse the conception of justice in the popular consciousness, and take no chance of running counter thereto. For these reasons the jury, as a part of such public opinion, in its judgments and considerations, takes account not alone of questions of fact but of prevailing notions of justice; and these likewise shape the verdicts of condemnation or acquittal. The jury thus becomes the judge not alone of the evidence but of the general question of culpability; and thereby exercises the dual function just alluded to. If the jury, speaking in behalf of common opinion, confirms the culpability, the cause of personal liberty will have been adequately safeguarded; it will, at all events, have been established that the exercise of justice in accord with the popular conception demands a condemnation. To thus express the popular sentiment is the complete function of the jury. It is not qualified to decide the question of choice and duration of punishment. The jury, representing public opinion, demands a condemnation and obtains it. The determination of the sentence involves technical questions beyond the jury's capacity, and issues in which popular opinion should not decide because it lacks the requisite knowledge. Hence the advisability of associating the jury with the court which is authorized to fix the penalty.

There remains in the system in vogue the fear of acquittals through mistrust or ill-will. That was the reason why in 1832 the decision relating to the admission of extenuating circumstances was assigned to the jury; and it might have been better in that case also to have adopted a compromise. But the procedure authorized in 1832 is still useful, particularly if ever there be established an intermediate jury for individualization. As at present the ordinary jury will re-

§ 76] LEGAL INDIVIDUALIZATION 235

tain the right of admitting extenuating circumstances, either in the present indefinite form or in some more precise form, such as that proposed in the Swiss draft; and such decision will bear upon the extenuation of punishment so far as pertains to the maximum set by the court. Why then, if the court may assign punishments of different nature and if the choice is not determined by the nature of the offense (as obtains in such cases as political offenses, or again in duelling, or in offenses due to negligence), why should not the jury be able to determine the kind of punishment and not merely its term? Assuredly the treatment should not be specified, for that would confer the control of individualization; but if there were an intermediate jury charged with the decision on that count, it could require the court to refer the issue to this special jury. This would be quite simple if but three principal groups of punishment be admitted. Whenever the jury makes no special recommendation, the ordinary common-law punishment would apply, by way of a corrective or reformatory punishment. However, the jury may be uncertain as to the choice of punishment. It may be that the defendant is an occasional offender who still remains a worthy man, for whom a different kind of punishment is appropriate, and it may be that he is an incorrigible who should be eliminated. In either case the jury has but to decide that there shall be a reference to the special jury for the choice of punishment. Such division of function would furnish all the necessary guarantees.

Yet this is but one possible procedure; there are others, and possibly the simplest would be, as is now proposed, to associate the jury and the court in the formulation of the punishment. Whether the last or some other more preferable procedure be adopted, it is clear that the difficulty does not lie there. Practical applications, as is always the case whenever progressive ideals are to be introduced, will develop their own institutions, and a practicable system will emerge. The main point is to become convinced of the need of reform and to desire its introduction. We thus reach the commanding consideration: How shall this reform be organized? What are its essential principles?

CHAPTER IX

JUDICIAL INDIVIDUALIZATION

§ 77. Older Forms of Individualization.
§ 78. The Analysis and Place of the Motive.
§ 79. A Second Interpretation of the Motive: the Psychological Factor.
§ 80. Difficulties in the Application of the Motive to Punishment.
§ 81. A Third Interpretation of the Motive: the Moral Status.
§ 82. Individualization and Political Crimes.
§ 83. Individualization in the Italian Penal Code.
§ 84. Principles underlying Individualization: Uniform Punishments.
§ 85. Legal Individualization for Special Offenses or Circumstances.
§ 86. The System of Parallel Punishments; Punishment and Social Dishonor.
§ 87. The Factors entering into the Classification of Criminals.
§ 88. A Tentative System of Individualization; Static and Dynamic Criminality.
§ 89. The detailed Classification of Criminals.
§ 90. Concessions to other Principles.
§ 91. Special Types of Individualization.
§ 92. Possible Extensions of Individualization; Relation to Preventive Measures.

§ 77. Older Forms of Individualization

WE shall now undertake a brief survey setting forth the basis on which judicial individualization shall proceed. This question cannot be solved independently. It is indissolubly bound up with a series of problems that relate to the regulation of punishment. Since individualization implies the introduction of punishments of a different character for the different kinds of criminals, a two-fold problem arises: first, to establish a classification of criminals; and second, to determine the punishments appropriate to the several classes. Let us review the principal measures that have been proposed in favor of permitting the judge to apply the most highly individualized punishments.

We begin with the principle which makes the extenuation or aggravation of the punishment depend upon the motives of the crime. This theory or system of "motives"[1] has been somewhat vaguely outlined in several modern legislations and projects; and it has received a precise and scholarly formulation in the Swiss preliminary draft, particularly in its first form.[2]

The Swiss preliminary draft does not adopt the French system of wholly indefinite extenuating circumstances, which commits their determination solely to the judge. It was held that this would make the extenuating circumtances play a double rôle, of which the second was that of granting a reduction of the legal punishment solely because, under the law, it seemed excessive. This was not compatible with the spirit of a new penal code, which, shaped by the demands of public sentiment, could not further limit the formulated consensus. It may be replied that codes once formulated do not change, while public opinion does; and that popular notions in regard to criminality may thus quickly come to be out of relation with the penalties of the code. The scale of penalties is based upon the social gravity of each infraction; and naturally according to the times and customs, a different conception will prevail. If punishments are to be neither too lenient nor too severe but remain in satisfactory accord with popular sentiment, there must be ways of maintaining the punishment at such a level. Ballast and a safety-valve must be provided. Extenuating circumstances in an indefinite form are well designed

[1] See the work, previously cited, of *Holtzendorff*, "Das Verbrechen des Mordes und die Todesstrafe."

[2] "Avant-projet Suisse," first edition, art. 37, and art. 39.

for this service. However, it may ensue that in regard to certain offenses the legal punishment will be deemed too severe even in the absence of condoning motives; and such bias will lead to acquittal. The Swiss preliminary draft in the scale of its penalties has not considered this point. It admits only specific extenuating circumstances. It holds that the law should arrange the different causes of extenuation or aggravation in very general classes. Accordingly it provides, particularly in its first form, a legal classification of the different motives that may give rise to crime. According as these motives imply a certain measure of persisting virtue, or on the other hand a deeper degree of perversity, the motive becomes a ground of extenuation or aggravation.

It is quite right that the consideration of the motive should affect the term, and through it the degree of punishment. But if it goes no further, the system is not adequate. The fixing of the term of the punishment in effect involves the determination of its character; and the point at issue is precisely whether the motive is a sufficient criterion whereby to determine the nature and the details of the punishment. For that purpose a true conception of the motive and what it involves is indispensable. Liszt has contributed a very acute and penetrating analysis of status of motives,[1] the influence of which will appear in the exposition to follow.

§ 78. The Analysis and Place of the Motive

In the sense commonly used the motive is confused primarily with the purpose sought, the end which the criminal

[1] *Liszt,* "Die psychologischen Grundlagen der Kriminalpolitik," in his Review (*Zeit. f. d. ges. Str. R. W.*, 1896, p. 477, particularly p. 483, *seq.*); and *Kraus,* "Das Motiv zur psychologischethischen Grundlegung des Strafrechts" (same Review, 1897, p. 467, *seq.*). Also the thesis, cited above, of *M. Legrand,* "De la préméditation," p. 186, *seq.*, and that of *M. Rigaud,* "De l'influence du motif," p. 7, *seq.*

had in mind. Take the case of a man who has killed another for purposes of robbery; robbery is then said to be the motive of the murder. Or take the case of an heir who poisons the man from whom he is to inherit; the motive of the crime is prematurely to secure the inheritance. In another instance a man sets fire to his house in order to obtain the insurance; or a thief breaks into the safe of a bank to pay his gambling debts. Such cases may be indefinitely varied. The motive is the advantage to be gained from committing the crime. Thus considered, the motive has no real value in criminal law except as a symptom. It serves to complete the account of the crime as planned; it illuminates and interprets it. It sets the crime in proper relation to the purpose of the criminal, for a crime is never an end in and by itself; it is almost always a means to effect a more remote purpose. Except under the sway of a purely diabolical passion, murder is not committed for the sake of killing; murder is a means to effect a definite purpose, and this purpose is the true end of the culprit. It is that which dominates the act. For the criminal resolve, meaning thereby the voluntary act that consummates the crime, never furnishes an adequate conception of the crime. The legal view of the intent detaches the crime from the true will of the individual, making it an independent act of will, while actually it is only a factor in an integral whole; and in the totality the commanding idea is the final purpose. Take the case of a thief caught in the act. To avoid arrest or prosecution he commits murder. Clearly as a deliberate intent he had no design of murder. He would not assassinate in cold blood. His purpose was to escape the police and the trial. To escape, it was necessary to get rid of a witness, and for that he had to murder; and so he committed the murder. The whole tragedy occurred in a moment; the three successive acts of will were instantly conceived and merged. The whole action expressed a single will; the steps were acts of will, determined by the purpose designed and accepted; they followed upon it. To understand and judge the crime, the situation as a whole with its psychological setting must be reproduced. The act of will must be regarded as a whole, and the part which the crime played therein duly noted. The purpose dominates the act. Clearly, however imperfectly, the purpose alone reveals the character of the agent. Yet without other considerations it would be totally inadequate to serve as the basis of a psychological classification of criminals. Let us consider the situation more in detail.

Take the case of a man who poisons the person from whom he expects to inherit. This is a sign of avarice, a greed for money. But the world is full of people thus affected, who, fortunately, are quite incapable of committing murder to satisfy their desires. The analysis of the case thus involves a step beyond this simple desire for wealth and gain; it must include all the motives associated with the purpose of the crime. Take the example of a faithless cashier who appropriates trust funds to pay a gambling debt. This is an abuse of confidence. What follows from the motive of the theft is that the cashier was possessed by the feeling that a gambling debt is a debt of honor, that must be paid at all costs. The majority of gamblers share this feeling without thereby becoming dishonest. To wish to pay one's debts, even if they are not gambling debts, is an honorable desire. If this principle goes so far as to lead to an act of indiscretion, a further examination of the chain of motives becomes necessary. It at once becomes clear that this desire to pay one's debts is not the definite purpose that determined action, for if this feeling is strong enough to lead to theft, it indicates that beside the desire to discharge an obligation there was the indirect or more immediate purpose of escaping arrest, ruin, or dishonor; and it is this final purpose that counts. But how does this final purpose enlighten us in regard to the criminality of the agent? Everybody, even the most honest of us, wishes to avoid ruin and dishonor; yet most men would be wholly incapable of committing theft to avoid such a calamity. To induce one to steal involves the presence of an additional quality, the possibility of bringing to the surface a tendency to dishonesty (the *improbità* of Garofalo), which in turn may be quite momentary and incidental, or may be a fundamental trait of character. An intense desire to escape ruin brings to the surface a dishonest streak, or, possibly, it discloses an underlying, latent trend of dishonesty ready to assert itself; and for the moment this dishonest tendency takes possession and overcomes all opposition. It is responsible for the action, and in it lies the mainspring of the crime. Yet clearly the purpose sought in the act in no manner reveals the existence of this dishonest streak.

Yet in the second example above given, that of murder, it appears that the motive is somewhat different from that in the other cases. In the case of the man who murders for money, the incentive, apparently, is greed; and the motive thus reveals an innate quality or trait. Yet this inference may be superficial. At all events the purpose for which the murderer wanted money is an essential consideration. It may be for the same reason that obtained in the case of the cashier, namely, to pay a gambling debt, or to avoid arrest and ruin. The complete account requires the attempt to find the motive for the motive; and even then we do not reach a motive that may serve as an adequate criterion of the subjective criminality of the agent. What we really find are two resolutions of a criminal character, one following upon the other, both demanding for their comprehension the consideration of yet further motives, which the end in view as above considered does not disclose. Thus the truly final purpose is to avoid arrest and ruin; and that necessitates robbery. Accordingly, it must be made plain through what trait of character the decision to steal becomes effective. It appeared, moreover, that to accomplish the theft, it became necessary to murder. It must similarly be explained upon the basis of what trait of character the decision to murder became effective. The trait which explains the murder may be not at all the same as that which explains the theft. The final purpose, which is to avoid arrest and to find the wherewithal to pay one's debts, gives no hint of these complex traits of character. Thus, once more, the final purpose becomes a motive which is quite non-committal in its bearing upon the conception of criminality. It reveals nothing essential in regard to the criminality of the agent.

To be thus serviceable a motive must be reached that unmistakably discloses a distinctive trait of character. Thus stealing for the professional thief is a business and he steals for the sake of stealing; his purpose is to get a living at the cost of others. The alleged motive has no other value than as a symptom and index of the lack of honesty, of the existence of the anti-social tendencies of the thief. From the penal point of view this trait of character, this condition of latent criminality, is the important thing. It constitutes the true motive to be considered; while the end pursued is to be taken into account only as an expression of the criminal state of mind.

§ 79. A Second Interpretation of the Motive: the Psychological Factor

For purposes of punishment the motive in the sense first considered has no real significance; and that for two reasons:

first, that commonly it reveals nothing in regard to the criminal; and second, that when it reveals a criminal trend, it is this trend, not the manner of its expression, that forms the essential basis of the criminality. We thus reach a second conception of motive which, in effect, agrees with that adopted by the Swiss preliminary draft.

This analysis shows that the purpose sought — for example the desire to get money or to avoid ruin — is not in itself criminal. Before such a purpose leads to crime, it must arouse or bring into play the impulse or trait of character or latent tendency that makes one resort to a criminal measure. A man in desperate straits may feel a growing desire to steal. He knows very well that he is contemplating a dishonest action, but the moment that the thought of theft is lodged in his mind the original purpose thereof drops out of sight. At first his one thought is to find money; later this vague and remote purpose becomes specialized, and takes a definite form; it appears as the thought of the immediate step to be taken, which is the act of theft. His entire reflection leads to this fixed idea of theft, and presently this engaging consideration brings into play impulses that are new in his experience in that they are not concerned with finding money in honest ways. There then ensues a contest between the instinct of uprightness and honesty, and its opposite, the suggestion that the duty of honesty may be set aside. The first suggestion of this possibility acts subconsciously, and, as it grows, it takes possession of the man, and finally, if it prevails, becomes the decisive and determining factor of the act. Psychologically the immediate cause of the criminal act is not the advantage to be gained, but the impulse or trait of character, which in turn yields to a general temptation rather than to the suggestion of a specific act. Such feelings or instincts form the true mainspring of the act. If the desired advantage had not awakened a criminal or immoral tendency the criminal act would never have been committed. An honest man, however urgently in need of money which he seeks in every legitimate way in the pursuit of his purpose, will never entertain the thought of stealing. Such a thought comes forward only if under the pressure of necessity it appeals to a latent tendency, which is allied to the impulse of dishonesty or criminality.

This psychological factor constitutes the motive in the second sense of the word. In place of considering the contemplated purpose which served to arouse and stimulate the inherent criminal tendency, it is the psychological factor thus aroused by the end in view that must be taken into consideration and regarded as the real motive.[1] The motive in the second sense may thus be defined as the reaction aroused by the final purpose which the agent has in view and which becomes the immediate and psychological cause of the criminal action. It is in this sense that the Swiss draft interprets the motive. Thus the first draft cites as a cause for the aggravation of punishment such circumstances as that the action was done through baseness of character, through deviltry, brutality, trickery, vengeance, greed, malice, or pleasure in crime. These motives as general grounds for aggravation were withdrawn from the second draft, but they reappear with reference to particular crimes or offenses, such as murder (Art. 52) or injury to property (Art. 79). As extenuating motives the Swiss draft speaks of honorable motives; the first draft calls them refined motives. The expression appears somewhat extreme as applied to a crime or misdemeanor. It seems out of place to speak of a crime as incited by refined or exalted motives.

[1] *Liszt*, "Die psychol. Grundlagen der Kriminalpolitik" p. 486.

It seems better to speak of them as honorable motives. Perhaps it would have been better, as was proposed in the commission, to use a negative form, and speak of motives that carry no dishonor or imply no degenerate trait. At all events it is evident that in all cases it is not the final end sought but the tendency or psychological factor which this purpose arouses or stimulates, that becomes the determining cause of the crime.

Here we are clearly in presence of a psychological fact that has a real value for penology, but its precise value is difficult to determine. The same objection as applies to the acceptance of the final purpose as a criterion may again be urged; namely, that such tendencies may exist apart from any criminal manifestation, and that thus they cannot be considered as necessarily containing the germ of a criminal trait. It is true that one may have a low character, be moved by feelings of vengeance or greed, without necessarily becoming criminal; and if, as the Italian school holds, punishment has no other end than the prevention of the repetition of crime, one could hardly accept the presence of a tendency to vice or greed as a probable indication of its becoming a source of crime in the future. Further evidence would be needed: it would have to be determined whether this tendency is strong enough to bring about a further criminal action, and, assuming it to be so, whether it would induce the habit of crime, or whether, perhaps, it may not in the first instance have been the issue of a passionate and momentary outburst under the pressure of circumstances; and secondly, it would have to be determined whether this psychological factor, supposing it sufficiently powerful to induce the habit of crime, was innate or at least antedated the crime committed, or whether it was incited solely by the momentary purpose entertained. In the one case there is a chance that this psychological factor will not reassert itself; in the other it forms part of the nature of the individual and must be treated as a permanent menace. These two proofs are in no way furnished by the existence of a tendency to greed or to evil passion as an efficient cause of crime.

§ 80. Difficulties in the Application of the Motive to Punishment

If this view is valid, this second conception of a motive will likewise fail to furnish a scientific classification of criminals, or at least fail to indicate the kind of punishment suitable to the individual. It is important to recognize that to be of service to penology by prescribing the character of punishment, this second conception of the motive must be developed more thoroughly. In proof thereof consider that it may well happen that wholly debased natures may at times commit crimes incited, to use the language of the Swiss draft, by honorable motives. Take the case of a professional criminal, a thief who, perhaps, has already been guilty of murder. He is led to commit a murder with the sole motive of preventing an evil deed. He is witness, for example, of a fray, in the course of which one of his companions calls upon him to commit a dastardly attack, — let us say that he proposes to assault a woman. The proposal arouses a feeling of moral revulsion. Considering what he is, this is clearly a generous sentiment. He may have the courage to come to the defense of the threatened victim and attack the fellow. If in the course of the fight he strikes a hard blow that kills his companion, he may have a legitimate defense; but if, in place of this, he takes him by surprise from behind and kills him in cold blood, knowing full well that he is attempting and committing a murder, then there will be no desperate situation, no legitimate defense to justify the crime. It becomes a clear case of murder. Yet it is proper to take account of the feeling of generosity that enters into such a case to mitigate the punishment. But suppose that the judge has at his disposal different kinds of punishment, some designed for those by nature honest who have no need of reformation, others designed for perverts whose re-education is to be attempted. It may indeed be extremely unwise by reason of the motive that accounts for the crime, to apply to an offender, who is a professional and at bottom an evil-doer, a discipline arranged for accidental offenders who stand in no need of reform. It would be a serious error to make capital of this sentiment of generosity as though it were a part of the habitual nature of the individual and to treat him as one unacquainted with any criminal impulse.

Conversely, one may suppose a respectable man by chance yielding to a low and vicious impulse; in this spirit, the Swiss draft deliberately places greed among the grosser impulses that aggravate punishment. Consider once more the case of the cashier who after a long career of honesty is led into a breach of confidence under the pressure of circumstances which have called forth a feeling of momentary but irresistible greed; we there decide it proper, if this impulse is a vicious one, to increase the punishment and impose the maximum sentence. But if the judge is convinced that he is dealing with a man momentarily led astray, intrinsically honest, would it be just to impose upon him a punishment designed for perverts, and suitable only to the worst types? Punishment of that kind tends to lower and debase morals rather than to maintain them.

It thus appears that the motive in the second sense of the word may well serve as the criterion for the degree of punishment, and yet remain inadequate to determine its nature and discipline.[1] It takes into account a momentary impulse and gives evidence only of the state of mind at the moment of the crime, and this momentary, transitory, and quite artificial aspect of the man is not sufficient as evidence of his true and general character. The feeling which he shows at the moment of the crime may be an exceptional condition, and in assigning his treatment according to the indications of this momentary condition there is danger of a radical mistake.

One may even go further. Very often, indeed, it would be wholly false to judge the morality of an act according to the sentiment that the purpose sought calls forth, without taking account of the latter. It has been seen that the purpose sought leads to crime only if the desire for it is supported by a criminal trend strong enough to induce the crime. This pressure must be such as to replace, at least momentarily, the man's sense of honesty, which until then was his true nature, by a sense of dishonesty. This is perfectly correct; but what is often quite false is to appraise the deed solely according to this dishonest impulse, to the neglect of the external pressure and the purpose that gave rise to the crime. For that, one must return once more to the example of the faithless cashier who stole to cover his obligations. Evidently there was a moment when the feeling of honesty was replaced by its opposite, by the decision to use fraudulent means, the willingness to become an instrument of fraud. But shall one say that this feeling, which in itself is low and perverse, should determine his character and his moral status in regard to the act committed? To use the terms of the Swiss draft, shall one say that this man stole because of greed? That would seem to be quite im-

[1] See Kraus, cited above, p. 481.

possible, because what here prevailed was the more remote purpose; and without this necessity to avoid ruin at whatever cost, the fraudulent impulse would never have entered into the mind of the unfortunate miscreant. It would be otherwise only if the feeling in favor of fraud and dishonesty had existed before the development of the situation which gave it the occasion to appear in a specific form.

Indeed, even when the case is one that indicates a criminal act — and independently of the question of determining the penal treatment — the dominant impulse of the crime is to be considered only if it were present in the criminal in a latent form previous to the crime; and if, furthermore, it came to be the dominant cause of the crime, while the purpose sought was only its occasion. We must accordingly return to the terms of the proposition that served as our former formula, if we wish to find a motive that may be considered as a criminal impulse, as the dominant motive of the criminality of the act, which in turn may serve to characterize it in terms of crime and to assign it its place in the scale of subjective criminality.

The final purpose, we say, determines the criminal impulse; and this impulse, in turn, determines the crime. Yet very commonly the reverse is true. It is the perverse impulse that determines the end to be gained and incites it; and it is the end that becomes the immediate occasion of the crime. Thus in case of the person who became an incendiary to obtain the insurance, it is not his necessity to get this money that aroused his feeling of greed; this was already present and urged him to attempt to obtain money by means of a crime. The same is true for the majority of cases of theft. Even in cases of murder involving brutality and cruelty and vengeance, these are sentiments that existed antecedent to the end sought; or rather, this end tended to satisfy these feelings. But these feelings may be said to be the true motive of the crime only under the supposition that the feeling of wanton lawlessness, which is sympathetic to crime, has given rise to the particular plan followed. This is no longer true when the feeling is but a reflex emotion that arises after the undertaking has begun and is incidental to the purpose sought. In order that the motive, in the second sense of the word, may be regarded as the determining cause, it must be merged with the end sought, and the crime must have no other object than to give satisfaction to this feeling of dishonesty, of perversity, or of cruel and savage passion, that existed before the crime — at least in a latent form — and in this form became part of the real nature of the criminal's personality.

§ 81. A Third Interpretation of the Motive; the Moral Status

We here come upon a third conception of motive. The motive is no longer the psychological factor aroused by the end to be gained which has become the immediate cause of the crime; it is the essential quality of the moral character, the satisfaction of which stands as the final purpose of the crime to be committed. Possibly this is the meaning of the Swiss draft; in speaking of a murder incited by cruelty or vengeance, it interprets that the murder was committed to satisfy this impulse of cruelty and desire for vengeance.

We thus reach the conclusion that the motive which penology must particularly consider is that embodied in the psychological factor that incited the crime and gave it its dominant character. It is the motive thus specified that nearly always serves to indicate the objective criminality of the act. It supplies the judge with one of the surest criteria of judgment in regard to the degree of punishment, and consequently of its duration.

In a theory that does not admit individualization based upon responsibility there is needed an individualization based upon the subjective criminality of the action: that is, upon the criminal act taken as a whole with all its psychological causes and judged as a unity and a totality. Punishment in regard to its duration should have two standards of measure: an objective and legal standard, according to the social gravity of the crime abstractly considered, and a subjective standard, derived from the criminality embodied in the action, which in turn is determined for the most part by the nature of the emotion or the moral factor which inspired the crime.

The value of the motive considered as a criterion of the subjective criminality of the act is thus established. It may be added that even in the third sense the motive is not the exclusive factor to be taken into consideration: which, in turn, may be thus made clear. One may suppose a murder incited by a motive that is not a perverse impulse, let us say a feeling of righteous indignation. Brutality does not enter, although the murder may have been committed under conditions that indicate a decided cruelty. Here the indignation brought forward the brutality, not alone such brutality as every intentional homicide implies and which may be assumed if one is capable of murder, but a peculiar brutality, quite irrelevant as a determining cause and foreign to the execution of the act, but evidenced in the refinement of the suffering inflicted. Would it be proper to say, in terms of motive, that there is present in this case but a weak degree of subjective criminality? Is it proper to speak of the honorable motives that the Swiss proposal admits? In short, side by side with the motive, must one not take account of the means, in order to present not alone the material circumstances of the deed but its subjective criminality? Surely, the most honorable murder — explaining this combination of terms by the interpretation already given to it — if vitriol is used in perpetrating the crime, is proven to be the act of a low and base criminal.

Thus considered the motive itself remains wholly inadequate to determine the subjective criminality of the act. If the act is to be characterized in terms of its prevailing sentiment, account must be taken of the entire complexity of impulses disclosed by it, which as a whole constitutes the moral nature. The subjective criminality of the act is the act considered in its psychological origin, and at the same time it is an expression of the feelings leading to its execution. It is the psychology of crime and of the particular crime judged by its causes and the manner of its execution.[1]

§ 82. Individualization and Political Crimes

The conclusion thus reached brings us merely to the determination of the scale of punishment. In the present issue this is but the secondary aspect of criminology; the main and serious problem is to determine upon what basis to differentiate suitable punishments and how to assign the proper punishment to each case.

To accomplish this the attractive plan of affording the judge several kinds of punishment differing in their character and discipline has been proposed; whatever the offense, the judge may thus have available two different kinds of punishment for any individual case. There will be two scales of punishment; and according to the character of the agent the judge can place him in one or other of the two

[1] See *Stooss*, "Das Motiv im Entwurf zu einem schweizerischen Strafgesetzbuch" (in the *Revue pénale suisse*, 1896, p. 167, *seq.*).

groups. This has been designated as the system of parallel punishments.[1]

That the requirements of modern individualization lead directly to the admission of a system of parallel punishments is clear. The difficulty lies in determining the basis upon which the judge shall assign one or the other type. Those favorable to the plan have found no other basis of distinction than that of the motive. The motive, as above interpreted, thus sets the standard for the term of punishment and determines as well its character and discipline. This conclusion must be carefully examined. Let us inquire into the nature of the doctrine of parallel punishments.

The criminologists who originated the theory started from a well-known precedent: the recognition, with reference to the material crime, of two standards of punishment, the one applicable to political crimes and the other to crimes of common law. The suggestive principle thus introduced is capable of considerable development. The social gravity of political and common-law crimes may be identical. Indeed, objectively the political crime often carries graver consequences than the common-law crime; for the latter carries direct injury only to a single individual. As political crimes disclose a different type of impulses it has been held that the character of the punishment should be different. Dostoiewsky's "House of the Dead" will acquaint one with the effect of promiscuous association of different kinds of offenders. Political offenders, those guilty of military in-

---

[1] The main contribution to this question is the learned report of *M. Garçon* to the Société générale des Prisons: "Les peines non déshonorantes," in the *Revue pénitentiaire*, 1896, p. 830, *seq.* See also a symposium upon the question, contributed by a number of criminologists, whose opinions are published in the *Revue pénitentiaire*, 1896, p. 1099, *seq.*; p. 1407, *seq.*; and Année 1897, p. 144, *seq.* See also the thesis, previously cited, of *M. Rigaud*, p. 49, *seq.*

subordination, and common criminals are thrown together in the same prison. This abuse is the best possible plea in favor of parallel punishments.

In differentiating the punishments of political criminals it was the criminal and not the crime that was considered. It was deemed unjust to subject the political offender to the same kinds of punishment as were provided for ordinary criminals, for such are regarded by the law as infamous. Political punishments are intended to be deterrent and by their severity and length to discourage plotters, while likewise they are regarded as measures of public welfare to hold agitators in check, but they were not intended to be infamous. The terms "infamous" and "non-infamous" refer only to the nature of the discipline and the attitude of public opinion. They do not necessarily refer to the weaknesses which occasioned the punishment, continue even after its execution, and are considered as true derelictions, either political or personal. All that has nothing to do with the notion of infamy. It is directed to the removal of a danger. For whether or not a punishment is infamous, a man who has been sentenced is regarded as a transgressor, as lacking in certain respects. To entrust him with a responsible position and place him in charge of the moral education of others would be a public danger; and the same applies to the restoration of his political rights without further evidence. While definitely eliminating the idea of disgrace we do not necessarily imply that all minor disabilities should be cancelled, and in proof thereof it is the case that political punishments, while not regarded as infamous, involve minor disabilities.[1] These appear in the conditional sentence, which is especially intended to avoid every im-

[1] For "infamy," in Anglo-American law, see *Professor Henry Schofield's* note in the *Illinois Law Review*, Vol. V, 1911. — ED.

plication of disgrace, yet which deprives the man under sentence, at least during his period of probation, of the exercise of his political rights. This distinction is quite definite.

§ 83. Individualization in the Italian Penal Code

We come now to the statement of the principle. But are the political criminals the only offenders who are likely to arouse interest? Common-law criminals do not all inspire the same aversion; there are some whose crime does not disclose any previous perversity. The Swiss draft assumes the existence of crimes committed for "honorable" motives. Obviously, among so-called crimes of passion, there are some that do not imply the perversity of the agent. Certain cases of homicide, from the ethical standard, approximate closely to cases of legitimate self-defense. Honor must be defended as well as life. The court proceedings show such cases as that of a father defending the honor of his daughter. Strictly speaking, justice must apply the law to such cases, but is it proper to regard persons thus involved as on a level with common murderers and subject them to the same punishment, not merely in length of term but in discipline? This is opposed to every sense of justice.

One of the first attempts thus to establish distinctions among offenders with reference to the application of punishment was made in the preparation of the Italian penal code. This was one of the most fruitful innovations accepted and developed by the penal code of 1889. This indebtedness should be clearly acknowledged.[1] One of the numerous proposals and drafts advanced two scales of punishment by imprisonment. The one entailed a discipline

[1] See the interesting and detailed study of *Ugo Conti* (*Supplemento alla Rivista penale*, vol. V, fasc. 3–4): "I moventi a delinquere e il Codice penale italiano."

§ 83] JUDICIAL INDIVIDUALIZATION 257

far more rigorous and of a different order from that prescribed for the other, but instead of deciding the punishment, as in France, wholly according to the objective gravity of the offense, it was the purpose to apply it in accord with the subjective criminality of which the criminal gave evidence. It was thus that deportation and detention were reserved for political transgressors and for so-called crimes of passion, — *I reati politici e d'impeto.*[1] This occurs in the draft of 1866. This draft met the fate of many legislative constructions; it was the subject of many changes and was replaced by other drafts. The principle of parallel punishments survived these parliamentary vicissitudes.

In the draft of Mancini it assumed an interesting form. This permitted the judge to take account of motives and to substitute one punishment for another. Such substitution was made, not as in France, by reason of extenuating circumstances which would warrant only a change in severity of punishment, but it permitted the substitution of a totally different type of discipline, even a discipline of an entirely different nature and character from the punishments prescribed by the law. It is true that in France, according to our system of extenuating circumstances, one discipline may be substituted for another; thus penal servitude may be substituted for hard labor, or hard labor for corrective imprisonment, but in the operation of this substitution the law considers only the presumptive severity of the discipline. It regards penal servitude as more rigorous than hard labor, and in cases of extenuating circumstances it is authorized to substitute one discipline for another. This is really a mistake, and those who have to undergo the punishments often think differently. They prefer the work out-of-doors in a colony, in a new environment, where the

[1] See *Conti*, cited above (special impression), pp. 10–11.

echoes of the normal life they have led and others are leading does not reach them, to the prison work-rooms which they never leave. It should be added that the penal code in prescribing penal servitude and in determining the relative scale of punishments, considered only the old-type convict prisons; indeed, the discipline in these was naturally different in severity from that obtaining in our jails. The introduction of deportation in 1854 changed this, — so much so, that, in spite of the edicts of 1891 and others that have attempted to re-establish the legal proportion, the order of preference is now inverted. Those concerned once more prefer penal servitude to hard labor. This indicates the spirit in which these distinctions of discipline were established. They were not designed to differentiate criminals in natural groups but to punish crimes according to their gravity. It may be said that penal servitude, hard labor, and even reformatory imprisonment were designed for persons of the same type. It is a fact that the more deserving characters are found among those deported and among convicts, rather than among the ordinary prisoners. When the law, by reason of extenuating circumstances, permitted a change of discipline, it was done solely to make the punishment less severe because it considered the crime as less serious. It was not done to afford the convict a discipline better adapted and more appropriate as a means of restoring him more certainly to a moral plane, or as an additional guarantee against the contamination to which he was exposed. Indeed, the contrary was more nearly true.

The several Italian proposals referred to have a different trend. The purpose of permitting the judge to substitute one punishment for another was not only to lessen the rigor of the discipline but to give it a different direction and character. The substituted punishment was not merely lighter

§ 83] JUDICIAL INDIVIDUALIZATION 259

but was designed for those who were not perverts and were to be punished without, however, involving their social degradation, without dishonoring them in the eyes of their fellow-citizens. Most of all were such offenders to be separated from congenital criminals. Without following the several changes which the Italian draft underwent, let us briefly review the final form of the provision.

The system adopted was composite; and the offenses were arranged in three groups. For some the only punishment set by the law was hard labor, a common-law punishment; for others the law provided only detention, a special punishment; and, thirdly, the law permitted the choice between the two. Thus in the Italian penal code the differentiating principle adopts, side by side, two systems, the one applied by the law and the other applied by the judge. For those offenses for which the punishment is unalterably fixed by the law, the law retains the choice, and applies one or other of the parallel punishments according to the character of the offense. On the other hand, for those offenses for which the choice between the two punishments is left to the judge, it is the judge who applies one or the other, according to the merit of the individual. The system is not fully developed; and the same may be said of the parallel punishments of the German penal code. According to Art. 20, in certain cases, as prescribed by the law, the judge has at his disposal two kinds of punishment by imprisonment. To justify the application of the more severe, the details of the crime must be peculiarly abhorrent. But in fact, since the law prescribes and determines the applications of these parallel punishments, it admits them only in cases not very different from political crimes and in certain offenses of state officials.[1]

As a result of the able report of M. Garçon the question

[1] See *Olshausen,* "Kommentar zum Strafgesetzbuch," I, p. 97.

has been taken up anew and thoroughly studied. It was presented before the Société générale des Prisons, and was followed by a general discussion by several men of authority. Expert opinion is thus available;[1] indeed this admirable and profitable method of securing scientific information should be more extensively adopted.

§ 84. Principles underlying Individualization; Uniform Punishments

The field for such discussions was prepared by the ideas advanced at the Congress at Stockholm in behalf of a uniform type of punishment. This view has since then made considerable progress. Recent drafts and codes tend in this direction, and the French revision, in its approximate adoption of the principle, presents one of its most successful innovations. This improvement is due to M. Leveillé. It was recognized that the so-called differences of discipline were little more than varieties of torture (using the word in no harsh sense) and were of little avail. It is a survival (and in so far justifies the use of the word " torture ") of the fertility of such devices in our ancient criminal practice. To apportion the suffering to the evil done was the traditional form of the system of penalty; and in principle this relation has persisted. Those who still hold to the conception of penalty have rejected the crude conception of injury for injury, particularly as circumstances do not permit any real equivalence and merely serve to bring about the striking inequalities of punishment. Penalty implies responsibility and the evidence of moral guilt; it implies as well the possibility of a moral effect, a moral action of the punishment, and this is confused with expiation; it effects a regeneration through suffering. Unquestionably suffering is experienced,

[1] See above, p. 254, note.

but the hope may be expressed that for some, if not for all, suffering will be resignedly accepted. Such is the implication of the word "penalty," — the end in view in expiation; but the conception of a fictitious proportion between the evil done and the moral injury realized is acceptable only as a religious doctrine of retribution, according to which the destiny of the human soul is regarded as predetermined, and past sins must be wiped out. But when the future is at stake, the past is negligible in comparison to the protection of a career and the reformation of a life. The notions of penalty and expiation are of value only in stimulating activity in the direction of moral reform. We are justified in asking how, in times of religious faith, these ideas of retributive justice were reconciled with the Christian conception, which is devoted to the saving of souls so long as life lasts, and regards past sins and penances merely as successive stations in the gradual ascent of the moral life. Under our present views such conceptions must be looked upon as survivals of the old conception of the law of retaliation — an eye for an eye, a tooth for a tooth. Morally this does not appeal to us, and practically it is becoming less and less realizable. The difficulty appears in the distinction between reformatory imprisonment and hard labor, which for the most part is vague and confused. Unquestionably a difference in punishment should be retained corresponding to the difference in crime; but this should be expressed in the term of sentence, and therein will the principle of proportionality be maintained so long as we hold to an objective scale of offenses. There will be no danger of the prevalent differences of judgment of court and prisoner with reference to the severity of penal servitude. There will be an approach towards a uniform type of punishment, applicable to all criminals through a reformatory discipline arranged in progressive stages. England has for some time afforded an example of such a system. The only distinction that remains is that between punishments that may be adapted to such a discipline and those that cannot; and this corresponds to the distinction between long-term and short-term punishments. These conclusions are now generally accepted.

If there is to be but a single type of punishment with an invariable discipline, it becomes illogical to put all kinds of offenders, as the expression goes, in the same boat. Such lack of discrimination runs counter to current opinion, well worthy of respect, which itself does not favor any extreme variety of disciplines. If the punishment is not to vary according to the external character of the crime, then punishment must be classified upon some other basis, which must be the consideration of the individual, — a subjective classification of punishments replacing the prevailing objective classification. In this way the system of uniform punishments leads insensibly to uniformity in each group of individualized punishments.

These steps in the development should be carefully noted; the system of parallel punishments forms one transition, and that of individualized punishments another. As appeared above, the difficult point in the combination of parallel punishments with the uniform type of punishment is to determine the criterion of application of the different parallel punishments; the punishment is uniform in terms of the objectivity of the crime, but variable according to its subjectivity. On what basis shall this distinction be established?

§ 85. Legal Individualization for Special Offenses or Circumstances

There are but two systems possible, as was seen in the case of the Italian penal code, — application by law or application by the judge. The former is proposed by the more hesitant innovators. It consists merely in separating, in the law, certain crimes or misdemeanors of a less infamous character, and applying to them the one of the two types of punishment by imprisonment, which is not considered infamous. Duelling is to be treated in this way, and the same obviously applies to offenses of negligence and infractions. There should likewise be placed in this privileged group the several offenses of intermediate status between deliberate offenses and those incurred through negligence, in which the intention was not directed to the result that ensued while however considering it as a possible outcome. Such would be the case of the hunter who fires while aware that there are passers-by within range. He considered the possibility of an accident, but this was present to his mind as a most unlikely chance. He fired and an accident occurred.[1] This is more than an offense of bad judgment. It is an offense of intent in the sense that the intent in its possibilities was in the direction of a possible murder. It is thus a contingent offense. It should be punished more severely than a simple offense of negligence but differently from an ordinary intentional offense that implies a true criminal intent. In this case a special punishment and not the common-law punishment should apply.[2]

In other words there will merely be extended to certain

[1] There may be added the case of the station-master who gives the signal for the departure of a train, although the track is not clear, and foresees the possibility of an accident, although there is but one chance in ten in favor of it. Having considered the contingency, it becomes a contingent offense. There is also the case of the physician, who in his scientific enthusiasm in attempting a new treatment, inoculates a hospital patient with the microbe of a disease that is nearly always fatal. He foresees very clearly that the patient may die. This involves more than bad judgment; there is an intent and a contingent crime.

[2] On this theory of contingent liability see above, p. 221, note 1.

common-law offenses the provisions now obtaining for political offenses. The law will thus regard certain common-law offenses, that in themselves and objectively do not imply a true subjective criminality, as similar in status, and in the appropriate punishments to be assigned them, to political offenses.

But such individualization by law is quite inadequate. A further step must be taken by allowing the law to provide a special punishment for the offenses just indicated; but in addition a similar provision must be made for all other offenses by affording the judge the choice between the two punishments according to the moral nature of the offense. This will be a system of judicial application, but it in turn may be understood in two ways, with or without legal prescription. The law may leave entire freedom to the judge, neither guiding nor prescribing his choice. The judge may thus make his own criterion of application, and in this case the criterion may be the consideration of the individual in his entire personality, in place of the individual considered solely in relation to the deed committed. But this excellent plan is not what is generally proposed. It is the intention to give the judge, whatever may be the crime or misdemeanor, a choice between two parallel punishments; but the law shall state the basis of choice to be employed. The law is thus to determine the criterion which is to serve as the indication to the judge to apply one or the other of two punishments; and this criterion will be precisely that of which we have spoken at some length, — the motive. The motive will be interpreted in the sense set forth in detail, as the emotional or moral factor which has incited either the end for which the crime was committed or the crime itself as a means of attaining the end. The psychological factor plays the determining part in the crime.

§ 85]   JUDICIAL INDIVIDUALIZATION   265

This amounts to affirming that the nature and the discipline of the punishment should depend upon the motive, that is, upon the moral attitude revealed by the crime, — or, rather, that which is revealed as the active force and incentive of the crime. There will be different punishments for those whose crime has been incited by low and perverse sentiments and for those whose crime was incited by sentiments that in themselves are not dishonorable. From this starting point the advocates of parallel punishments propose to classify punishments in two groups: the one corresponding to infamous punishments, like hard labor in the Italian penal code; and the other corresponding to punishments that are not infamous, like detention as it is set forth in the same code. That is the whole of the system. It is clearly a step in advance. It evidences the growing movement towards a subjective penal law, that is, towards a penal law that is more humane and more considerate of the individual. The eyes of Justice have too long been bandaged and prevented from seeing the position of her scales; and this has given rise to many an injustice. The bandage must be removed. Justice must be given sight and insight that shall be adequate to probe the human conscience, not to find the proof of freedom of action — for this, Justice is not equipped — but to sound the moral depth of the offender, a service to be readily and even scientifically performed. The system of parallel punishments is a protest against abstract impersonal justice, which was the ideal of a former generation, but which we reject because we know its results: criminals by birth who scorn it, or chance offenders whom it brands and ruins. The bandage on the eyes of Justice protects the perverts and degrades the chance offender. The former welcome and find support in it; the latter find in it their despair. We demand a Justice that sees clearly, that treats perverts as perverts, and the wayward as wayward — as redeemable members of society.

§ 86. The System of Parallel Punishments; Punishment and Social Dishonor

The system of parallel punishments is a first step in this direction, but is, as yet, inadequate. From two points of view it remains too superficial: as a system of punishments, from the punitive point of view; and as a criterion of application, from the psychological point of view. So far as concerns the discipline but two things seem to have been considered: to make punishment less infamous, and to make it less severe and thereby less deterrent. The former is valueless and the latter altogether inadequate. The question of the infamous character of punishment should never have been raised. The purpose of punishment is never to destroy honor but to restore it. What constitutes infamy is the corruption disclosed by the crime and which makes the criminal an outcast. Condemnation disgraces him in that it reveals officially and judicially his psychological criminality, and in that it fixes his attitude and position with reference to the social group. But the feeling of honor is one of the impulses least amenable to reason because it is of purely social origin. It belongs to the subconscious relations of the individual with his social group. It is not a feeling capable of conscious and reasoned analysis. It is the sense of being a member of a group, an equal amongst equals. This becomes the standard of social normality. Crime throws a man out of relation and makes him abnormal; he becomes an outcast and an alien. The sense of dishonor presents an inner and an outer aspect, and it is well to observe — in opposition to the common opinion — that it begins from within, in a sense of abnormality and degradation which the crime has brought about. Is this feeling shame or is it remorse? It cannot be remorse, for this is an elevated moral conception, — although it is often misunderstood as though it were a sort of brooding upon the past, while rightly it should be a source of energy for future regeneration. It more nearly approaches shame, although the strong consciousness of abnormality may develop into the consciousness of a deeper personality, of a more serious and stronger initiative. The transition from one group to the other is accompanied by the self-bestowed honors of war. Criminals have the courage of their crime.[1]

Let us hold to this direct influence disclosed by a psychological and social analysis, namely, the consciousness of social loss of caste. Though strange, it is true that, as outwardly reflected, such loss of honor is slow to appear. The social estrangement of the criminal will not be seriously reflected by the treatment of his associates if he himself puts up a bold front and gives no suspicion of his inner disgrace. One knows him to be a dishonest man but continues to pay him respect and consideration; he remains a part of the social group; he is not ostracized nor excommunicated. Infamy does not depend upon morality but upon social equality. So long as the dishonest man holds his own and remains within the group of his equals, one ignores what he is. Social consciousness and social unity are so strongly embedded in our nature, that no one individual takes it upon himself to exercise the social authority and excommunicate another. In order to render infamy effective the social organism, here expressed in the judicial power, must pronounce the loss of caste. Contrary to the familiar saying, "It is the scaffold and not the crime that disgraces,"

[1] On this subject, and from an analogous point of view, see the recent volume of *Sighele*, "Littérature et criminalité."

it is really society that disgraces. Honor and esteem should not be confused. Esteem is conferred by one individual upon another; honor is conferred by society alone.

Condemnation by means of a legal sentence becomes a social excommunication, and as such it dishonors. But wherein consists the infamy of the punishment that follows? The dishonor is already incurred, and honor is now to be restored. Lost ground must be recovered and a new opening found through which an entrance and adjustment to a social status may be brought about. The social ban must be lifted; the convict must make himself socially acceptable, and thereby regain his sense of honor. The purpose of punishment is to facilitate such reinstatement and to restore the sense of social equality.

Punishment should not be designed to intensify the dishonor inherent in condemnation: and that for two practical reasons, first, because it would intensify the depravity prevalent among criminals; and second, because it would impede the social reinstatement. There are two sources of corruption: the hardships of the environment, which re-enforce evil impulses; and the loss of the sense of honor, or rather of self-esteem. Of the two, the more serious is certainly the second. The hardships of the environment can never quite destroy the moral sense, never wholly destroy regret for the past and hope for the future. The loss of self-esteem is the definite abandonment of oneself and the acceptance of one's downfall. The man who knows and feels himself lost is, socially speaking, "done for." He is beyond the pale, fallen to the level of those whom society has dishonored and rejected. He is degraded in his own eyes and in the eyes of others. Nothing more is to be expected of him; and thus the disgrace of punishment acts as the most powerful means of corruption. The serious

§ 86]   JUDICIAL INDIVIDUALIZATION   269

obstacle to social reinstatement is obvious. How is society to accept one whom it has already rejected? To him all doors are closed, particularly the door of the workshop. Refused by society, the only world that is open to him is that underworld frequented by his prison chums.

Such is the effect of infamous punishments. Punishment, to accomplish its end, must not involve the loss of honor. It must aid in its restoration. Far from exerting its present influence, punishment must be made to support self-esteem by aiming to weaken the immoral impulses which have led to its loss, and by replacing these with tendencies opposed thereto. For this purpose the discipline must arouse in those affected a clear appreciation of their possibilities, a new conception of life, in which energy and personal initiative, the habit of work and effort, should be dominant. The effect of the discipline should be to make a man feel worthy of the social life, and thus restore his sense of honor. For the sense of honor, like that of dishonor, must be worked upon subjectively; it must exist within the man before others can be asked to recognize and sanction it. Punishment must bring about a spiritual regeneration, and thus make liberty the consecration of honor regained, the beginning of social rehabilitation which the test of life confirms. To this end punishment should prepare and give assurance of social reinstatement and never impose an indelible stigma. In this respect there is at present a fair agreement. There is a growing sentiment in favor of abolishing punishments that dishonor,[1] and of discarding the distinction made between infamous and non-infamous punishments.

[1] It has been indicated above that this is not necessarily connected with the removal of the disabilities accessory to punishment. See above, pp. 255-256.

§ 87. The Factors entering into the Classification of Criminals

The disposition of the severity of punishment is likewise unsatisfactory. Obviously punishment should be severe; otherwise it would not be a penalty, and would not stimulate reflection nor regret. It must work upon the individual to rebuild him spiritually. Again, if the prison discipline is not severe it ceases to intimidate; it would become a form of hospitality of which, apart from the moral effect, advantage would be taken. We must avoid all false sentimentality; punishment should be severe, if need be, very severe, and perhaps it should be imposed according to the nature of the criminal. Yet this is not enough. The relative severity of discipline is inadequate to place the punishment in proper relation to the corrective education and moral reform of those condemned. It is the mode of organizing the discipline itself, independently of the question of severity, that must characterize the punishment and constitute its true nature.

It has for some time been recognized that there should be three chief groups of punishments: (1) punishments organized with reference to a prospect of a social reinstatement; (2) punishments applicable to incorrigibles, where there is no such prospect; (3) punishments for those morally certain to make good. For the last, the question of morality does not really arise; for such offenders remain honest and there is no occasion to reform them morally or spiritually, or to provide a new environment. For them punishment has no moral or educational purpose but is simply a penalty of a deterrent nature. Apart from these two latter classes, there are punishments, reformatory punishments, applicable to offenders who stand in need of and are susceptible

§ 87]   JUDICIAL INDIVIDUALIZATION   271

of moral reform. Thus the three following classes: punishments for intimidation, for reform, and for social protection.

How shall the parallelism of punishments based upon the relative dishonor or severity of the punishment be assimilated to this three-fold classification? The fundamental basis of the classification should be the mode of organizing the discipline, or, better, the intrinsic spirit of the punitive treatment, and such classification should lead to a corresponding classification of criminals. Psychologically the question becomes the determination of a rational classification of criminals on the basis of parallel punishments.

In the theory of parallel punishments the classification is made according to the motive. But it has been shown that the motive is nothing else than the psychological factor dominant in the crime. It is the decisive cause of the crime, either in that it provided the object of which the crime was the realization; or that it itself was the issue of the end to be obtained and thus suggested the crime; or that it gave rise to the moral energy needed to translate the thought into deed. But the motive thus understood is but a peculiar and specialized sentiment, though also a part of character and the index of a dominant trait. Nine times out of ten it has a true symptomatic value, but not necessarily so. Rascals may on occasion act on generous impulses and commit crimes that are like the "crimes of respectable men,"— of the existence of which juries seem to be convinced, and which the Swiss draft does not hesitate to recognize legally. On the other hand criminals by accident may have committed a crime under the impulse of base sentiments, which, if alone regarded, would suggest a hardened and perverted professional. When we consider the motive we begin to obtain insight into the depths of human nature. But our considerations are still superficial. It is still too much the crime and not enough the criminal that is uppermost.

There are three stages in the psychological analysis of punishment, which the evolution of penal law discloses. At first the material fact alone was considered; so long as the crime was the same, the subjective criminality was deemed to be the same. A deeper analysis brought forward the question of responsibility. By using the criterion of accountability and freedom, the attempt was made to measure and gauge the moral status of the agent; but the act committed was ever uppermost, and the decision turned upon the amount of deliberate intent which the act disclosed, upon the responsibility attaching to the act itself. Whether this responsibility was exercised by a debased criminal or by a respectable man made no difference; indeed the punishment imposed was heavy for the respectable man, and seemed light to the hardened criminal. At length a further step was taken. Instead of undertaking to measure or estimate the degree of intent or freedom, which ever escape quantitative measurement, the quality of the will was looked into. Instead of a quantitative, a qualitative valuation was attempted, and the motive thus emerged, — that is, the relative depravity of the emotion that incited the resolve and gave it its character.

We thus reach not the degree of intent or freedom but the degree of perversity expressed in the action. This may be called the subjective criminality of the action and is to be substituted for responsibility. It is a decided advance. We are no longer exposed to confusions of terms such as those involved in the theory of responsibility, — the lesser punishments being assigned to the worst offenders. The criminality of the act remains in direct relation with the perversity with which it was conceived and executed. Even

§ 87] JUDICIAL INDIVIDUALIZATION 273

if we consider only the criminality of the act itself, the worst offenders have slight chance to escape the maximum degree in the scale of subjective criminality. Moreover, quite apart from the personality of the criminal, it is a large step in advance to assign the maximum of penalty to the maximum of perversity. The theory of responsibility might lead to a quite opposite result. But it is altogether likely that the perversity inherent in the act corresponds to the natural perversity of the individual. If the case is one of murder incited by pure cruelty there is considerable probability that the agent is by nature passionate and cruel.

However there are more or less exceptional cases in which this is not true; and if the law, according to the theory of parallel punishments, must necessarily make the particular punishment assigned depend upon the particular motive involved, the judge will have no choice and will be obliged to apply the punishment attached by the law itself to a crime committed under that particular motive. This is unfortunate; even in such a case, the judge should not have his hands tied.

We may accept the theory of parallel punishments but on the condition that the criterion of the selection of punishment must not necessarily be the motive of the crime. Without a further analysis the motive is nothing more than a part of the circumstance and closely related to the act committed. It affects the penalty, and the penalty is translated into the duration of the punishment. So far as the permanent and fundamental character is concerned, the motive expresses itself only indirectly and as a symptom. The special and individual adjustment of the punishment must be made according to the entire personality, not to the fragment thereof revealed in the crime. Among such motives a distinction should be made between a motive directly aroused by the end to be obtained and an impulse which has itself called forth this end. In the latter case the motive is due to a moral attitude that is antecedent not alone to the crime but to the details and circumstances that explain the crime, or which came to exist under pressure from without. With the motive as a criterion there will always be this ambiguity; and the two conflicting points of view will be liable to confusion.

Let us then still further extend the theory, and speak not of parallel punishments to be applied according to the motive of the crime, but of specialized punishments to be applied according to the moral temperament of the criminal.[1] We shall now see how such a system is to be constructed.

§ 88. A Tentative System of Individualization; Static and Dynamic Criminality

Having thus reached the heart of the question our further task is to supply a definite constructive system.[2] An early step in the direction of the newer view dates from the Congress of Stockholm,[3] where the plea for the uniform type of punishment was made. Opposed thereto was the cherished notion of our traditional law, that punishments must vary in discipline, and consequently in severity, according to the nature of the crime. The more serious crimes demand the more serious penalties, in length as well as in discipline. Hence the large variety of criminal punishments in which the penal code of 1810 abounds. It appears, however, that the opinion of criminals does not always agree

[1] On these measures see the just comments of *M. Alfred Gautier* in his comparative study of the revised French draft and the Swiss draft. *A. Gautier*, "Deux projets," in the *Revue pénale suisse*, 1894, pp. 105–107.

[2] For what follows see *L. Rivière*, "De l'individualisation des peines" in the *Revue pénitentiaire*, 1897, p. 1043, *seq.*

[3] See the account of the International Prison Congress at Stockholm, Vol. I, p. 139, *seq.*

§ 88] JUDICIAL INDIVIDUALIZATION 275

with that of the law and that frequently punishments intended to be formidable and deterrent are in fact preferred. The hardship of a punishment is determined less by the severity of the discipline than by the previous sensibility and education of the subject. It is thus quite useless to set the punishment according to the crime. The duration of the punishment must intimidate and stand as the penalty of the crime, and since it is the nature of the criminal that determines how the punishment is felt and regarded, and since this also conditions the psychological effect, it is according to the moral nature of the criminal that the nature of the discipline and the reformatory status of the punishment should be graded.

This then is our conclusion: the penalty aspect of punishment remains. Punishment remains a penalty because the conception of responsibility persists and because satisfaction is due to the sentiment of popular and social justice, which insists that society shall pronounce upon and reprove moral evil whenever it is injurious to the community. Punishment is an evidence of responsibility because responsibility alone makes salvation possible. It is not sin that degrades, because if it evidences the freedom of the sinner in sinning, it likewise attests his freedom to restrain. In any other theory the criminal becomes a lost being, an outcast and an alien, recalling the primitive savage described by Lombroso. Yet though possibly more degraded, he shares with all men the liability to sin; it is but a matter of degree. As a free agent, responsible for his actions, he may utilize this human privilege to effect his moral and social reinstatement, as well as his ruin. Not all is lost, and reform is ever possible. The conception of responsibility should be incorporated with that of punishment; without it the criminal is a creature despised, ostracized, abnormal, and even monstrous; with it self-esteem remains, or at least may be regained. The possible criminal, feeling himself free in his actions, is conscious of his power to act rightly as well as to act wrongly. He feels his community with all sinners, for no one is without some measure of innate depravity, and he feels particularly that he may again become the equal of the regenerate. So valuable a moral lever should not be interfered with.

But penalty, thus justified by responsibility, is not measured thereby. It must be apportioned to the subjective criminality of the agent and made to reflect not a quantitative but a qualitative factor of the will. This subjective criminality of the agent presents two aspects. There is the latent and passive criminality in the static condition, so to speak, which is one with the essence of the character. It expresses itself through this or that innate bent, or through hereditary or acquired vice. It appears in every action and every tendency of the individual, as well as in such actions as are not in any sense criminal. It represents the vicious aspect of the personality. The law does not punish this, for if it punished persons by reason of their character, it would be necessary to imprison them before they perpetrated crimes.

There is a second aspect of criminality. Besides the passive, there is the active dynamic criminality considered as a psychic factor, which on occasion sets free an impulse, which in turn breaks out into action. This active criminality is often but the expression and operation of the passive; the one reveals the other. Yet it is not always necessarily so. Every personality has several phases; each one of us harbors several conflicting personalities. St. Paul's cry of despair is true of all. At any given moment one of these several personalities becomes dominant, and through such dominance manifests the inherent morality or perversity of the individual or discloses his potential latent criminality. But there are other occasional phases of our personality which may come to the front; and there may arise immoral criminal suggestions which are quite exceptional and accidental, unconnected with our past and with little chance of a return in the future. Such active criminality does not necessarily represent the passive criminality of our moral nature and should not be identified therewith.

But it is this criminality in its active effective state that determines the act for which the law holds us accountable. Socially it constitutes the moral danger of which we give evidence, which the law recognizes, and for which it holds us accountable. The responsibility that law and common sense ascribes to us does not refer to the free will of the act but only to the extent and intensity of the subjective criminality. If the will, merging with the character, issues in a criminal impulse, then for such issue we are held responsible. For society, the criminality thus expressed and made manifest constitutes the crime. It is the cause of the disturbance and produces the injury for which we are held accountable.

Such active criminality, representing the subjective criminality of the crime, should determine the penalty. It is revealed in the motive considered as the psychological factor from which flows the direct impulse of the crime, and it is by the motive that the term of punishment should be regulated; for the term of sentence reflects the phase of the penalty proportional thereto.

But when we come to determine the discipline of the punishment, we need no longer consider the particular and detailed variety of criminality inherent in the act. Character must determine the discipline. The nature of the punishment should be determined by the passive criminality in its latent and static condition.

The judge must thus apply two points of view and two very different principles. He must determine the length of the punishment according to the active criminality that characterizes the crime, thus considering the principle of penalty; and he must determine the nature of the punishment according to the passive criminality of the agent, according to his character, thus considering the principle of the underlying purpose and of the individualization of punishment. The degree of passive criminality may quite often be determined through the motives and the subjective criminality of the act, but this does not necessarily follow; and here the judge must exercise large discretion. In some cases the two forms of criminality are quite certain to be contradictory, as in the case, for instance, of the recidivist who may be guilty of many infractions and thus reveals himself incorrigible and unimpressionable, yet whose latest offense may imply but the minimum degree of criminality.

§ 89. The Detailed Classification of Criminals

Such are the principles which should determine the application of the scale of punishment. We must now attempt a classification of criminals according to their psychological nature, and, corresponding thereto, reach an adequate classification of punishments.

Leaving the consideration of the term of punishment, which depends upon judiciary procedures not likely to differ markedly from current practice, let us briefly survey the nature of punishment and the resulting choice of the penal discipline.[1]

---

[1] See *Wahlberg*, "Das Princip der Individualisirung," principally chapters i and ii; and "Kleinere Schriften," passim, particularly I, p. 136, *seq.*; II,

This choice should be made according to the nature of the agent, or rather according to such criminal impulses as he may exhibit, and according to the direction, variety, and detailed nature of such criminal impulses. The object is to establish classes of punishment corresponding to the different classes of criminals. Here there is a serious primary difficulty to be avoided, namely, not to lose oneself in minutiæ of details and distinctions. There should be no attempt to establish on a legal basis a complete classification of criminals with all their characteristic types and varieties. This was the error of the anthropological school. Thus Ferri, in his Criminal Sociology, has pushed the distinction of types too far; his position involves a mistake and a faulty perspective, or rather, an error in the selection of the point of view. It is easy to multiply varieties, and indeed there will be a great many of them if one is bent upon establishing psychologically detailed differences of individual temperaments, and if these in turn are to be classified according to the causes influencing the origin of criminality, such as heredity, environment, degeneracy, etc. The criminal would thus be studied much as the botanist studies plants, classifying and subclassifying them as soon as a new variety is discovered; or as the zoologist follows a similar plan in classifying animal species. It is such an anthropological point of view that the sociological school assumes towards criminality.

p. 138, *seq.*; III, p. 18, *seq.* p. 55, *seq.* Also his excellent essay "Das Mass und der mittlere Mensch im Strafrecht" (in *Grünhut's Zeitschrift für das privat und öffentliche Recht der Gegenwart*, 1878, p. 465); *Colajanni*, "La sociologia criminale," *passim; Ferri*, "Sociologie criminelle," p. 80, *seq.*; *Garofalo*, "Criminologie," *passim; Tarde*, "Études pénales et sociales," p. 115, *seq.*, p. 117, *seq.*, p. 273, *seq.*; "Philosophie pénale," p. 215, *seq.* See especially *Liszt*, "Die psychologischen Grundlagen der Kriminalpolitik" (Z., 1896), p. 479, *seq.*, p. 488, *seq.* Also *U. Conti*, "Il delinquente nel diritto criminale," in the *Archivio giuridico*, 1894, p. 266, *seq.*

But this is not and should not be the point of view of the law. Its purpose is not merely the establishment of the facts and conditions but the investigation of principles, the testing of results, the conformity of the law to social standards. From this point of view a classification should be adapted to the results which the law seeks to secure. Criminals should be classified with reference to the provisions at our command, and such provisions are of a quite limited range, — measures of repression together with suitable varieties of discipline.

In this connection two observations may be urged: the first that for various reasons, of which perhaps the most obvious is the financial one, the variety of punitive treatments cannot be multiplied indefinitely; and the second, that even supposing we were in a position to establish varieties of discipline corresponding to every new variety of criminal, we altogether lack the scientific criterion to determine for each of the offenders appearing before the courts the exact class to which he belongs. Ideal classifications may be worked out on paper. We do not command a method of moral diagnosis that definitely establishes the type to which every individual properly belongs. Let us not aspire to the impossible lest we descend to the ridiculous. Most sociological classifications confuse two points of view which should be kept distinct. The one is that of the origin or source of the criminality — such as atavism, degeneracy, influence of the environment — to which there correspond criminals by birth or heredity, the degenerates, and others. The second is that of the type of criminality; such are the wanton, the crooks, the depraved, and many others which Garofalo has well characterized.[1] Finally, for each of the types, there are those amenable to reform

[1] *Garofalo*, "La Criminologie" (Paris, F. Alcan).

and the incorrigible. The former are such as have retained the sense of morality or a surviving vestige thereof, and thus are still capable of appreciating the immorality of their actions; they lack an incentive to effort, and this may be supplied. The latter are such as have lost all moral sense and can be but slightly influenced; their habit is set and their character is wholly depraved; their feelings have ceased to accord with those of normal men. There thus appear three aspects and classifications of crime, different in kind and scope: the first, in terms of the origin, the second, of the type, and the third, of the degree of criminality. In its bearing upon the law the first has no decided import. Whatever the origin of the criminal instinct, the kind of criminality which it produces may be quite the same. Whether the criminality be inherited or acquired, its psychological type may be similar. The born murderer, supposing there are such, and the murderer by acquired habit, are alike murderers so far as the law is concerned. The material distinction in such cases is the degree of cruelty, violence, or brutality involved. Yet in this respect a differentiation in terms of the origin of criminality may afford some valuable suggestions.[1] Although it may have no proper legal status, nevertheless it is indirectly useful. It will be found that the criminal by birth, if such really exist in Lombroso's sense of the word, will transgress differently from the criminal whose depravity is acquired and not innate. The impulses of the latter need only be redirected; his original nature is sound and may be appealed to. But it remains no less certain that there are three distinct aspects which should not be confused, and which the majority of classifications have wrongly presented as parts of one classification.

[1] See above, p. 131.

From the legal side, in its bearing upon penal law, the third aspect, that of the degree of criminality, is clearly of greatest import, since all repressive measures are to be directed towards its eradication. The two other classifications, the one in terms of the type of criminality and the other in terms of its origin, have value only in so far as they may furnish useful suggestions, either as to the degree of criminality or as to the measures that may counteract it.

The three-fold classification is an ancient one, classic in its traditions, even before it was officially applied; and it has not as yet been replaced. It includes the group of offenders without true criminality, offenders whose criminality is but superficial, and offenders tainted with a fundamental, and thus ineradicable criminality, — the incorrigibles. This is a fundamental division; to it should correspond the three classes of punishment repeatedly cited in former discussions, — deterrent, corrective, and protective.

§ 90. Concessions to other Principles

While contending that this classification should serve as the basis and point of departure for future criminal law, it must yet be conceded that for certain offenders some account should be taken of the type of criminality, or even at times, of the origin of criminality. This applies to certain varieties of criminality of definite nature and origin, which experience has shown may be relieved and counteracted by special measures. By way of illustration one may refer to certain types of delinquency, for which special institutions are now provided, wherein the discipline is directed towards the counteraction of the specific tendencies which produce this type of transgression. Such are asylums for drunkards and inebriates, workhouses and institutions for vagrants. These have been successfully established in other countries.

§ 90]   JUDICIAL INDIVIDUALIZATION   283

Experience has shown that in such institutions it is not sufficient to direct the discipline towards the formation of habits to counteract tendencies exhibited in the one constantly repeated transgression. The provisions should also afford scope for the influence of good example and intimidation. This method has been applied to vagrants who, in Germany for example, are sent to special institutions where they are trained to work and to regular habits. Yet no very marked results have been obtained, because the discipline is too lenient and the detention too short. One cannot hope to rebuild habits without ample time. Nor is there any need to avoid intimidation. In view of experience at home and abroad, it is now proposed in France to place vagrants in solitary confinement.[1] These vagrants are free-footed and irregular, devoted to the highway and an open-air life, and they are far less afraid of fatigue and hardship than of a steady and regular job. Advantage must be taken of their weak point by imposing solitary confinement; they must be subjected to what they most dread.[2] This is well enough, provided that solitary confinement is not made the sole factor in the punishment; for solitary confinement does not amount to a complete punitive measure. It is more a protection than a punishment;

[1] See the report of *M. Crisenoy* on the "Repression du vagabondage" presented at the meeting of December 15, 1897, of the Société générale des Prisons (*Revue pénitentiaire*, 1898, p. 4, *seq.*); and the ensuing discussion at the meeting in March, 1898.

[2] See the article in the *Temps* (Thursday, January 20, 1898): "La Police rurale et le vagabondage." The question of vagrancy has been made the subject of many proposed laws since 1898. The latest is that of *M. Etienne Flandin*, January 20, 1908, relative to the "Révision des lois pénales concernant le vagabondage et le mendicité." The text with a résumé of the previous proposals and with references is to be found in the *Revue pénitentiaire*, February, 1908, p. 292. Likewise see the current discussion before the Société des Prisons on the "Réorganization de la police en province" (*Revue pénitentiaire*, 1908, Nos. 3 and 4).

it puts an abrupt stop to an irregular existence, suspends the social life, encourages reflection, and facilitates thoughts of reform. As a means of terminating the old life it is efficient, but the problem of preparing the way to the new life remains. Solitary confinement is but the negative side of penal reform. There will be no advance unless a positive side is added. A reliance upon solitary confinement is a policy similar to that applied to children with delicate lungs whose anxious parents do not allow them to go out of doors in winter; they may escape bronchitis but their lungs will never be able to resist the cold air. But that is the real object. Convicts must be given a character capable of resisting contact with the open air of social life. The discipline of long solitary confinement (as in Belgium) is appropriate only if, as Lombroso maintains, the failure of penitentiary reform and the hopelessness of the convict's moral improvement are conceded. These views are not shared by the supporters of penitentiary discipline who regard solitary confinement as one of their most inviolable tenets. In hopeless cases there is nothing left but to inspire fear; and it may be granted that solitary confinement is the best means of intimidation. But once condemned to such punishment let the detention be a long one; when once prisoners have been cut off from life, there is nothing gained through their return. They have no fitness for social life, and this is as true of vagrants as of others. After trying out the discipline of isolation the convict should be released from his solitary confinement and resume social contact, but resume it through a discipline of work, — a policy applied to vagrants sent to workhouses.[1]

[1] On these points, and on the operation of the new Belgium system, see the interesting communication of *M. Batardy* at the meeting of March, 1898, of the Société générale des Prisons (*Revue pénitentiare*, 1898).

§ 91. Special Types of Individualization

One cannot touch upon this problem of vagrancy, which however belongs to the province of the police, without observing how decidedly it contradicts the principles derived from the doctrine of "responsibility." If punishment is to be inflicted only for the commission of crime, by what right shall the vagrant be punished who is but employing his freedom as he chooses? It is obvious that he is punished as a matter of prevention; and that is just. He is really punished for offenses which he *may* commit and which it is assumed definitely that he *will* commit, — clearly a preventive punishment and nothing else. Indeed some criminologists of the classic school urge that the vagrant's punishment should be most severe, — solitary confinement under the most rigorous conditions which our penitentiaries afford. In so holding they are right; but what becomes of the principles of their school? Even the adherents of the Italian school have not gone quite so far. The conclusion that follows from this situation is that the classic tenet of the distinction between prevention and repression has never been more than an abstract formula without practical application. Accordingly, when we urge that repressive punishment shall be made a preventive measure, we have in our favor the facts and the laws and, despite their principles, the support of the classic school itself.

Certain special disciplines have been cited, established in view of special offenses; and these take account of the varieties of criminality. In other directions the sources of criminality must be considered; for example, the neurotic, the degenerate, and such other classes as are affected with partial responsibility. Their criminality has no special type; they belong to any of the different varieties. They may include murderers and thieves, and particularly criminals of passion. Their common trait is that their criminality is bound up with their temperament. What they require is medical care in special institutions which combine hospital with prison treatment. There is a fair agreement as to this need, which, in case of minors, is met by houses of correction and reform.[1]

Apart from these exceptional classes we return to our general three-fold classification together with the three classes of punishments corresponding thereto. This classification has two advantages: it rests upon data that may be relatively simply determined; and it involves an easily provided type of discipline.

Its application is simple. Let us take the two extreme classes, the incorrigibles and the offenders without natural criminality. As affecting incorrigibles, we have an approximate provision in the law of 1885 on deportation, in so far as this applies to the recidivist. This is not the provision of the older penal code for a repeated offense; for that increased the punishment because it considered that there is an added culpability in again transgressing after a first condemnation. Yet such a measure issues from the conception of responsibility as the basis of punishment, which is not in question here. It is proper that the responsibility involved in a second offense should influence the term of sentence. But the law of 1885 makes a novel provision for habitual crime; it views such repeated transgression as a basis of individualization, as a symptom of incorrigibility. It is this new view of the habitual offender which is now in question, and it is the only one that should influence the character of the

[1] Upon an attempt in England to apply a special treatment for minors, the "Borstal System," see the article, already cited, of *Sir Alfred Wills*, in the *Nineteenth Century*, December, 1907, p. 881, *seq.*

punishment. It is significant solely as a symptom. Yet the provisions of the law of 1885 are worthy of support for several reasons, particularly because this law does away with the necessary enforcement of protective punishments on a basis definitely set by the law. It is important to retain a large discretion for the judge. There is no legal criterion of incorrigibility. Doubtless there may be certain factors designated by the law to guide the decision of the judge, but the Swiss draft leaves the judge wholly free. At best there should be but an initial limit set by the law, and on no account an enforced application. The law is concerned only with laying down principles and establishing the larger outlines, but leaves the details to other authorities.

At the other extreme, that is, at the upper end of the classification, are the offenders who stand in no need of reform because they are not perverts and present no innate criminality. Here also the bases of classification will be relatively simple; they will be furnished, as above noted,[1] by the nature of the transgression, and again — which is the chief factor — by the antecedents of the offender. In principle, the first consideration will be the absence of a previous sentence, or rather the absence of a previous offense. The classic distinction between the recidivist and the sum total of an individual's criminal record is significant only if we regard the habitual offense in the traditional sense as reflecting responsibility; it has no pertinence in regard to individualization.[2] There should be no misunderstanding in regard to the two different attitudes just noted, the one wholly objective, viewing the nature of the infraction, and

[1] See above, pp. 261-262.
[2] See the draft of the Norwegian penal code and the article which *M. Andréas Urbye* has devoted to it: "Les Sentences indéterminées dans le nouveau projet de Code pénal norvégien," in the *Revue pénale suisse*, 1898, p. 76.

the other purely subjective, although in principle depending upon the condition that the crime is a first offense. There is no question of the possibility of a cumulative charge in the sense that if the charge be an offense not indicative of subjective criminality, the defendant may be examined in regard to his character, and may be liable to a punishment of different nature from that prescribed by the law. It would hardly be fair, when the defendant is sentenced in court to a reformatory punishment, to plead that the sentence be altered on the ground that the case concerns a criminal by birth. That would be a purely preventive measure after the manner of those supported by the arguments of the Italian school. Such extreme conclusions we have declined to accept.[1] Common-law punishments should be applied to those convicted of common-law offenses, yet even in such cases one should be able to impose a mere reformatory punishment. But the converse would not apply. Unless we resort to the extreme conclusions of the Italian school, we should not consent to have a political offender subjected to the discipline of an ordinary criminal on the ground that he happens not to be a worthy man. Such a paradox should certainly not be countenanced.

§ 92. Possible Extensions of Individualization; Relation to Preventive Measures

As just noted these principles are thus applied to all first offenders, yet here likewise distinctions must be made between individuals, at all events in cases of common-law offense. But these distinctions are now well drawn by the courts under the application of the Bérenger law, though under conditions presenting difficulties in other respects. Why should not the same be done in cases of a choice be-

[1] See above, pp. 122–124, p. 137.

§ 92] JUDICIAL INDIVIDUALIZATION 289

tween a reformatory and a deterrent punishment? This would be but a compromise with the existing situation. As things are at present, it is all or none, — either imprisonment in its ordinary form or the entire omission of punishment. We urge an additional option between the two, that, before reaching the remission of punishment, there be instituted an intermediate stage — a substitution of punishment. It is true that abuses of parole are readily cited, but these are no more pertinently cited with reference to parole than to acquittals by juries in cases of crimes which the law punishes too severely. Impunity is preferred to a punishment that runs counter to public conscience. It would appear that only the lay judges, as they are called, are open to guidance by humane considerations or common-sense justice. But in so far as professional judges follow the precedent, is it not to their credit? What influences the verdict in such cases is not the injustice of the minimum limit of the punishment (since this no longer applies to "mitigated" sentences to reformatories); the jury take umbrage at the discrepancy between the punishment and the individual. To express their indignation at the crime they pronounce a severe sentence, but in sympathy for the individual they grant parole. This recalls the nominal punishments of the ecclesiastical law. There are cases, however, in which the punishment seems excessive even to the judges; they ask that a new statute give them an additional alternative. This new statute will not curtail the field of application of parole; that would be regrettable. It will provide an exceptional punishment having none of the disadvantages of ordinary imprisonment, which they may impose at their discretion.

There remains the intermediate class of true criminals, who are however amenable to reform; they result from the elimination of the two other classes, — a point that needs no further explanation. All this may be practically, simply, and readily introduced, without violence to the general policy of our laws and our penal organization. It requires no radical innovation, and still less a complete reversal of policy; it requires the special direction of existing provisions. We already have the three-fold classification;[1] we plead for its more rational application; and the same applies to the regulation of the punitive discipline.

Deterrent punishments are not directed to the reform or re-education of the vicious. Their purpose is to set an example that shall at once intimidate those upon whom sentence is pronounced (which the Germans call an individual prevention), and intimidate others as well by way of general prevention. This is the purpose of awards of compensation and fines and their development as advocated by Garofalo,— which are commendable provisions worthy of favorable application. Such is likewise the function of solitary confinement. This is decidedly deterrent, but yet a punishment subject to a special discipline somewhat analogous to that which detention provides for political criminals. Without entering into details, it is sufficient to recall the question actively discussed at the Paris Congress of 1895 on the extension of "enforced" labor even to political punishments, — a question that here comes up anew. Will not the best solution consist in a combination of the two, an enforced labor but a free choice of the kind of labor? In this way manual labor will not necessarily be imposed if the prisoner can show himself fit for other occupation; yet this must not be a parody of real work. Such measures are peculiarly appropriate to the class now under consideration, —persons who at all costs must be saved from contact with others, from the common work-room, from all that degrades

[1] See above, p. 209.

and contaminates. As to fines, if they are proportioned to the resources of the defendant, they present the advantages set forth by Garofalo. They are the least dishonoring, and present the great advantage that they do not interrupt a man's business or injure him professionally.

Punishments in behalf of public security are directed to elimination, with no great expectations of influencing those affected. They should consist in a discipline similar to that enforced in jails, while reserving deportation to the colonies for the more worthy and as a reward of good conduct. Even incorrigibles need not be despaired of. Such "colonial" punishments must be accepted in the light in which they are considered by those who undergo them; if considered as a lenient punishment, it should be the privilege of those partly released. Colonization should be reserved for the better class and not for the worst. The convict must entertain the hope of freedom by absorbing a different view of life. Saved from the promiscuous association of the prison he may be regenerated; he may come to believe that on the frontiers of civilization he may still serve society, no longer his enemy but his benefactor, to whom he repays his debt of obligation.

Corrective punishments are unquestionably the most difficult of all to organize. Very promising of worthy results is the progressive Irish system, or some proper adaptation thereof, with its variety of progressive disciplines carried out, if need be, in different institutions; thus solitary confinement at the outset, next occupation in the workshop, then transfer to an agricultural colony, and lastly conditional freedom with considerable discretion of the administration as to conditions. This plan seems to exclude deportation, but not altogether. There should be reserved for the worst crimes, those that carry a long-term sentence,

— after the period of solitary confinement and a certain period of probation, — the possibility of the conversion of the punishment. This likewise should be offered as an encouragement for good conduct, affording a transfer to the colonies under discipline of varied privileges, which means colonization for the more worthy, though a long-term if not permanent colonization. A similar alternative was attempted in 1852, before the law of 1854. Possibly deportation may thus be made to afford all the advantages which were, and still are, expected of it, without the disadvantages that have brought it into disfavor. It is in this direction that the commission for the revision of the penal code should proceed. The draft favors the uniform type of punishment with successive stages; unfortunately, it restricts far too much the period of conditional liberation.[1] It limits transfer to the colonies to the incorrigible under the form of deportation. We should have more confidence in the success of penal colonies if they were composed of first offenders, even though these had committed serious crimes, to whom the life in the colonies is offered as a means of reinstatement, but with definitive expatriation. It is probable that those who will thus choose expatriation will be the energetic individuals, who feel the burden of their transgressions and are anxious to take up a new career. All these, however, are details in regard to which an agreement can readily be reached.

Such are the general outlines of the system. As affecting those amenable to reform by suitable punishments, there still remains the difficulty resulting from the provision of the fixed term, — the difficulty of reconciling a moral regeneration with the certainty of liberation at a definite date. Thus we reach the last part of this series of considerations,

[1] See *Le Poittevin*, cited above (*Revue pénitentiaire*, 1893, pp. 160–161).

relating to the administrative individualization under the form of the indeterminate sentence.[1]

[1] As to the procedure considered above on page 233, it may be noted that if this combination appears a little complicated one may, as an intermediate stage, associate the jury in the determination of the sentence, — as is demanded in the recent draft of the Garde des sceaux (Keeper of Seals). This reform seems to be gaining favor. The distinction — in itself logical, and thoroughly legal as an abstract formula — between the function of the Jury and that of the Court has been tested, weighed and found wanting. It does not adjust itself to practice and conditions. In France present experience condemns it. (See the draft of the law having for its object the conferring upon the criminal jury of the power to participate in the application of the punishment: Officiel 1908, Documents parlementaires, Chambre des députés, No. 1605.)

To return to the question which constituted the principal theme of this chapter, we may record that since 1898 the advance of opinion has been tending in favor of the influences attaching to the recognition of the motive, not alone upon the duration of punishment, its mitigation or aggravation — as in the Swiss draft — but also upon its nature, — as in the Italian penal code of 1889. See *Andréadès*, "Les peines alternatives ou parallèles" (Thesis, Paris, 1899).

Pertinent to the legislative point of view is article 24, Norwegian penal code, which reads: "When hard labor is the only punishment depriving one of liberty prescribed by the law, it may be replaced by a punishment of imprisonment of equal duration, if the circumstances permit of the supposition that the act was not the result of an evil intent."

On the nature of the regulation of hard labor and imprisonment respectively, according to the Norwegian penal code, see, in the translation of this code, the note under article 24; and for a critical estimate of the interpretation of the text, see the preface of *M. Garçon*, p. xiii, *seq.*

Even in the domain of French jurisprudence one can observe a tendency to take the motive into consideration. See *Vidal*, "Cours de droit criminel et de science pénitentiaire" (edition of 1906), p. 183, note 1. On the influence of the motive, see the *Bulletin de l'Union intern. du droit pénal*, 1908, p. 287.

Perhaps after due deliberation it may seem that the detailed system presented in the above chapter would prove most difficult of application, especially on the part of the judges; and that frequent and serious errors would occur. The system is based upon the view that the judge can always determine the true character of the delinquent from the antecedents and factors of the case, and will have available sufficient data to classify him in one or another group, and to apply to him one or another kind of punishment. But it is evident that often such a decision will be impossible to the judge, who can then hardly escape the risk of making sad mistakes. How will he, relying solely upon the briefs and the impressions in court, come into possession of sufficient evidence to determine positively the moral and psychological nature of the agent; and particularly how shall he know in advance the effect of such and such a punishment of such or other character? This can only be determined by experience. Will it not necessarily result, so far as concerns the duration of punishment, in leaving it to the choice of the administration, under the form of an indeterminate sentence; so that in course of punishment one may pass from one punishment to another, if the first seems to be working contrarily to what was anticipated? But even in this event we are in the presence of a decision less vague and less arbitrary than when the issue was that of leaving to the administration the fixation of the term. The many objections made to the latter system will now be found to disappear, especially under the system of alternative sentences introduced in England, and now proposed for minors. It is considered in the draft now under discussion in Parliament, "The Prevention of Crime Bill" (see the *Times*, June 13, 1908, p. 15, and the *Daily Express*, June 13, 1908). Thus for minors, to whom a lenient discipline is to be applied, the Borstal system permits the administration, if it considers by its experience that this discipline is not adapted to the individual in question, to apply to the judge who issued the original sentence, to substitute a common-law imprisonment for the rest of the term. It thus results for minors — so far as concerns the nature of the punishment and not the duration — that every sentence which prescribes a special discipline becomes only a provisional sentence liable to be replaced in course of punishment by a different sentence. The judge has at his disposal the one or the other, but the second is not to be substituted for the first except upon actual experience, and not at the time of commitment, as is proposed in our parallel punishments. Hence the name of alternative sentences. It is evident that such a system may likewise be applied to adults in a system of punishments that adopts several parallel types of punishments even for adults.

Finally to complete the evolution, we must indicate the several laws and drafts relative to children and minors in general. In regard to them every one is agreed, even the most conservative classicists, that it is the principle of individualization that alone should be taken into consideration. Under the technical expression of "discretion," understood formerly solely in terms of responsibility, it is now the entire personality that is regarded. One may also speak in this connection of the Juvenile Courts as they have been organized in the United States, and of the valuable and successful movement undertaken by M. Ed. Julhiet with the purpose of establishing the same improvements in France. Some account of the views expressed in various quarters on the subject of reform schools and in favor of the application of indeterminate sentences in the cases of minors should also be given. For an account of the important movement relative to measures affecting minors, it is sufficient to refer to the Congrès national de droit pénal de Toulouse, 1907, of which a report will be found in the *Bulletin de l'Union internationale de droit pénal*, 1908, p. 3, seq. (See also in the same bulletin in the same number in the Appendix, the draft of the Austrian law on the penal treatment of minor criminals and on the protection of minors, 1907.)

CHAPTER X

Administrative Individualization

§ 93. The Administrative Treatment.
§ 94. The Principle of Indeterminate Sentences: the Elmira System.
§ 95. Modified Indeterminate Sentences adapted to European Conditions.
§ 96. Difficulties in the Extension of the System.
§ 97. The Personal and Religious Factors in Reform.

§ 93. The Administrative Treatment

IN matters of law, even more than in other fields, logic asserts its demands. As soon as one enters on a plan of individualization of punishment it appears that judicially individualization must ever be approximate, and thus inadequate, both as affects the term of punishment (which alone is ordinarily considered) and the nature of the discipline in which the movement had its origin.

The classification of offenders and appropriate punishments must be general, for it is impossible to consider an indefinite variety of punishments for the purpose of adjusting them in every group to the precise moral temperament of each individual. Judiciary individualization is but a form of diagnosis. It is an individual classification based upon an actual situation,— that is, an actual subject — instead of upon an abstract personality, as is the case in individualization by law. But in practical morals, as in medical therapeutics, mere diagnosis is not sufficient; a remedy must be applied, and that varies in each case. Now in matters of criminology the application belongs not to the official pronouncing the sentence but to the one administering it, the penitentiary administration. The law must grant to the administration sufficient initiative and flexibility in the adjustment of the discipline, so that it may, in turn, adjust the application of the punishment to the educational and moral requirements; and that is what is meant by administrative individualization.

As concerns the term of sentence, administrative individualization raises two questions: that of the discipline, and that of the term. Practically the two are one. It is clear that moral regeneration cannot be compatible with the certainty of a release at a fixed date. If punishment is to be primarily a reformative measure, a moral treatment, its length cannot be determined in advance. One cannot anticipate the time needed for a re-education; and it is quite as absurd to limit the period to so many months or years, as it would be for the physician, when summoned to a serious case of illness, to predict a cure at a fixed date. Moreover the case is not one of a true disease, for a disease presents an acute crisis which has its set period. The penal treatment is applied to a condition which is nearly always chronic, a condition which is part of the moral nature; so that, in fact, it is not a question of curing a disease, but of rebuilding a temperament. The physician may anticipate the period of an acute crisis, but can he judge how long will be required to alter the temperament of a neurotic, or to overcome the taint of congenital phthisis? The case of a criminal under a reformatory punishment is no different. From his knowledge of the case the judge can determine the most appropriate punishment. Possibly he can tell whether the defendant is a true or a false criminal, and whether he is susceptible to reform or incorrigible, and accordingly select the discipline and apply the appropriate punishment. But how can he at the same time set its term, and foresee how

§ 93] ADMINISTRATIVE INDIVIDUALIZATION 297

long will be required to convert the criminal into an honest man? It is as though the alienist who signs a commitment to an asylum, or the ordinary physician when he places a patient in the hospital, were to indicate at that time what is to be the date of discharge. The patient's discharge must depend upon his cure, that is, upon his restoration to physical health. The same should apply to the criminal. He should not be restored to liberty and the life of society until he has ceased to be a menace to society and has recovered his moral health.

But it is not the province of the judge to decide this. The decision can be reached only in the course of the administration of punishment through the judgment of those who closely follow the progress of the convict, observe him at work, and witness the regeneration that is taking place. It is not the judge who can determine the time of a discharge from the penitentiary, but the penitentiary administration itself. The judge signs the warrant and makes the choice of punishment; he determines the institution to which the individual is to be sent; but he does not endorse the discharge. This is a matter for the administration to which the convict has been assigned. Accordingly the judge has to determine not the length but only the nature and choice of the punishment. It has been noted in behalf of judiciary individualization that the judge should fix the length of the punishment according to the subjective criminality of the crime, and fix the nature thereof according to the general criminality of the agent. Henceforth the first of these two formulæ may be omitted. The judge has but to set the nature of the punishment, and thus need consider only the general criminality of the agent. The criminality of the act is a matter of indifference. However this fixation of the term of punishment according to the criminality of the act remains as the necessary consequence of the conception of penalty, which under all circumstances is bound to persist. Must there then remain an irreconcilable antagonism between the conception of penalty and of individualization? As yet we have found no objection, in principle, in ranging them side by side, the one serving as the justification and the validation of the other. Will it follow, if we carry out the plan to its logical conclusion, that the reconciliation will become impossible, and that the policy cannot be consistently carried through?

§ 94. The Principle of Indeterminate Sentences: the Elmira System

If then we reject the determination by the judge of the length of punishment, the last trace of the conception of penalty and responsibility will disappear and the notion of justice will have no place. It becomes a matter of a moral cure and hospital treatment. In this system the sentence will carry no date of expiration of the punishment; that is, the judge will not determine in advance in the sentence the fixed term of the punishment. This is called the system of the indeterminate sentence. By this provision there is a double individualization, assigned to two authorities: one part falls to the judge, who retains the choice of the punishment, — judiciary individualization; and the other falls to the administration, — administrative individualization; the latter alone determining the length of the punishment and terminating it when it is no longer considered necessary.

It thus becomes clear that the two points of view converge, for there can be no indeterminateness as to duration unless there is also an appropriate and individualized adjustment as to discipline. We cannot presume to detain inmates in prison or in analogous institutions for an indeterminate period unless we subject them to a discipline to effect such moral reform as their character permits. The system is in practical operation, and in practice the two phases are merged and the two principles applied conjointly.

It must not be supposed that this is but a dream, or an invention of closet philosophers. The dream has been realized and the credit does not belong to the philosophers. Indeterminate sentences are not an invention of doctrinaires and idealists; they are an accomplished fact. They originated in the mind, or rather in the heart, of an apostle; but this apostle was American, and Americans are not in the habit of keeping their ideas in the abstract: they transform them into deeds.[1]

About 1876 the director of a reformatory institution in New York State, Mr. Brockway, discouraged by the unsatisfactory results obtained under the traditional method, conceived the plan to make moral reform, which was generally agreed to be the function of punishment, the sole and constant purpose not alone of the administration but of the prisoners themselves. The preaching of good conduct to prisoners is carried on unceasingly, but what does it amount to? They know that at a set time they will be released and that, whether the punishment has been effective or not, their liberation is assured. What needs to be guaranteed is not the release but the moral improvement. Such improvement is made the very condition of release, and thereby gives a definite interest to the endeavors and efforts of moral reform which the prisoner himself exercises.

The great difficulty in such a system is to devise a reliable test. It would be easy for a prisoner to pretend a conversion. This seems peculiarly true in America, in an environment

[1] *Frédéric Lévy,* "Les Sentences indéterminées" (Paris, 1896); the bibliography of the subject will also be found there.

strongly imbued with the religious spirit. If any such demonstrations of attained salvation were to be readily accepted, would not the system place a premium on hypocrisy?[1]

Mr. Brockway is too well acquainted with the inmates of American prisons not to have foreseen this danger; he has organized the discipline so that it itself shall serve as a test and evidence of the moral progress of those subjected thereto. There must be certain definite indications to mark these stages of progress. The system of indeterminate sentences is not compatible with the discipline of State penitentiaries. It is practicable only under a specially devised system, one that departs as little as possible from the life of a free society with the initiative that it involves and the efforts which it enforces. Thus alone may the attitude of the prisoner towards a regular life be stimulated, may he serve an apprenticeship to a regular life, and be readapted to the life of society. This double advantage Mr. Brockway based on the data and experience of a penal community at Elmira in the State of New York.

This place was not a penitentiary properly so called, but a house of correction, a reformatory, a private institution. But Mr. Brockway secured from the State of New York the concession that the courts should be authorized to commit to his charge certain offenders, — in general, first offenders and young men who seemed particularly promising. To this the State and courts agreed; and under this arrangement the judge could avail himself of two kinds of punishment, either the ordinary punishment in the penitentiary with a fixed term, or a special punishment at Elmira under an indeterminate sentence. Thus private initiative and public authority combined for the most effective organization of

[1] See what *Mr. Montgomery* has said in regard to English conditions in the article cited above (*Nineteenth Century*, January, 1908, pp. 82-83).

punishment. To us, who are committed to the policy of State prerogative, this seems rather upsetting. We hold that punishment belongs exclusively to the State and to public authority. This axiom, like many another, if made an invariable rule may prove to be a mistake. The province of the State is to pronounce sentence, but the execution of the punishment belongs to those to whom the State is willing to entrust it; and these may well be private institutions due to individual initiative. The plan has the distinct advantage of making private individuals patrons of those who stand in need of social reinstatement and of released prisoners. Respectable persons are apt to assume an attitude of distrust or aversion towards those who have served time; the prejudice against those who have been inmates of prisons is familiar. But if these same respectable persons undertake to interest themselves in the public penal problems, as Mr. Brockway has done, they will come in contact with prisoners and constitute themselves their moral sponsors. When this occurs, as in America (for example in Massachusetts), these quasi-guardians, instead of impeding the social reinstatement of released prisoners, facilitate it in every way; and prejudices are removed.

§ 95. Modified Indeterminate Sentences adapted to European Conditions

It is upon such facts and conceptions that the institution at Elmira is based. Its success is practically established. M. Lévy's thesis gives the statistics and details of the system. It is sufficient here to indicate the combination of the two points of view in regard to administrative individualization which it embodies, the elasticity and flexibility of the treatments fitting in well with the indeterminateness of the sentence. It is indispensable, if the treatment is to have a fair test and if the evidence of its success is to be furnished by the authorities of the reformatory, that the director thereof retain large discretion in adapting occupation to ability, and the nature of the work to the severity of the discipline. Accordingly, the individualization is made in the course of punishment, not by larger or smaller groups and classes, as would be done by the Court, but for each individual in particular, according to the personal experience resulting from the first application of the punishment.

Judiciary individualization, which deals with large numbers, is supplemented by administrative individualization, which deals concretely with individuals. The first determines only the manner of punishment; the second, for the same class of punishments, determines the discipline, — an ideal combination.

Somewhat anticipating the system of indeterminate sentences, it was urged so long ago as at the Congress of Stockholm, that the punishment should be set only in its general outlines, not in detail; and that the administration should have large freedom and initiative in determining the individual adjustment. It was the most comprehensive plea advanced in behalf of administrative individualization.[1] The indeterminateness of the sentence was but a further license following upon the discretionary right, as we may say; for it was discretion in the sense used in ancient law, assigned to the penitentiary administration.

The reformatory at Elmira has in some respects realized what was advocated at the Congress of Stockholm. The system has attracted general attention and stimulated reflection. It has called forth strong opposition, but it like-

[1] See the account given of the meetings of the Congrès pénitentiaire international de Stockholm, Vol. I, p. 110, *seq.*; for the proposed solutions see pp. 137–138.

§ 95] ADMINISTRATIVE INDIVIDUALIZATION 303

wise has its enthusiastic supporters. Some are not satisfied with this partial experiment with a selected number, but would like to see the system extended and applied to all promising cases. This would make an ideal type of reformatory punishment. Its general organization would be about as follows: the sentence would fall into two parts, the first considering the evidence and the choice of punishment; and then in course of punishment and upon the initiative of the reformatory administration, a second sentence as to the term thereof. The first would consider only the crime and the criminality of the criminal at the time of the crime; the second would have nothing to do with the crime and would consider only the presumable morality of the prisoner at the period when the sentence is imposed.[1] The decision of the judge would still influence the period of the punishment, but it would be operative at two points: first, in the order of commitment, and second, in the order of discharge. This system affords a reply to the objections that have been made against the possible abuses of the system if all is left to the discretion of the administration.

To complete the account of the system it should be mentioned that several degrees of indeterminateness have been devised. If the first sentence, that of commitment, does not set either a minimum or a maximum limit of length there will be an absolute indeterminateness. This may seem somewhat startling because theoretically there is the possibility of holding a man for life. But a relative indeterminate sentence is possible in one of several forms. It may have merely a maximum limit to avoid the danger of arbitrarily prolonged detentions; but even then the indeterminate sentence is quite different from the ordinary fixed-term

[1] *Sternau*, "Die Abschaffung der Strafmasse," *Zeit. f. d. Ges. Str. R. W.*, XIII, pp. 29-30.

sentences, for the reason that within the limit of the maximum period a discharge may at any time be granted when it shall appear that a reform is accomplished; and again, in that it is held that such limit may properly exceed the legal term of the punishment under a fixed-term sentence. It may be that only a lower limit is set to satisfy the notion of penalty and to guarantee at least a minimum period of the punishment, — a period in some general relation to the fixed-term sentence. It has also been suggested to combine the two and permit a discharge only within the two limits. It is also possible to suppose, — and this would be more in accord with the logic of the system — instead of a maximum set in each particular case, a general maximum applicable to the punishment, as in the present law certain crimes carry a maximum penalty. In the last hypothesis the indeterminate sentence comes decidedly nearer to our actual fixed-term sentences, but with conditional discharge; yet there remains this difference, that the maximum necessarily exceeds the normal length of punishment and that discharging a prisoner brings about a definite liberation, while under the conditional release the punishment continues under a system of virtual freedom.

If we were to make an attempt to introduce indeterminate sentences, it should be done under this modified form. It is true that this form retains the disadvantage that the prisoner is sure of his release at a set time, but it should be noted that the time is remote and that he retains an interest in effecting his reform. On the other hand, if his conduct indicates his classification among the incorrigible, he may be transferred by a new sentence to the class of hopeless cases and undergo a protective punishment.

The retention of the conception of penalty requires that a minimum limit of incarceration be imposed. Inasmuch as such minimum limit maintains its relation to the term of punishment under fixed sentence, it follows that the judge continues to apportion the punishment to the criminality of the act, and that the principles involved in the conceptions of penalty and responsibility are safeguarded quite as much as in the present system of conditional release. The system of indeterminate sentence has the distinct advantage above that of conditional release both by reason of the discipline it imposes and by the more favorable condition attaching to the prisoner after his release; and especially because of its power in cases of manifest incorrigibility to prolong the sentence to its maximum term.

It would seem that the French adherents of the principles of penalty and responsibility should find acceptable a plan of indeterminate sentence under this form, which provides a minimum limit as a part of the judicial sentence, or, if preferable, both an upper and a lower limit. Indeed, under this form, it is difficult to see what objections in principle could be raised against the system. Unquestionably, it may involve serious practical difficulties in any general scheme of application; but this is another question which in conclusion may be briefly considered.

§ 96. Difficulties in the Extension of the System

Under the form specified, the indeterminate sentence may be widely extended with due consideration of the objections and without entering the field of experiment. It is applicable, for example, to cases of commitment to educative or reformatory institutions; to houses of correction or colonies for minors, asylums for the treatment of neurotics, workhouses, homes for inebriates. For all these the suitability of the plan is conceded.

In cases of protective punishments the system seems acceptable as a corrective of a possible mistake in diagnosis. Consider the case of incorrigibles who are definitely to be eliminated. They are sentenced for life. On no account should a prisoner deported to a penal colony be eligible to return to the mother country; otherwise, as M. Leveillé has well said, he will make a poor colonist, if such he can be called, for he will never settle in a permanent way. This applies all the more to a system which makes such life in a foreign colony a premium for the more desirable and worthy, but only on condition that those thus privileged should become true colonists and pioneers. They are given their freedom, accorded privileges, and find available a new and more independent environment ready to accept persons with a blot upon their past, but upon the condition that this be for life and upon a definite status. This is well enough; but if it appears that a mistake has been made, if before reaching the period of deportation to the colonies, it is found that the case is capable of reform, should not the administration be empowered to take the initiative, not necessarily for a revision of the sentence but for a conversion of the punishment? This may well be exceptional, as clemency now is for the deported, but still this exceptional course should not be excluded by the law. A system in which conditions are not set in advance is better than a system depending wholly upon administrative clemency.[1]

[1] See the interesting and suggestive study of *M. Andréas Urbye*, "Les Sentences indéterminées dans le nouveau projet de Code pénal norvégien." (*Revue pénale suisse*, 1898, p. 71, *seq.*) In it is described the first attempt at a systematic and extended organization of the indeterminate system. It is considered as the necessary consequence of a system of subjective classification, — at all events, so far as relates to punishments designed for dangerous criminals; and in the Norwegian draft that corresponds, with certain important differences, to what we call incorrigibles. What I have just said on the subject of indeterminate sentences applied to protective punishments, was already written, when I received *M. Urbye's* study in the *Revue suisse*. It wholly confirms the opinions I expressed.

§ 96] ADMINISTRATIVE INDIVIDUALIZATION 307

It is obvious that the system is not applicable to deterrent punishments, since they apply to persons who stand in no need of reform. In regard to corrective punishments the situation is uncertain. The theory is admirable, but practically it is the administration that determines the sentence; so that the procedure is one of administrative regulation, although the court is called upon to determine the release. The extension of such a system to the punishments imposed in our State institutions would be a very serious matter, if not wholly impracticable in the present state of affairs.

It has been thus shown that the system involves a complex and sensitive treatment, a flexibility of individual application. It assumes institutions or colonies of restricted capacity, arranged, as at Elmira, upon the pattern of a manufactory with compulsory residence; or, it may be, with provisions for outside work during the day under the superintendence of an employer; and indeed with other similar arrangements. But whether such a system is possible for the great mass of offenders dealt with in our prisons is another question, for the personality of the officials of such institutions must be considered. We concede that the higher officials of the prison administration are in every way worthy. M. Coppée's delineations in "*La Coupable*" must not be taken too literally. Nevertheless it is an administrative staff bound together through its routine and without habit of initiative, or authority to think independently or to inaugurate experiments. Innovations can be made only by way of general regulations. This is not the system at Elmira. It would be difficult to introduce a similar system for the majority of our State prisons; even in America this has not been done.

But if it were possible in France in connection with the

administrative regulation of punishments to establish an experimental reformatory institution on the American plan, in which affairs are entrusted to a selected staff, governed by a man of initiative and original ideas, such as Mr. Brockway, the plan would find general and enthusiastic approval. If such an institution were established, the privilege would readily be obtained to permit the courts, as in New York State, to choose between the ordinary commitment to common-law institutions and a special commitment to a reformatory under indeterminate sentence. This would give the courts an additional option, — something between parole at the time of sentence and the common-law commitment to ordinary penitentiaries. If the experiment is adjusted to our conditions, it is sure to be extended. Reformatories will be multiplied, and we shall have individualization of punishment brought to its most complete perfection.[1]

§ 97. The Personal and Religious Factors in Reform

The religious element must likewise be considered. In America the religious spirit has been actively maintained. It serves as a personal incentive, as a source of individual inspiration and fruitful initiative. To create missionaries for the work of social regeneration, conferring upon them a humane disposition and an enthusiastic faith seems, indeed, to have been the mission of the Protestant spirit. This personal spirit is necessary to bring about such a movement as that at Elmira, and equally to ensure its general success and to accomplish a special service in each individual case, by

---

[1] The following references may be added to the bibliography cited by *M. Lévy* in his thesis, cited above, on "Les Sentences indéterminées": *Vargha*, cited above, II, p. 506, *seq.*, and *Schmidt*, "Die Aufgaben der Strafrechtspflege" (1895), p. 290, *seq.*

stimulating endeavor and a regeneration from within on the part of these unfortunates tainted by crime, who are nevertheless candidates for re-entrance into life under new auspices. All such reforms are the work of personal initiative and individual character. In matters of moral reform such initiative can but be a work of the religious life in the large sense of the word. This spirit of personal influence in the field of the religious conscience appears at the present time to be gaining among all Christian churches. The movement, in America, has spread even to the inclusion of Catholicism. It leaves untouched the dogmas of the Church and the feeling of inspiration attaching to indemonstrable truths, yet, in all that bears upon the essentials of the inner life and the individual attitude thereto, it becomes infused with a regeneration of that spirit of high aspiration and free initiative which characterized the faithful in mediæval times.[1] In some respects we, in France, may have the same opportunity to further free initiative in religious matters, and, what is more urgent, to facilitate the rebirth of a personal and individualized religious life. Such a confession should become, on the part of those whose moral regeneration is to be effected, the earnest and permanent work of their own consciences, in place of being, as is too commonly the case, a readily repeated and promptly forgotten lesson imitatively learned. When this spirit shall have entered such of our reformatory institutions as may then properly be called select, it will become peculiarly easy to reproduce in France what has been accomplished at Elmira. This moral factor is one which each may appraise as he prefers in terms of its real nature, but whose reformatory value no criminologist can

[1] See particularly the "Vie du P. Hecker," published (in translation) by Lecoffre, 1897, and the "Vie du cardinal Manning," by *M. de Pressensé*. See also my review of Fogazzaro's novel "Il Santo," in *La Quinzaine*, February 1 and 15, 1906.

afford to neglect, for there can be no more powerful lever for the reform of conscience and the return to a moral attitude. The *Zweckstrafe*, which considers punishment for its future benefit, has precisely this purpose.

The appeal to personal initiative, which is made by individualization and other social measures incorporated in the penal régime, is at length becoming the watchword for all seriously concerned with the need of a change in the public attitude towards these questions. Without exaggerating the analogy, it is proper to recognize that between the obligations which material distress imposes upon society and those due to moral distress, there is an unmistakable resemblance, at all events in the resulting conditions. They are the shortcomings of humanity in general and of our civilization in particular. It would be objectionable to hold that distress is a vice of those afflicted by it, for it is equally a vice of society. This is true of poverty, and it comes near to being true of criminality. Moral and material wretchedness so commonly associated are often the issues of one another.[1] The present tendency is to relieve material poverty by measures of true individualization and personal initiative; these replace administrative and even sectarian charity, which is but a charity administered by rule, apt to make paupers instead of making poverty an incidental misfortune. Poverty requires the aid that relieves and does not encourage the condition itself. There are at present societies guided by this spirit of individualization; they dispense with any regular form of administering charity and leave to their members the duty of assisting the poor and unemployed to such positions as they are capable of filling. They do this through personal interest and through the

[1] See the excellent address of *M. l'abbé Maurice de Baets*, "Les Influences de la misère sur la criminalité" (Gand, 1895).

§ 97] ADMINISTRATIVE INDIVIDUALIZATION 311

various provisions that the organization of their work places at their disposal.[1]

The provisions for relief of material distress must be applied to moral distress; and in place of punishment administered by rule and with an invariable uniformity, we ask for a system of individual superintendence through which the individual initiative may be appealed to, and the most suitable measures of assistance provided for each case. There are many offenders, and equally many of the unfortunate poor, whose contact with crime is but a phase of their existence, who pass through it without belonging to it body and soul. They experience a crisis and must be helped through it. In this service punishment should be one of the most effective measures. It must be wisely utilized, but, to be thus utilized, there should be no concealment of the need of repentance and expiation, for that alone can effect a revival of conscience. If the interests of social protection were alone considered, convicts might be treated like hounded animals and not like men; but that is not the way to bring about their reformation.

Of all the theories proposed as a basis of punishment, to the exposition of which this book is devoted, this last seems the only one likely to enlist the good will of all and to involve no abandonment of principle.

The classic system will be acceptable only to those — and they are few in number — who hold to the belief in free will in its traditional form. The extreme position of the Italian school appeals only to the determinists of a materialistic trend. This irreconcilable difference of view will

[1] See the fine address of *M. Jules Lemaitre* at the general meeting of January 30, 1898, of the "Société charitable des visiteurs pour le relèvement des familles malheureuses" (in *Figaro*, January 31, 1898; reprinted, with the report of *M. Bazin*, in the *Bulletin de l'Union pour l'action morale*, March 1, 1898, p. 411, *seq.*).

continue. If the problem be shifted to the field of practical results, while still holding to the authority of the principle of responsibility, a common ground seems available. Responsibility is adhered to, but it involves no conclusion incompatible with the conceptions of the positivist school; and in turn, among the tenets of this school, there is none that need be so interpreted as to be opposed to the idea of responsibility. The difference is one of theory and belongs to the field of individual opinions and convictions of conscience. In either case, the punishment as applied and in the nature of its discipline will be the same and similarly organized. The one system looks upon punishment as a penalty directed to the interest of social defense, and the other regards it wholly as a measure of social security; but this difference will not affect the practical measures in regard to which men of science and philanthropists are in full accord. This is substantially the point of view and the watchword of the International Union of Criminal Law; and it has been the purpose of this book to set forth the evidence of its worth.[1]

[1] Since 1898 the system of indeterminate sentences has stimulated many discussions and publications, in addition to the general works on criminology and penal science which necessarily consider it; notably *Prins*, "Science pénale et droit positif," pp. 453-460.

We mention first of all, especially on the application of the system in America, *Teutsch*, "Méthodes pénales et pénitentiaires des États-Unis" (*Revue pénitentiaire*, 1905). Articles devoted entirely to indeterminate sentences are (in chronological order), *Tarde* (*Revue pénitentiaire*, 1899), p. 1087; *Malpel*, "Essai sur la mise en pratique de la sentence indéterminée" (Thesis, Toulouse, 1900); *Salomon Rapoport*, "Les sentences indéterminées" (*Revue internationale de sociologie*, Giard et Brière, 1904); *Gras*, "Des sentences indéterminées" (Thesis, Paris, 1905); *Roux*, "Les sentences indéterminées et l'idée de justice" (*Revue pénitentiaire*, 1905), p. 3.660.

At the International Prison Congress held at Washington, in October, 1910, the First Section formally voted to "approve the scientific principle of the indeterminate sentence." This was the first occasion on which an International Congress had given such approval, and demonstrates the progress of thought on this subject. — ED.

One may say that the general tendency nowadays is to discard the absolute indeterminateness of the sentence by reason of its possible encroachment of personal liberty through the autocracy of the administration. A relative indeterminateness is preferred, that is, the fixation by law and the judge of a minimum and a maximum sentence. This system of relative indeterminateness has been legally authorized by the Norwegian penal code. According to the terms of Article 65 of that code, when a person is guilty of one of several crimes which the law specifies, "the court may put to the jury the question of determining whether the author of these acts, by reason of the nature of the crime, of the motives which have directed it, of the impulses which it discloses, may be considered as peculiarly harmful to society or to the life, health, and welfare of particular persons." In case of an affirmative, the sentence may specify, at the expiration of the punishment, a supplementary detention which must not exceed the three-fold period of the punishment, or in any case be more than fifteen years. (For a critical opinion of Art. 65, see the preface of *M. Garçon*, p. xviii.)

For the points of resemblance between indeterminate and alternative sentences, such as obtain in England, see the final note of the preceding chapter, p. 293, note.

To return to disciplines applicable to individuals undergoing reformatory punishment in appropriate institutions, it seems likely that there will be established experimentally and for certain types of offenders, what may be called an out-door prison, which is to serve as a gradation between imprisonment and freedom under surveillance. For one of the greatest disadvantages even of a short-term detention is that it takes a man away from his work, and consequently from his source of livelihood. And in another respect this is a most unequal punishment, because in the case of those who have a manual trade or who practice an industrial or commercial vocation, it often amounts to ruin; while it has no effect at all upon those who have a sufficient fortune not to be dependent upon a lucrative calling. Would it not be possible to permit these persons to exercise their vocation with nothing to mark them off from their companions except the requirement to return to the institution at evening? The experiment would carry a more general advantage, namely, that of accustoming their employers, and as well their fellow-employees, respectively to employ and to be considerate to those who have served a sentence for an accidental transgression.

INDEX

INDEX

[REFERENCES ARE TO PAGES]

A

Adickes, Erich, 180 n.
Alienation, see Crime and abnormal condition.
Alimena, 69 n., 125 n., 165 n., 223 n.
Ancyrus, Council of, 201.
Anderson, Sir Robert, 19 n., 34 n., 136 n.
Andréadès, 293 n.
Aquinas, Thomas, 40 n. 2, 66 n. 2.
Aschrott, 110 n., 214 n. 1.
Aubry, Octave, 114 n., 215 n.

B

Bachem, 218 n.
Baer, 130 n.
Baets, Maurice de, 310 n.
Balfour, 179 n. 2.
Ballet, Gilbert, ii n., vi n., 98 n.
Ballvé, Antoine, 136 n.
Bartmann, 36 n. 1.
Batardy, 284 n.
Bazin, 311 n.
Beaudouin, 24 n. 4, 27 n. 2.
Beccaria, 52, 100.
Bentham, 52.
Bérenger, Law of, see Law.
Bernhöft, 24 n. 3.
Binding, 49 n.
Birkmeyer, 138 n. 3.
Blondel, Maurice, 173 n., 179 n. 2.
Borstal System, 286 n.
Boudinhon, A., 199 n. 2.
Bouton, R., 201 n. 2.
Briand, 96 n.
Brockway, 299, 300, 301, 308.
Brunetière, 179 n. 2.
Brunner, 24 n. 3, 27 n. 1, 32 n. 1.
Bufnoir, vi, viii, ix, xii n.

C

Calvin, 36 n. 2.
Carnevale, E., 125 n., 126 n., 227 n. 1.
Carrara, 100.

Cathrein, 152 n.
Chiaroni, 215 n.
Circumstances,
  extenuating, see Extenuation.
  of crime, see Crime, circumstances of.
Classic School, see School, Classic.
Clement XI, Pope, 203 n. 3.
Coconnier, P., 172 n. 2.
Colajanni, 132 n., 278 n.
Complicity, see Crime, complicity in.
Comte, xi.
Conti, Ugo, 62 n., 256 n., 257 n., 278 n.
Contingent liability, see Crime, contingent.
Coppée, 307.
Coulanges, Fustel de, 24 n. 3, 27 n. 2.
Crime,
  and abnormal condition, 77–79, 80–82, 142, 143.
  and criminology, 84.
  and pathology, 4.
  and punishment, 13, 117, 120, 193.
  and sin, 33, 197, 198.
  and society, 13, 186, 187.
  and sociology, 4.
  as symptom, 117, 133.
  circumstances of, see Crime, objective.
  complicity in, 221, 225.
  contingent, 221, 263, 263 n. 1, 3.
  classic conception of, 7.
  factors of, 102, 279.
  materiality of, 5.
  objective, 5, 31–33, 46, 47, 186, 187.
  of passion, 256–258.
  political, 205, 253–256.
  subjective, 31, 33, 84, 205.
Criminal and Criminality,
  accidental, 271.
  and premeditation, 69.

317

318　INDEX

Criminal and Criminality — *Cont.*
　as abnormal, 83, 130, 131.
　as alien, 94, 155–157, 268.
　confirmed, 103, 207.
　diagnosis of, 127–132, 133, 296, 297.
　dynamic and static, 276–278.
　making of, 104–106, 121, 148–149, 216, 217, 310, 311.
　prevention of, 123.
　promiscuity of, 106, 112.
　protection against, 123.
　reform of, 131, 287, 289.
　subjective aspect of, 45.
　types of, 118–122, 127, 128, 144, 270–274, 278–282.
Crisenoy, de, 283 n.
Crofton, Walter, 110.
Cruppi, 228 n.
Cuche, xii, 17 n., 18 n., 136 n., 181 n.
Curel, de, 154 n.

D

Dantec, Félix le, 169 n. 1.
Delaquis, Ernest, v.
Deportation, see Punishment, as deportation; Individualization.
Desdouits, 179 n. 1.
Desjardins, Albert, 129 n.
Desjardins, Paul, 231 n.
Determinism, 57, 67, 151, 177–179.
Dobresco, 156 n. 1.
Dostoiewsky, 130 n., 213 n. 2, 254.
Dubois, ii n., vi n.
Durkheim, 20 n., 24 n. 1.
Duval, Raoul, 42 n., 221 n. 1.

E

Ecclesiastical law, see Law, ecclesiastical.
Eliot, George, 88 n.
Elmira system, 298–301.
Encyclopedists, 53.
Engelmann, 35 n. 1, 40 n. 1.
Esmein, 20 n., 27 n. 1, 51 n.
Extenuation of circumstances, 58, 76, 79, 82.
Eycken, Paul van der, 19 n.

F

Ferri, 102, 102 n., 103, 116, 136 n., 278 n.
Ferriani, L., 130 n.
Feuerbach, 52.

Flandin, Etienne, 283 n. 2.
Fogazarro, 309 n.
Fonsegrive, 40 n. 2, 66 n. 1, 175 n., 179 n. 1.
Fouillée, xiii, 67, 105 n., 175 n.
France, 50, 51.
Franck, Reinhard, 19 n., 98 n., 136 n.
Frassati, 129 n.
Fredus, 27, 28.
Freedom, see Responsibility and freedom.
Free Will, 64, 175–177, 197, 198.
　analysis of, 65–67, 170–172.
　conditions of, 71, 72, 85, 178.
　see also Punishment; Responsibility and freedom.
French Empire, 50.
French Revolution, 50, 54.
Frins, P., 179 n. 1, 199 n. 1.
Fulliquet, 139 n.
Fustel de Coulanges, see Coulanges.

G

Garçon, iv, v, 19 n., 62 n., 98 n., 223 n., 254 n., 259, 293 n., 312 n.
Garofalo, 102, 135, 242, 278 n., 280 n.
Garraud, v, 19 n., 62 n., 139 n., 169 n. 2, 221 n. 3.
Gauckler, 136 n.
Gautier, Alfred, 274 n. 1.
Gény, 19 n.
Giddings, 157 n.
Glasson, 27 n. 1.
Gospel, see St. John, St. Luke, St. Mark, St. Matthew, St. Paul.
Granier, 129 n.
Gras, 312 n.
Grasset, ii, 98 n., 181 n.
Gretener, 78 n., 143 n.
Gumplowicz, 28 n. 2, 157 n., 164 n.
Günther, 30 n., 35 n. 1, 203 n. 2.
Guyho, Corentin, 96 n., 126.

H

Hamel, van, 144 n.
Haracourt, 38 n.
Hatzfeld, 36 n. 2.
Hecker, 309 n.
Hefele, 201 n. 1.
Hinschius, 35 n. 1, 203 n. 2.
Historical School, see School, Historical.
Holtzendorff, 223 n., 238 n. 1.
Hymans, Paul, 213 n. 2.

INDEX

I

Ihering, 49 n.
Imbert, 46 n.
Individualization,
  administrative, 12, 294 n., 295 seq.
  and responsibility, 183, 272, 276.
  and the jury, 95–97, 232–236.
  in deportation, 206–209.
  in political crime, 253–256; see also Crime, political.
  judicial, 12, 48, 50, 223, 227–230, 237 seq., 293 n.
  legal, 12, 220 seq., 262–266.
  moral aspects of, 192–195.
  of the Italian School, 119.
  principles of, 260–262.
    types of (including false), 11, 12, 44–47, 220, 223–226, 235, 237–239, 298, 303.
Infamy, see Punishment and infamy.
Infanticide, 200, 201, 223.
Ingegnieros, José, 136 n.
Insanity and crime, see Crime and abnormal condition.
Intimidation, see Punishment, deterrent.
Irresponsibility, see Responsibility and irresponsibility.
Italian School, see School, Italian.

J

Jansen, 36 n. 2.
Joly, Henry, 62 n., 105 n., 130 n.
Jousse, 46 n.
Judge,
  discretion of, 57, 227–229.
  education of, 231.
  functions of, 47, 48.
Julhiet, Ed., 294 n.
Jury,
  history of, 11.
  in individualization, 232–236.
  attitude of, 10, 11, 93–95.
  special types of, 233.

K

Keller, 174 n. 1.
Kohler, 30 n.
Kovalevsky, 24 n. 3.
Kraus, 239 n., 249 n.
Krohne, 111 n.

L

Laberthonnière, P., 179 n. 2.
Law
  and minors, 76, 294 n.
  and social protection, etc., see Social, etc.
  Bérenger, xvi, 195, 212, 213, 216, 217, 229, 288.
  ecclesiastical, 191, 192.
  French, of 1854, 110.
    of 1875, 113, 211.
    of 1885, 17, 223, 286.
    of 1891, 210, 212.
  Germanic, 24, 199.
  responsibility in, 39–42.
  Roman, 27.
  Salic, 26, 34, 54, 55, 199.
Lea, Henry C., 199 n. 2.
Legrand, 69 n., 98 n., 223 n., 239 n.
Lemaitre, Jules, 311 n.
Le Play, xi.
Le Poittevin, A., iv, 62 n., 98 n., 216 n., 292 n.
Leredu, 98 n.
Leveillé, 62 n., 111 n., 113, 208 n., 260, 306.
Lévy, Frédéric, 299 n., 301, 308 n.
Lévy-Bruhl, 175 n., 179 n. 1.
Liepmann, 53 n.
Lippert, 24 n. 3.
Liszt, von, 9 n., 49 n., 56, 87, 98 n., 129 n., 136 n., 137, 138, 138 n. 1, 2, 139 n., 141 n. 1, 142 n., 147 n., 150, 165 n., 184, 218 n., 219 n., 221 n. 1, 239 n., 245 n., 278 n.
  Theory of Rechtsgüter, 49.
Löffler, 30 n., 32 n. 1, 3, 35 n. 1, 41 n. 1, 165 n.
Lombard, Peter, 66 n. 2.
Lombroso, 19 n., 101 n., 102, 103, 103 n., 116, 118, 122, 127, 128, 129, 130, 132, 137, 275, 284.
Louis XIV, edict of, 48.
Lucchini, 129 n.
Luther, 36 n. 2.

M

Mabille, G., 181 n.
Magistrate, see Judge.
Makarawicz, 4 n., 16 n. 3.
Mallieux, 19 n.
Malpel, 312 n.
Mancini, 257.
Manning, 309 n.
Marx, Karl, xi.

320 INDEX

Maudsley, 143 n.
Merkel, 16 n. 2, 35 n. 2, 160 n., 172 n. 1.
Meynial, 19 n.
Minors, see Law and minors.
Mitigation, see Extenuation.
Mittlestädt, 16 n. 2, 213 n. 1.
Molinists, 40 n. 2.
Montgomery, H. J. B., 136 n., 145 n. 1, 213 n. 2, 300 n.
Morality, see Punishment, moral issues in.
Moriaud, Paul, xii, 85 n.
Morin, Gaston, iv.
Morlot, Emile, 219 n.
Morrison, 130 n.
Motive, 224, 239–253, 264; see also Responsibility, moral nature of.
Mumm, 214 n. 1.
Muyart de Vouglans, 153.

N

Néret, 98 n.
Normality, see Punishment and normality.

O

Offender and offense,
 first, 59; see also Recidivist.
Olshausen, 259 n.
Oppenheim, 214 n. 2.
Ortolan, 62 n.

P

Pardon, see Parole and Pardon.
Parole and Pardon, 192, 204, 212–214, 215–218, 219 n., 229, 230, 289.
Payot, 179 n. 2.
Pellizari, 37 n.
Penal Code,
 Austrian, 80.
 Dutch, 186, 227 n. 2.
 French, 6 n., 10, 18, 76, 79, 203.
  of 1810, xiv, 56–58, 73, 74, 182, 183.
  of 1791, 54.
 German, 80, 259.
 Italian, 6, 7 n., 80, 100, 101, 224 n., 256–260, 262.
 Norwegian, 19 n., 293 n., 313.
 Swiss, 78 n., 146 n., 222 n.
Penalty, see Punishment.
Penance, 198, 199–203.
Penitentials, 199, 199 n. 2.
Penology, see Crime; also School.

Personality, see Responsibility and personality.
Picard, L., 196 n. 1.
Post, 24 n. 3.
Premeditation, 68, 69, 72, 223 n.
Pressensé, de, 309 n.
Prins, 18 n., 132 n., 177 n., 312 n.
Progressive system, see Punishment, progressive system.
Promiscuity, see Criminal and Criminality, promiscuity of.
Punishment,
 and free will, 179–181, 188, 189, 212; see also Responsibility.
 and infamy, 206, 255, 267–269, 269 n.
 and motive, 247–251; see also Motive.
 and normality, 140–144, 162, 163, 164.
 as deportation, 110, 204, 206–209, 258, 292, 306.
 as expiation, 29, 37–39.
 as private vengeance, 21.
 as reparation, 59–61.
 as risk incurred, 33, 190.
 as solitary confinement, 109, 113, 211, 283.
 as Wergild, see Wergild.
 conception of, 187–189.
 degrees of, 187, 238, 275.
 deterrent, 125, 126, 145–147, 165 n., 208, 270, 271, 284, 285, 288, 290.
 divine, see Punishment as expiation.
 equality of, see Punishment, uniform.
 exemption from, 83.
 indeterminate, 298–301, 301–305, 312 n.
 in the primitive clan, 25, 26.
 long-term and short-term, 109, 209 seq.
 mitigation of, 201, 224–226, 257–259; see also Extenuation.
 moral issues in, 139, 193–195, 213, 251–253, 268, 309.
 parallel, 259, 262, 265–268, 271, 273.
 preventive, see Punishment, deterrent.
 private and public, 28.
 progressive system, 110, 291.
 purpose of, 116–118, 195, 218.
 reformatory, 194, 270, 291, 307.
 special, 263–266, 283, 285.

INDEX 321

Punishment — *Cont.*
 uniform, 59, 61, 112, 261, 262.
 variable between limits, 58.
Puybaraud, 130 n.

R

Rapoport, Salomon, 312 n.
Rechtsgüter, 49; see Liszt.
Recidivist, see Criminal and Criminality.
Relegation, see Punishment as deportation.
Reparation, see Punishment as reparation.
Responsibility,
 and crime, xiv, xvi, 33, 75.
 and freedom, 56, 96, 166, 168–172; see also Free Will; Punishment.
 and irresponsibility, 77–79.
 and moral nature, 159–162, 164, 191, 192.
 and normality, see Punishment and normality.
 and personality, 173, 174.
 and punishment, see Responsibility and crime.
 and reason, 158, 159.
 and will, 43.
 conception of, 35, 87.
  in Christianity, 35–37, 55, 191, 192.
 degrees of, 81, 82, 168.
 individualization and, see Individualization.
 in ecclesiastical law, see Law, ecclesiastical.
 partial, 142, 226.
 practical, 158–160.
 remote and immediate, 87–90.
Richard, Pierre, 111 n.
Rigaud, 223 n., 239 n., 254 n.
Rivière, L., 274 n. 2.
Rossi, 62 n., 100, 103.
Rostand, Eugéne, 105 n.
Rousseau, 20, 52, 53, 53 n., 54.
Rousseau de la Combe, 153.
Roux, 141 n. 1, 312 n.

S

Sabatier, A., 36 n. 1, 174 n. 2.
Sacharoff, C., 219 n.
Salic Law, see Law, Salic.
Schmidt, 308 n.
Schmitz, 199 n. 2, 201 n. 1, 3.

Schofield, Henry, 255 n.
Scholastics, 39, 44.
School,
 Classic, 51, 52 *seq.*, 114.
 Historical, 51.
 Italian, 16, 99 *seq.*, 115, 119, 132, 134, 135, 150.
 and individualization, see Individualization of the Italian School.
 Neo-Classic, 63 *seq.*
 "Third Italian," 125.
Schröder, 30 n.
Schwinderem, van, 26 n.
Seigneux, de, 96 n.
Sentence, see Punishment.
Siéyès, 116.
Sighele, 102, 156 n. 2, 267 n.
Sin, see Crime.
Social,
 interests, 49, 189.
  in punishment, 89, 90, 219.
 regulation, 73.
 responsibility, 90–93, 155, 156, 185, 186; see also Sociology.
Sociology,
 purpose of, 2, 115; see also Crime and sociology; Social.
Sohm, 22 n., 27 n. 1.
Speyr, D. von, 83 n.
Stammler, 174 n. 1.
St. Augustine, 36 n. 2.
St. Bernard, 40 n. 2, 197 n. 2.
St. John, 197 n. 1, 198 n. 1, 2.
St. Luke, 35 n. 2, 198 n. 1, 2.
St. Mark, 196 n. 2, 198 n. 1.
St. Matthew, 35 n. 2, 198 n. 1, 2.
St. Paul, 36 n. 1, 195 n., 198 n. 3, 4.
Sternau, 303 n.
Stooss, 87 n., 142 n., 145 n. 2, 146 n., 224, 253 n.
Sumien, 81 n.

T

Tacitus, 24 n. 2.
Taine, 50 n.
Tarde, Gabriel, v, vi, ix, xi n., 2 n., 16 n. 1, 28 n. 1, 102, 126, 130 n., 136 n., 148 n., 155, 156, 185, 278 n., 312 n.
 Introduction by, xi, xvii.
Temibilità, 69, 117, 150.
Teutsch, 312 n.
Thaller, iv.
Thibierge, 221 n. 2.
Thonissen, 30 n.

U

Urbye, Andréas, 287 n. 2, 306 n.

V

Vagrant and Vagabond, 283.
Vargha, 125 n., 134 n. 1, 203 n. 1, 213 n. 1, 308 n.
Vence, C. de, 227 n. 1.
Vergeltungsstrafe, 5, 8, 9.
Vidal, 129 n., 293 n.
Viollet, 27 n. 1, 199 n. 2.
Volition, see Responsibility and will.

W

Wahlberg, 39 n., 86 n., 134 n. 2, 278 n.
Wergild, 23–27, 30 n., 31, 33, 190, 199.
Wernle, 36 n. 1.
Will, see Responsibility and will.
Wills, Sir Alfred, 136 n., 286 n.

Z

Zurcher, 78 n.
Zweckstrafe, 8, 9, 310.